LIBRARY
UNIVERSITY OF NEW HAVEN

The Politics of School Desegregation

The Metropolitan Remedy in Delaware

Temple
University
Press
Philadelphia

The Politics of
School Desegregation

The Metropolitan Remedy in Delaware

Jeffrey A. Raffel

LC
214.23
W54
R33

Temple University Press, Philadelphia 19122
© 1980 by Temple University. All rights reserved
Published 1980
Printed in the United States of America

Library of Congress Cataloging in Publication Data

Raffel, Jeffrey A
    The politics of school desegregation.

    Includes bibliographical references and index.
    1. School integration—Delaware—Wilmington metropolitan area.   I. Title.
LC214.23.W54R33   370.19′342   80-10840
ISBN 0-87722-176-6

Contents

Acknowledgments

This book reflects the work, influence, and help of many people. Jon Chace, Win Cleland, Susan Greenblatt, Betty Lewis, Daniel Monti, Dorry Ross, David Schulz, Charles Willie, and Frederick Wirt struggled through early drafts and made many cogent comments. Barry Morstain suggested scores of ways to improve the manuscript. C. Harold Brown and Daniel Rich constantly supplied ideas and moral support. Priscilla Crowder Edward Ratledge, Norfleet Rives, Jr., Linda Sasser, and Julie Schmidt read portions of this manuscript and made helpful suggestions. Kathy Turkel served ably as a research assistant for the survey analyses. Elise Harvey not only skillfully edited the bulk of this volume but also furnished inspiration, ideas, and encouragement. I am grateful to all of these people for helping me to finish this book.

If I personally thanked all the people who helped me to consider the process of desegregation, I would have to list several hundred names and would certainly forget scores more. The individuals who most regularly stimulated my thinking, those to whom I owe the most special thanks, are Jon Chace, Debbi Donovan, Helen Foss, Cheryl Graham, Ruth Graham, Lynn Kaufman, Betty Lewis, Thomas Luce, Robert Moore, Larry Nagengast, David Weber, and Sandra Worthen. I also must thank the hundreds of people, many anonymous, who worked with me and against me, helping me to understand the nature of the process in which I was involved. I also appreciate those school and public officials who talked frankly with me about desegregation in Delaware.

The financial support for the polls reported in this book came from the Delaware Postsecondary Education Commission and the Wilmington News Journal Company. In addition, the University of

Delaware and the College of Urban Affairs and Public Policy provided support for my participation in the desegregation process and my writing of this volume. To each of these organizations, my thanks.

Without the major assistance of Gloria Stover, who typed the entire first draft of this manuscript in record time, this volume might not yet have been in your hands. Learis Donovan, Jackie Noakes, Florence Torri, and Libby Stewart spent hours deciphering my handwriting and editorial directions. Their excellent typing and patience are greatly appreciated. Bonnie Topper helped to organize my files and my working hours. Her help was crucial.

During my work on desegregation, family support has been even more vital than financial support. I have had to be away from home for early morning breakfast meetings, evening meetings, and various out-of-town trips. Further, even when I was home in early 1978 writing this book, I was usually unavailable for talking and listening. The support of my wife, Joanne, and my children, Allison, Lori, and Kenny, has been invaluable. I hope that my work in the desegregation process in Delaware has benefited them, and others. I will be glad if this book helps others to make similar contributions elsewhere.

The Politics of School Desegregation
The Metropolitan Remedy in Delaware

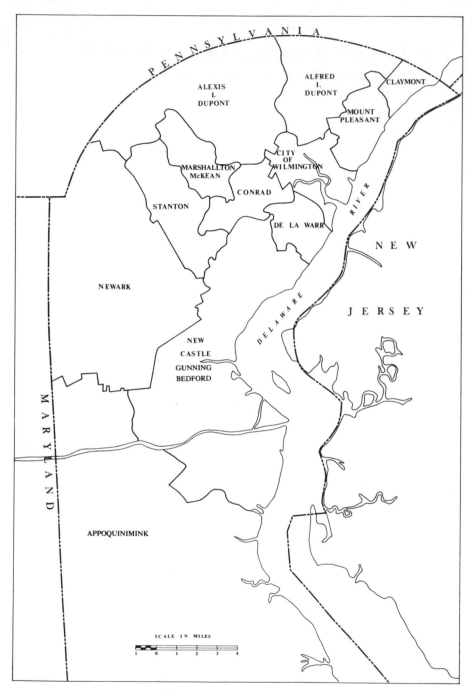

Wilmington Area School Districts. Drawn by Mark Wnoroski, Geography Department, University of Delaware.

1 / Introduction

In September 1978 the Wilmington, Delaware, city schools were combined with those of ten surrounding suburban school districts. Over twenty thousand students were bused to achieve desegregation of the metropolitan area schools. This reorganization and transportation were carried out by federal court order despite the opposition of most local officials and widespread public hostility. This book is a political analysis of what took place and of who gained and who lost by the decisions.

There are several reasons for examining the Wilmington desegregation case. First, the area exhibited the classic pattern of metropolitan school problems. As in many other population centers around the country, the central city's public schools held a concentration of disadvantaged, minority, underachieving children while most of the adjacent suburban schools served mostly, white, middle-class, academically oriented youngsters. The remedy ordered in Wilmington may also be prescribed in places like Los Angeles, St. Louis, Kansas City, Atlanta, and Indianapolis.[1] Gary Orfield, a well-known analyst of school desegregation, believes that metropolitan situations are likely to dominate national school policy discussions in years ahead.[2]

Second, as the first instance of court-ordered metropolitan interdistrict school desegregation, Wilmington became something of a proving ground for proponents and opponents alike. National attention focused on the case as the *New York Times*, the *Los Angeles Times*, and the *Washington Post* published articles on the extensive preparations for the opening of school in 1978.[3] National interest groups entered the Wilmington arena. They included the NAACP Legal Defense Fund (litigation), the National Center for Policy Review (litigation), the United States Department of Justice (litigation and desegregation planning), the National Association for Neighborhood Schools (congressional lobbying), the Lamar Society (consultation for a community coalition), the Rockefeller Foundation (funding for a study of the effects of desegregation), the Ford Foundation (funding for a community coalition to consult other coalitions), and the Rand Corporation (a study of the role of community groups).

Third, as Charles Willie and Susan Greenblatt have noted, "only sparse information has been published concerning the success or failure of communities in their efforts to gain popular support for desegregation plans."[4] Daniel Monti has seen a "genuine need to know how school systems implement a desegregation plan and cope with the rancor and bitterness that often accompany desegregation."[5] I hope that a close look at the events in Wilmington will illuminate the process of complying with court-ordered desegregation not only to help make it less divisive in other communities but also to increase the likelihood of positive educational results.

There is a final reason that I undertook an analysis of the Wilmington case. Quite simply, I was there. As a social scientist and as a participant, I had access to data and a strong interest in what was happening. I first became involved in November 1974. Since then, I have served as staff director of a group ordered by the governor to work for peaceful implementation of the federal court order. This has led to my playing a variety of other formal and informal roles. I chaired a secret desegregation planning group composed of governmental, school, religious, and community leaders that met about twice a month to discuss the status of implementation. I helped to develop both a countywide desegregation information center and an alliance of community groups concerned about public education. I directed a small-group discussion program that went into homes, churches, and meetings of organizations to encourage discussion of desegregation issues. I codirected two public opinion polls on the subject. I gave numerous talks. I advised many people (including teachers, parents, and students) on preparations for desegregation. I observed school board–teacher association collective bargaining sessions and worked with parent groups and the governor's office to end a long strike in the fall of 1978.

Christine H. Rossell has criticized most of the academic research and writing on school desegregation for taking an apolitical, technocratic viewpoint.[6] The result of this detached, efficient approach is that the extensive literature on the subject offers little help to a school system faced with a federal court order.[7] I can testify from my own experience that the critical issues, the problems and difficulties both great and small, are best understood within a political framework. They affect basic community relationships and the process of working them out is political through and through.

This book is not a tract on the pros and cons of busing. Others have kept up that debate.[8] My position is that, when ordered to do so by the courts, schools should be desegregated peacefully and effectively. Robert Crain has written that, to be useful, policy research on this topic must address the question, "How can desegregation be done better?"[9] That is what I have tried to do in this work.[10]

A BRIEF SKETCH OF THE WILMINGTON METROPOLITAN CASE

A few dates and events provide a helpful historical background for analysis of the complex Wilmington metropolitan case (Figure 1-1). The original Delaware school desegregation case was consolidated with several others in the historic U.S. Supreme Court *Brown* v. *Board of Education* decision in 1954. In 1957 black parents began a new suit charging that the State Board of Education had failed to desegregate Delaware's schools despite the court order to dismantle its *de jure* segregated school system. The new suit was named *Evans* v. *Buchanan*. Although the two rural southern counties of Delaware were desegregated in the 1960s, the Wilmington public schools in 1971 were still serving a majority of black children while students in the surrounding eleven school districts of New Castle County were almost exclusively white. Indeed, the state legislature passed a school district consolidation law in 1968 which prohibited the merger of the city school district with any other system. This, said the black parents in their suit, prevented the desegregation of Wilmington schools.

In July 1974, a three-judge federal panel ruled that the Wilmington public schools were segregated. In August, a decision by the U.S. Supreme Court reversed a metropolitan order in the Detroit metropolitan area case and sent the Delaware case back to the three-judge panel. The panel ruled in March 1975 that a metropolitan remedy was permissible in Delaware despite the Detroit ruling. But by then, government officials had appointed a citizens' group to work toward a smooth transition, the State Legislature had established a special committee to determine its own role, the corporate business community had analyzed possible response to the situation, and an antibusing group had recruited over 10,000 members.

In May 1976, the three-judge panel (1) rejected the desegregation plans that had been submitted and ordered the establishment of an Interim Board, which through state legislative action had thirteen

Figure 1-1
Key Events in the Wilmington Metropolitan Case, July 1974–November 1978

COURTS						
Milliken Reconsidered July 1974–June 1975	Phase 1: Free-for-All July 1975–June 1976	Phase 2: Interim Board July 1976–June 1977	Phase 3: "But For" July 1977	Phase 4: New Board Aug. 1977–Feb. 1978	Phase 5: Final Order March 1978–June 1978	Desegregation July 1978–Nov. 1978
District Court						
• Wilmington schools segregated • Planning halted; suburban districts invited to be intervenors	• Milliken not restrictive in Delaware case • Deadline for submission of plans from State Board	• Interim Board established; 10–35% minority ratio. Secondary school desegregation to begin in Sept. 1977, elementary in Sept. 1978		• But For Plan rejected; stay issued. New Board established • State Treasurer named as defendant • Sept. 1978 set for desegregation	• Final order: 9–3 plan, includes remedial plan, sets tax rate	• Accepts tax cap
Court of Appeals						
			• Upholds all but 10–35% ratio			• Upholds all but rejection of tax cap

	Milliken Reconsidered July 1974–June 1975	Phase 1: Free-for-All July 1975–June 1976	Phase 2: Interim Board July 1976–June 1977	Phase 3: "But For" July 1977	Phase 4: New Board Aug. 1977–Feb. 1978	Phase 5: Final Order March 1978–June 1978	Desegregation July 1978–Nov. 1978
Supreme Court	• Milliken decision limits metropolitan busing	• Affirms Delaware Judgment • Denies State Board request for new hearing	• Refuses to hear Delaware case for want of jurisdiction	• Upholds remedial programs in the Detroit case	• Refuses to grant certiorari • Refuses request for rehearing		• Brennan refuses stay • Rehnquist refuses stay after consideration

SCHOOL OFFICIALS

	Milliken Reconsidered July 1974–June 1975	Phase 1: Free-for-All July 1975–June 1976	Phase 2: Interim Board July 1976–June 1977	Phase 3: "But For" July 1977	Phase 4: New Board Aug. 1977–Feb. 1978	Phase 5: Final Order March 1978–June 1978	Desegregation July 1978–Nov. 1978
State Officials	• Agree to comply with whatever ordered	• Submit 5 District and Zone Transfer plans		• Submit One-way Voluntary Plan • Submit 10-2 Plan			
Suburban Officials	• Enter case as intervening defendants						

Figure 1-1: School Officials (cont.)

	Milliken Reconsidered July 1974–June 1975	Phase 1: Free-for-All July 1975–June 1976	Phase 2: Interim Board July 1976–June 1977	Phase 3: "But For" July 1977	Phase 4: New Board Aug. 1977–Feb. 1978	Phase 5: Final Order March 1978–June 1978	Desegregation July 1978–Nov. 1978
City Officials					• Submits 8-4 Plan		**Suburban and City Officials** • Schools open without incident • Teachers Strike • Teachers Strike ends after 5 weeks
Court-Related Officials			• Interim Board established • Appoints supts. council and administrative director • Appoints citizens to advise Task Forces	• Interim Board dissolved	• Supt. designated • NCCEA wins bargaining election	• Open house attracts 10,000+ in city	• Staff inservice and open house • ESAA funds • Disposition on stay filed
				• Votes for Intermediate School Authority and 5,9 Grade Center Plan			

	Milliken Reconsidered July 1974–June 1975	Phase 1: Free-for-All July 1975–June 1976	Phase 2: Interim Board July 1976–June 1977	Phase 3: "But For" July 1977	Phase 4: New Board Aug. 1977–Feb. 1978	Phase 5: Final Order March 1978–June 1978	Desegregation July 1978–Nov. 1978
Legislature		• 1st Legislative Committee on Desegregation forms • Leg. Com. requests appearance of federal judges • Leg. Com. recommends not entering case at this time • Filing of Joint Resolution for Inquiry of Judge Gibbons • 2nd Legislative Committee forms; $50,000 authorized for counsel • Prof. Kurland addresses General Assembly	• Interim Board expanded • Voluntary transfer plan approved • Zelon Magnet School Report released	• But For Reverse Volunteerism Plan developed	• Resolution passed to disclaim New Board • Court names state treasurer as defendant • Resolution passed to ask president to remove judge • Governor's 4 District Plan rejected	• 4 District Plan passed • Tax cap passed	

Figure 1-1: Governmental Officials (cont.)

Milliken Reconsidered July 1974–June 1975	Phase 1: Free-for-All July 1975–June 1976	Phase 2: Interim Board July 1976–June 1977	Phase 3: "But For" July 1977	Phase 4: New Board Aug. 1977–Feb. 1978	Phase 5: Final Order March 1978–June 1978	Desegregation July 1978–Nov. 1978
Executives						
• Mayor Maloney speaks favorably of decision	• Slawik asks DCSD to request stay	• Mayor Maloney campaigns against busing		• Mary Jornlin becomes county executive	• Gov. du Pont and Mayor McLaughlin take office	• Simulation, Media Center opened
	• PAC asks gov. to dissolve DCSD			• New executives elected	• Info. Center opened	
• Governor and mayor adopt DCSD	• Gov. refuses PAC request		• Gov. says busing inevitable			• Gov. names Effective Transition Committee
	• Gov. says he will ask for antibusing amendment		• Intergovernmental Task Force on Desegregation established			
	• Slawik removed from office		• Information Center opened and closed			
	• Gov. agrees to establish Information Center; state police given charge over desegregation					

Milliken Reconsidered July 1974–June 1975	Phase 1: Free-for-All July 1975–June 1976	Phase 2: Interim Board July 1976–June 1977	Phase 3: "But For" July 1977	Phase 4: New Board Aug. 1977–Feb. 1978	Phase 5: Final Order March 1978–June 1978	Desegregation July 1978–Nov. 1978
• DCSD hires staff • DCSD holds public meetings on desegregation • Governor and mayor adopt DCSD	• Meetings begun to plan Information Center • PTA and DCSD hold hearing on Desegregation Plans • DCSD proposes Information Center Plan • Community leaders visit Louisville–Jefferson County • News Journal sponsors desegregation coverage meeting • First Breakfast Meeting	• Washington Conference on Coalitions in desegregation • Clergy leaders make joint desegregation statement • Black leaders form group to monitor desegregation • 1st Alliance meeting • Marshallton–McKean Group witnesses Interim Board–Legislative Committee clash • DEEP discontinues programming • Alliance communications plan presented to Interim Board	• Executives announce task force at NCCJ luncheon • Info. Center established • Info. Center closed • DCSD calls for blue ribbon panel to supercede it • Blacks demonstrate against 10-2 plan • DCSD abolished • Interfaith Task Force established • School/Police/Clergy Workshop held			• Alliance receives funds from Newark and Wilmington City Councils

Figure 1-1: Community (cont.)

Milliken Reconsidered July 1974–June 1975	Phase 1: Free-for-All July 1975–June 1976	Phase 2: Interim Board July 1976–June 1977	Phase 3: "But For" July 1977	Phase 4: New Board Aug. 1977–Feb. 1978	Phase 5: Final Order March 1978–June 1978	Desegregation July 1978–Nov. 1978
	• NCCJ Conference at Longwood Gardens • SANE formed	• Interim Board establishes task forces and holds public hearings • SANE hires Spiro and Associates • 1,000 people attend Interim Board meeting to debate desegregation plans				
• PAC formed	• PAC tells Gov. to fight federal courts				• PAC President Venema announces candidacy as Republican against Senator Biden	

members representing the city and the ten surrounding school districts in the "desegregation area"; (2) ruled that each school in this desegregation area should have been between 10 and 35 percent minority students; (3) ordered that a single, reorganized school district, be established if the State Legislature failed to enact an acceptable alternative reorganization plan; and (4) ordered implementation in September 1977. The Interim Board struggled for a year to design a desegregation and reorganization plan, despite efforts by the legislature to avoid busing and pressures from the large antibusing organization. Concurrently, several community coalitions were formed to work for effective desegregation and more extensive preparation for implementation.

In June 1977, the Third Circuit of the U.S. Court of Appeals upheld the three-judge panel's decision, except for the 10 to 35 percent minority ratio, and state officials offered the district court a one-way busing plan that would meet the requirement of the Third Circuit. In August 1977, Judge Murray M. Schwartz, the federal district court judge in charge of implementation, granted a stay until the U.S. Supreme Court had considered the state's appeal. At the same time, Judge Schwartz ordered a five-member New Board to design a desegregation and reorganization plan for a single school district.

In January 1978, three months after the U.S. Supreme Court refused to hear the Delaware case, Judge Schwartz ordered the eleven school districts merged, city children to attend suburban schools for nine years, and suburban children to attend city schools for three consecutive years. In July 1978, the New Castle County School District officially replaced the city and ten suburban school districts. Over 24,000 children were reassigned as the 1978–1979 school year began. In September 1978, the schools opened without incident. The Wilmington metropolitan area thus became the first community to undergo court-ordered, interdistrict, metropolitan desegregation.

As the reader will see, many sectors of the state were involved (the courts, schools, governments, community), there were many actors in each sector (for example, there were several courts—District, Appeals, Supreme), and the relationships among many of the activities were complicated and often unclear. To add to the complexity, the history of school desegregation began long before the first court decision on the metropolitan aspects of the case. And during the period covered by this volume—1974 to 1978—there was a continuous shifting of actors and groups in relation to one another.

In the chapters that follow I will focus on four straightforward questions. 1. What had to be done? (Why did the federal courts order

Delaware's officials to alter the pattern of racial separation in New Castle County's schools, and what was the nature of these orders?) 2. What was done? (How did public officials and community leaders respond to the court's challenge?) 3. What resulted? (To what extent did school desegregation result from these responses, and what were the early effects of the desegregation process on blacks and whites?) 4. What can we learn from analyzing these events?

2 / Racial Separation and Public Opinion

WILMINGTON METROPOLITAN AREA

The Wilmington metropolitan area lies squarely in the center of the eastern megalopolis. It is a stop on the New York-to-Washington Amtrak railroad. Wilmington is divided by Interstate 95 as that super-highway connects Maryland and Pennsylvania. The city has been reshaped by the same forces that have affected other eastern cities.[1]

The City of Wilmington has been losing population to its suburban ring for several decades. According to 1975 Census Bureau estimates, 76,654 residents lived in the City of Wilmington, down almost one-third from 110,356 in 1950 (Table 2-1). During the same period, the suburban population tripled.

Most residents in the Wilmington metropolitan area (as defined by the U.S. Census Bureau) live in New Castle County, which had a 1975 population of 393,648. The population of the surrounding out-of-state counties in the Standard Metropolitan Statistical Area (SMSA) was slightly over 100,000. The focus of this study, New Castle County, thus includes about 80 percent of the population within the official Wilmington SMSA.

New Castle County covers 435 square miles, about 42 percent of which (185 square miles) is rural area, the Appoquinimink School District. The heart of the metropolitan area, the City of Wilmington, is 15 square miles in size. The area of the surrounding suburbs is more than ten times the size of the city.

As did other cities, Wilmington changed character with suburban-ization. From 1950 to 1975, the percentage of blacks in the city increased from 7.6 to 55.5 percent, while in the suburbs, the black population dropped from 16.1 to 3.9.[2] Like most of America's metro-politan areas, the Wilmington area comprises a small central city with a high perentage of low income and minority residents, surrounded by affluent white suburbs with very few minority residents.[3]

Political Divisions

Political divisions mirror and maintain the demographic separations. While many politicians and community leaders have talked about somehow consolidating the city and county governments, Wilmington's government remains separate from that of New Castle County. The county includes nearly a dozen small incorporated municipalities. Largest in 1975 was the City of Newark with 25,829 residents, of whom over 6,700 were students.[4] Most of the residents of New Castle County, however, live neither in Wilmington nor in the incorporated municipalities but rather in the unincorporated areas that are dependent on the county for services. As the population grew in these areas, the structure and sophistication of county government changed. Today the county executive serves like a mayor, six county council members are elected by district, and a council president is elected at large every four years. Despite the number of people who live outside the boundaries of the City of Wilmington, media attention remains fixed on the city government and the mayor. The City of Wilmington has a mayor-council form of government. Blacks have

Table 2-1
Total Population Trends and
Black Population Trends, 1950–1975

Area	1950	1960	1970	1975
Population (no. and %):				
Delaware	318,085	446,292	548,104	574,692
New Castle County (including Wilmington)	218,879	307,446	385,511	393,648
Wilmington	110,356	95,827	80,386	76,654
Suburban New Castle County	108,523	211,619	305,125	316,994
Wilmington, percentage of New Castle County	50.4%	31.2%	20.7%	19.4%
Wilmington, percentage of Delaware	34.6%	21.5%	14.6%	13.3%
Black Population (%):				
New Castle County (including Wilmington)	11.8%	11.8%	12.7%	13.9%
Wilmington	7.6%	26.0%	43.6%	55.5%
Suburban New Castle County	16.1%	5.3%	4.5%	3.9%

had virtually no political power in the county and very little in the city government. Their activity has been limited to holding a few seats on the City Council and occasionally running for citywide office.

The city is dependent upon the State Legislature for the authority to levy taxes. In 1970 the State Legislature agreed to allow the city to establish a wage tax at the rate of 1.5 percent. This tax, which applies to wages earned in the city by people who live in the suburbs, has been a constant political issue since its adoption.

This separation of city and suburban government reflects its setting: in Delaware, metropolitan and rural representatives have clashed for decades. Like Illinois and New York, Delaware has downstate and upstate political cultures. The downstate climate is influenced by the two rural southern counties, which are isolated from the major routes of eastern seaboard transportation. The southern counties are historically strong, politically. Despite reapportionment, the downstaters appear to wield more power than their 31.5 percent of the state population would suggest. They are split between the two parties, while the city tends to vote Democratic and the suburbs are mainly Republican. During the 1970s, all of the executive positions in Wilmington, New Castle County, and the state changed party hands at least once.

Delaware has been called a microcosm of the nation. It is divided into southern and northern segments that include city, suburban, and rural areas. Its political party system is strongly competitive. The metropolitan area within this microcosm has the characteristic problems of other American metropolises, including racial segregation and severe problems in urban education.

PUBLIC EDUCATION

School Governance

At first glance, Delaware education appears to be strongly directed from the top: the six-member governor-appointed State Board, which serves without pay for three years; the president of the Board, who serves at the governor's pleasure; and the superintendent of public instruction, who is selected by the State Board. Further, the state funds 70 percent of the cost of public schools.

Nevertheless, it is localism and not state control that dominates the public education system. This reinforces the divisions between city and suburban schools[5] In a recent study, Frederick M. Wirt found Delaware educational policy to be the nation's twelfth most decentralized.[6] Neither the State Board of Education nor the State Department of Public Instruction (DPI) exert any measure of control over local school districts. State DPI officials are highly deferential to local school boards and superintendents. Being composed of all local superintendents, the Advisory Council to the State Board reflects local power. I saw this power exhibited at a meeting that purportedly was called to review federal proposals in the context of general state needs and goals. When the local superintendent who represented all of the twenty-three superintendents in the state made it clear that he did not appreciate the implications of the review procedure, one DPI official responded (and I paraphrase), "Well, we'll put together a possible policy and then submit it to the local superintendents to have them approve it." In other words, local superintendents often can veto state educational policy.

There are a number of reasons for local domination. Local control has dominated public education throughout the history of the nation. In Delaware, this tendency is reinforced by the small size of the state; superintendents, school board members, and their constituents have no trouble reaching state legislators and officials to complain about state "interference" in public education.[7] State DPI officials have local school district backgrounds. The state superintendent is a former superintendent of a rural school district in Delaware; the president of the State Board was the head of the Newark Board. It is locally oriented school people who are in power at the state level. To further strengthen this orientation the legislature recently required that at least four members of the State Board of Education be former or current local school board members.

In New Castle County, DPI has often been seen as a minor annoyance. It has rarely been viewed as a help or as a strong directing force. Major changes in state educational policy (such as educational assessment and competency-based education) were often modified or watered down by local forces. DPI was seen as inadequate by large districts, who believed that they could perform sophisticated tasks on their own, and as unnecessary by smaller districts, who were unconcerned with elaborate state programs of any kind.

Part of the cause, and some of the effects, of local control were the broad diversity of local school districts and the great influence of each local superintendent on the style of the local district.[8] In nearly all of the school districts, the local superintendent dominated the decision-making process.[9] Local forces long have been successful in keeping education out of the governor's cabinet, in minimizing the influence of state education officials on their local districts, and in keeping the redistribution of funds to a minimum.

In all this, Delaware follows the national pattern. As in many other communities in the United States, the effect of such localism has been to perpetuate segregated schools. Residential patterns have determined the makeup of a community's schools. Although the suburbs of Wilmington are diverse, the basic fact remains: before the desegregation plan was implemented, the public schools of Wilmington primarily served black and poor children and the suburban school districts served white middle-income children.[10]

Suburban Schools

Delaware's most prestigious school districts are the three suburban districts on Wilmington's northern border—the Alexis I. duPont, Alfred I. duPont, and Mt. Pleasant School Districts (see Figure 2-1). Approximately 20 percent of the public school children in the county attend these public schools (Table 2-2). Most come from middle-class and upper-middle-class white families (many headed by DuPont professionals and executives); almost all are college-bound.

These suburban districts differ in character. The Mt. Pleasant district is a relatively old and well-preserved residential area with a long history of excellent public schools; Alfred I. is composed mainly of suburban developments built in the last two decades along the Concord Pike, a major road of shopping centers; Alexis I. lies in the heart of wealthy "Chateau country," sprinkled with nationally known historic sites such as the Winterthur and Hagley museums.

The Alexis I. district serves about 3,000 pupils, Mt. Pleasant about 4,500, and Alfred I. over 9,000. In 1975–1976, 1 percent of the pupils in Alfred I., 4 percent in Alexis I., and 6 percent in Mt. Pleasant were black. About 98 percent of the population of these areas is white.

Students in these three school districts outscore students in other New Castle County school districts on standardized achievement tests. Alfred I., Alexis I., and Mt. Pleasant eighth graders ranked highest on average test scores in the spring 1973 Delaware Education Assessment Program.[11]

To the west of Wilmington lie the predominantly middle-class suburbs of Marshallton-McKean, Stanton, and Newark. These districts are composed primarily of suburban developments built in the 1960s. The Newark School District has the state's largest student enrollment, serving about 20 percent of the county's students. The City of Newark, where the University of Delaware is situated, is the center of the school district, but only a third of the residents served by the district live within the city limits. Stanton (with 5,000 pupils) and

Marshallton-McKean (with 3,500 pupils) lie close to the second major suburban shopping-center road in the county, the Kirkwood Highway.

All three districts have pockets of working-class families, but each district serves predominantly middle-class students. Newark and Marshallton-McKean also have very small black communities within their boundaries, but neither had a black enrollment beyond 5 percent in 1975. With the stated purpose of solving facilities problems, Marshallton-McKean desegregated its elementary schools by using the Princeton Plan in the early 1970s. Newark's desegregation has been described in an article by Herbert Barringer.[12] Stanton had less than 1 percent black students.

Given recent research on the effects of family background on school achievement, it is not surprising to find that students in these three middle class districts score just below the three upper-middle class districts on standardized tests. In 1973 they all scored above the mean.

Table 2-2
1975–1976 Pupil Enrollments

School District	Percentage Black	Percentage White	Percentage Spanish/ Oriental	Total
Alexis I. duPont	3.9	93.8	2.3	3,258
Alfred I. duPont	1.0	97.8	1.2	10,261
Appoquinimink	27.1	72.2	.7	2,401
Claymont	4.3	94.9	.8	3,306
Conrad	3.2	95.6	.9	5,334
De La Warr	54.9	43.9	1.2	3,172
Marshallton-McKean	4.8	94.9	.3	3,713
Mt. Pleasant	2.7	96.0	1.3	4,868
New Castle–Gunning Bedford	5.9	92.9	1.2	9.016
Newark	4.3	94.2	1.5	16,923
Stanton	.7	98.1	1.2	5,237
Wilmington	84.7	9.8	4.5	13,852
Total	19.7	78.4	1.9	83,079

Source: Delaware State Department of Public Instruction, "Racial and Ethnic Report Pupil Enrollment: September 30, 1975," by Anne T. Jones, December 1975. The 1975–1976 enrollments are presented as being relatively unaffected by forces related to the desegregation case. White flight and the effects on enrollment of the voluntary transfer plans are discussed below, in Chapter 9.

About 20 percent of the public school students attend schools in the working-class districts of Claymont, New Castle–Gunning Bedford, and Conrad. The last two are located south of the city. These districts contain a mixture of industrial areas, apartment buildings and town-houses, and modest homes. Enrollment in each of these districts was less than 6 percent black in 1975–1976. The Claymont students have on the average scored above the mean on the DEAP tests; the students in the other districts score almost exactly at the average.

The De La Warr School District is the anomaly; it is a suburb with a majority of black students. In 1975–1976, 54.9 percent of the 3,172 students were black. De La Warr is next to one of the poorest areas of Wilmington and is divided by access roads to the Delaware Memorial Bridge that links Delaware to New Jersey. Major tax-exempt prop-erties within the district include these access roads, the Greater Wilm-ington airport, and the Wilmington Marine Terminal. De La Warr has suffered from racial conflict, lack of funds, and high administrative turnover. Wilmington is the only district in the county that has ranked below De La Warr on the DEAP test scores.

Finally, the Appoquinimink School District covers the rural south-ern-most part of the county. Like the school districts in Delaware's southern counties, all of Appoquinimink's schools contain 69 to 77 percent white students; that is, they had been desegregated. However, Appoquinimink served the fewest students in the county—only about 2,400 in 1975–1976.

Throughout the suburban school districts, neighborhood schools have been the rule. Those elementary students living more than a mile from their assigned schools, as well as secondary school students living more than two miles away, have been bused to school at state expense. In the small and compact Claymont School District, only about 10 percent were bused; only 15 percent of the students in Wilmington rode school buses; and in the Alexis I. district 96.6 percent of the students were bused. The 1975–1976 average of the twelve districts was 52.9 percent bused.[13]

Wilmington Schools

Wilmington is surrounded by these eleven suburban school dis-tricts. As Table 2-2 shows, during 1975–1976 in Wilmington about 85 percent of the public school children were black, 10 percent white, and 5 percent Spanish. Although a small majority (53 percent) of the total population of Wilmington is black, the white age distribution and attendance in private and parochial schools have lowered the percentage of white students in the public schools.[14] In 1975–1976 the almost 14,000 Wilmington pupils attended three high schools, four middle schools, fourteen elementary schools, and one special school for handicapped students. Nine of these twenty-two schools were almost 95 percent black, a major point brought out in the court case. The Drew, Elbert, Stubbs, Bancroft, and Howard facilities, for example, have been almost entirely black since the 1954 *Brown* decision. In 1957 two-thirds of Wilmington students were white, but by 1964 almost two-thirds were black. By 1975, the minority group enrollment was approaching 100 percent and the Wilmington schools mentioned above remained almost totally black. In the mid 1970s, in New Castle County as a whole, only about 20 percent of the students were black and 80 percent were white. The percentage of black children in the suburban areas remained small, increasing from 4 percent in 1954 to 6 percent in 1973.

The Wilmington public schools have faced educational problems like those of other cities in the nation. In March 1973, Mark Shedd, exsuperintendent of the Philadelphia public schools, with a field team from the Harvard Graduate School of Education, conducted a one-week needs assessment of the Wilmington public schools.[15] The criticisms and recommendations in their report could be made to other city school districts:

> Eighty-six percent of Wilmington's children are reading below grade level by grade three. Subsequent to grade three, gains average only four to six months per school year, resulting in growing cumulative deficits for most children. By grade six, 80 percent of the children are reading more than one year behind grade level and 60 percent read two or more years behind. By grade ten, the mean reading achievement level is 6.5 citywide and three quarters of the students are reading more than two years behind grade level. Thus, the extent of the reading problem is all-pervasive in the Wilmington schools.
>
> Reading achievement was proclaimed the first priority of the Wilmington public schools in 1970. Since then a coordinator has been instituted and an excellent comprehensive program has been drawn up. Funding of the program has not yet taken place, however, and without materials and staff the reading effort has little change of success.[16]
>
> Administrators, teachers, parents, and community residents agree that there exists a lack of parental involvement in the operations of the schools; and, more specifically, a lack of attendance on their part in the school's various parent councils and boards. Although generally supportive of the school system, community residents felt frustrated with the available lines of communications and do not feel that they are informed or included in the decision-making mechanisms in the

schools. As a result, schools tend to operate and plan in isolation from their surrounding communities.[17]

An overwhelming majority of persons interviewed, both inside and outside the system, expressed dissatisfaction with the present organizational structure of the schools.

The feeling was that there are too many administrators in the central office, that areas of responsibility are overlapping, that lines of responsibility are unclear, that central office administrators do not spend enough time in the schools, and therefore that the central office does not effectively direct or support what takes place in the schools.

Throughout the schools there was a concern that the services presently offered by the middle level central office administrators, especially the supervisors, were not being effectively delivered at the school level and were not being effectively supported at the higher levels of the central administration. Support was said to be particularly lacking in the area of curriculum development and implementation.

In the schools the feeling was that principals were overburdened with administrative and disciplinary responsibilities, that curriculum and supervision were being neglected, and that the administration of the community schools lacked coordination with the regular school principals.[18]

Like other urban school districts in the 1960s and 1970s, Wilmington had its share of political conflict. It has been under pressure from the city administration to reveal more of its financial affairs. The city government controls the tax rate for the school district through a tax commission that includes the mayor and three members of the City Council.[19] Because the city spent about a third of its budget—$9.1 million—on education in 1975, the cost-conscious city administration demanded more fiscal accountability from the school district.

Relations between the teacher union and the school district have also been marked by conflict. Before desegregation implementation, Wilmington teacher salaries were higher than salaries in suburban New Castle County, and higher even than those of many city districts throughout the nation. Affiliated with the American Federation of Teachers, the Wilmington Federation of Teachers has pressed for better wages while the city administration has fought to keep a lid on the school budget. A bitter strike in 1975 lasted twenty-seven school days. The school board (four members appointed by the governor, three by the mayor, all for four-year terms) has been caught up in interracial conflict, partly as a result of the movement for black power and control. The most publicized example occurred in February 1974, when a new black majority elected the president and vice-president of the board. One white member quit; a second declared that she was too

mission but it is little help in racial matters. It has the power to investigate complaints only on a case basis, not to act, and it must regularly fight for its life at appropriations time. There are no official human relations commissions at the city or county levels.

An example of government indifference to social problems is the nature of state aid to education. While the state provides a great deal of funds to education, the equalizing formula is unequal to the inequalities. The equalization fund contained only $3.8 million in 1973–1974, about 3 percent of the state's $121.7 million appropriations. Public housing is no more popular. The County Council's failure to support public housing efforts in the 1960s was a substantive point in the school desegregation suit.

Even the state's highest office has not always acted in a way that would further good race relations. In April 1968, fearing that racial conflict would develop in the wake of the assassination of Martin Luther King, Jr., Governor Charles L. Terry ordered the national guard into Wilmington. City residents, particularly those in black sectors, lived with the incursion of armed guardsmen, jeeps, and military paraphernalia until January 1969, when Russell Peterson took office as the new governor.

This political inertia in the face of social problems, overcome only by attempts to maintain the status quo when change threatened, reflected a widespread public attitude. Race and racial feelings were inextricably intertwined with the formal division of city and suburban areas of New Castle County, Delaware. Wilmington city lines divide the county by race and wealth. As Long observed:

> The suburb is the Northern way to insure separate and unequal. It has the advantage of being legal. If housing, education, jobs, and matrimony are to remain a charmed circle among formally equal citizens in the era of public goods, there is a powerful logic behind the existing fragmentation and the basis for considerable resistance to the creation of really general governments.[24]

This fragmentation was particularly evident in the great disparties between the school systems. State aid helped to perpetuate the differences by giving each school district approximately the same funds per pupil, regardless of need. And housing patterns insured the separation of students by race as effectively as the state constitution once had done.

THE PUBLIC'S VIEW OF NEW CASTLE COUNTY SCHOOLS
In spring 1977 and winter 1978, opinion polls showed that both city and suburban parents deplored the conditions in the city schools

(Table 2-4).[25] There was even general support for desegregation among white suburban parents. This support, however, did not translate into support for busing, and there was almost unanimous opposition to any desegregation plan that would involve the city and the suburbs.

Table 2-4
Comparative Ratings of Schools

School of Children	Wilmington Better	Suburban Better	Same	Don't Know
Wilmington Public	3%	36%	31%	30%
Suburban Public	2%	35%	18%	45%
Private/Parochial	1%	45%	16%	38%

Source: Spring 1977 poll. Question: "How would you compare the quality of education in the Wilmington public schools with that of the schools out of the city? Are the city schools better; are the suburban schools better; or are they about the same?"

The estimates of public school quality among those polled were related to their social and economic class. Four groups of school districts were established: Wilmington; four blue-collar districts (Claymont, Conrad Area, De La Warr, and New Castle–Gunning Bedford); three middle-class districts (Marshallton-McKean, Newark, and Stanton); and three affluent districts (Alexis I. duPont, Alfred I. duPont, and Mount Pleasant). As Table 2-5 shows, the more affluent the school district, the more parents rated their schools as good or excellent.

Table 2-5
School District Ratings

Type of School District	Poor	Fair	Good	Excellent	Don't Know
Wilmington	13%	38%	40%	3%	6%
Blue Collar	12%	27%	37%	16%	8%
Middle Class	5%	14%	54%	28%	0%
Affluent	2%	6%	48%	40%	4%

Source: Spring 1977 poll. Question: "We'd like to know what you think of the public schools in your school district. Are they POOR, FAIR, GOOD, or EXCELLENT?"

Opinions on Busing

In spring 1977, 93 percent of the suburban parents sampled agreed with the statement: "It is a good idea for children to attend school with children of other races." They were also virtually unanimous in their opposition to busing to achieve desegregation (Table 2-6). Ninety percent of the suburban parents interviewed opposed busing between city and suburbs to achieve school desegregation. Two-thirds were "strongly" opposed. (Of suburban non-public school parents questioned in the spring 1977 poll, over 83 percent also opposed busing. Those without children in schools, however, were only 70 percent opposed to busing.)

Table 2-6
Attitudes toward Busing

	Suburban Parents		Wilmington Parents	
	1977	1978	1977	1978
Attitude	(N = 300)	(N = 303)	(N = 317)	(N = 195)
Strongly Favor	1%	2%	8%	9%
Favor	8%	7%	31%	39%
Oppose	25%	23%	16%	32%
Strongly Oppose	65%	66%	26%	11%
Don't Know	1%	2%	19%	9%

Source: Spring 1977 poll. Question: "In general, do you favor or oppose busing both black and white children between Wilmington and suburban schools to achieve school desgregation?"

Wilmington parents were divided evenly on the busing issue. Forty-two percent favored busing, and 39 percent were opposed in 1977. In the next poll 48 percent were favorable and 43 percent opposed. But of those in favor of busing, only about 20 percent felt strongly in favor. These attitudes reflect black concerns that their children and "their" Wilmington School District would be hurt by the desegregation process.

In short, the only individuals favorable to busing were almost exclusively black residents of Wilmington, and of these, only a small percentage reported feeling strongly about their position. On the other hand, suburbanites were nearly unanimous in opposition. If the samples were weighted to reflect the true proportions of surburban and city parents in the desegregation area, then we would find only about

15 percent of the parents in the desegregation area as a whole in favor of busing and over 80 percent opposed in 1978. In fact, using this weighting procedure, only about 3 percent of the area's population would be strongly in favor of busing.

The results of similar polls conducted on a national basis indicate that support for busing was probably less in Delaware in 1977 than elsewhere in the nation. In summarizing attitudes toward busing, Gary Orfield argued that by 1972 opinion in the nation against busing had stabilized at 70 percent opposed to busing, 21 percent in favor, and 9 percent with no opinion. Opposition was no longer affected by the exact wording of the question.[26]

Perceptions of the Effects of Busing

The spring 1977 poll included a number of questions about the likely outcomes of busing. The results indicated large city-suburban disagreements (see Table 2-7).

Suburban parents did not think that desegregation would produce positive outcomes either for their children or for black children. As one respondent said, "I don't feel that the mere moving about of children is going to have any effect on the quality of education." About two-thirds of the suburban parents did not think that black children would get a better education or that racial prejudice would be reduced. One suburbanite said, "The [black] children may feel too uncomfortable to learn." Suburbanites were even more skeptical about desegregation having positive effects on white children, and worried about their child's safety and the lessening of their own influence as parents. A majority of suburbanites also saw academic harm in the future and accepted the statement that white achievement test scores would drop as a result of desegregation.

In the city, on the other hand, a small majority of city parents did think that desegregation would provide a better education for black students. Some agreed with the black parent who said, "[Busing is] the best way for race relations to improve." Other black parents wanted their children to attend suburban schools because of their better facilities. Several black parents thought that desegregation would improve the motivation of black children. However, a majority of the Wilmington respondents agreed with five of the seven negative statements.

While comparisons should be treated with caution because of differences in time and place, it is clear that at best New Castle County was no more hospitable than most other communities in the United States to a busing order. For example, while a majority of respondents

Table 2-7
Parental Views of Desegregation Outcomes

Outcome	Suburban Parents		Wilmington Parents	
	Agree	Disagree	Agree	Disagree
Positive:				
Desegregation will provide a better education for most white students	11%	85%	37%	34%
Desegregation will reduce racial prejudice	24%	72%	42%	38%
Desegregation will provide a better education for most black students	30%	67%	52%	33%
Negative:				
Desegregation will lead to an increase in discipline problems in the schools	73%	23%	52%	30%
Desegregation will risk the safety of students when on buses	79%	18%	56%	28%
Desegregation will lead to parents having less say as to how the schools are run	73%	24%	36%	29%
Desegregation will bring a drop in achievement test scores for white students	51%	40%	13%	48%
Desegregation will cause parents to have problems when a child is sick or hurt at school	73%	25%	57%	29%
Desegregation will reduce after school activities	78%	19%	54%	31%
Desegregation will cost a great deal	97%	2%	80%	8%

Source: Spring 1977 poll.

in a 1971 Gallup Poll agreed that integration would improve education for blacks, only a slim majority of Wilmington and less than a third of suburban New Castle County parents agreed.[27] New Castle County respondents were also more skeptical about the benefits of desegregation for whites. In a more recent poll, 65 percent of white respondents in a national sample agreed that desegregation would risk the safety of students.[28] In the 1977 poll in New Castle County, 79 percent of the white respondents feared this outcome.

THE BASIS OF OPPOSITION TO BUSING

Self-interest, lack of knowledge, and prejudicial racial attitudes have all been proposed as possible bases of attitudes against busing.

In a poll of 1,049 white residents of the Louisville–Jefferson County, Kentucky, area in spring 1976, McConahy and Hawley found that self-interest (as measured by variables such as the number of children in public school and whether children were to be bused to the city or not) was not related to attitudes toward busing. Instead "symbolic racism" and a belief in the existence of discrimination were highly related.[29]

Cataldo and others, studying attitudes toward busing in Florida counties in 1972–1973, found that the incidence and distance of busing did not determine whether families would enroll their children in non-public schools in order to avoid it. The critical variable was whether or not a child was to attend a school with 30 percent or more black children.[30] Racial and class prejudice were related, although only slightly, to avoidance. Avoiders tended to be those with higher social status, that is, those with the financial resources to send their children to private schools.[31]

Opinions about busing may also reflect the available information. Orfield found that knowledge about busing among parents was positively related to favorable feelings toward busing in a 1972 poll.[32]

For those trying to design desegregation plans and to prepare the public to accept them, the basis of attitudes about desegregation is very important. If attitudes are based on self-interest, compromises among the collective interests may increase acceptance. If attitudes are based upon a lack of knowledge, an information campaign may help. If attitudes are based upon racial prejudice, however, the alternatives are more limited. Emotionally based attitudes are harder to change. Below I examine the relationship of knowledge, self-interest, and racial feelings to attitudes toward busing. Since almost all suburbanites opposed busing, I supplemented their answers to pro-con busing questions (see Table 2-6) with their responses to questions about their antibusing activities and feelings about obeying the plan.[33]

Knowledge and Self-Interest

In the 1977 and 1978 polls, respondents were asked ten desegregation information questions.[34] Both polls indicated a low level of public knowledge, especially among Wilmington parents. For example, only half the suburban parents could answer half the true-false questions correctly in both polls, the same as if they had answered at random. In the 1977 poll, a majority of Wilmington parents responded "Don't know" to each question.

Not surprisingly, educational background, presumably a measure of people's ability and inclination to use and understand the mass media and other communication forms, is related to information level. In the total sample, the percentage answering more than half the questions correctly begins at 10 percent for those lacking a high school diploma and increases to 71 percent for those with graduate degrees (Table 2-8). Any analysis of the correlates of information level thus must take into account educational level.

Table 2-8
Parent Desegregation Knowledge
by Educational Level

Educational Level	Percentage High in Desegregation Knowledge
Under High School (258)	10%
High School Graduates (311)	25%
Some College (168)	43%
College Graduates (93)	66%
Post-graduates (56)	71%
	$\gamma = .56$

Source: Spring 1977 poll.

It was found that Wilmington parents, who were primarily black, had a much lower level of information than suburban parents, who were primarily white. This difference relates almost entirely to levels of education.[35] (It should be noted that race, level of education, and being in the Wilmington School District are highly interrelated and thus the relation of each of these factors to information level cannot be separated.) Similarly, in the suburbs, parents in the blue-collar school districts were least informed, those in middle-class districts next, and those in the affluent districts were the most informed.

Parents were least knowledgeable about the costs of busing. In both polls, fewer realized how little the added cost of transportation would be. In 1978, about half the suburban parents did not reject an exaggeration about the extent to which property taxes would be raised (tripled) because of busing. In both polls, a substantial number were aware of the details of the student assignment plans being discussed—with one major exception: in both polls, only a minority of suburbanites correctly rejected the assertion that after desegregation some white students would be in majority black schools. Research has suggested that the percentage of black students in a school is important in white parent decisions about whether to flee to or to leave their children in newly desegregated schools (see Chapter 8). Thus many suburbanites exaggerated the costs of busing and the degree to which their children would be in the minority in desegregated schools. In these areas, at least, parents overestimated the degree to which their self-interest would be threatened by busing.[36]

Racial Attitudes

Few of the white respondents exhibited overt racism. Almost all (84 percent) agreed that it was a good idea to have people of different races going to school together and living in the same neighborhoods. In fact, two-thirds said they would like to live in an integrated neighborhood. These statements, however, masked feelings of racial unease.

A majority of white parents rejected the contention that blacks are being discriminated against. More than half of the white parents surveyed agreed that "the amount of prejudice against minority groups in this country is highly exaggerated" (Table 2-9). Most white parents said only "few" or "no" (as opposed to "many" or "some") blacks in New Castle County miss out on job and housing opportunities because of discrimination. Almost two-thirds of the whites (62 percent) said that the government has been paying too much attention recently to blacks and minorities.

There are thus a number of whites who are not openly prejudiced but who are not sympathetic to the status of blacks in the local community or nation. Not surprisingly, blacks are much more likely to perceive discrimination and to disagree that they have received "too much attention" from government.

When these variables are considered simultaneously for whites in a multiple regression analysis, an index combining these more subtle racial attitudes is the largest single basis of busing opposition.[37] Self-interest, that is, whether the respondent has children in public school, is also related, but to a lesser degree. The extent to which racial attitudes are related to opposition to busing among whites suggests a difficult time for those who must implement desegregation.

Among blacks, only information level is statistically related to busing attitudes; those with more information are more likely to favor busing.

PUBLIC COMPLIANCE

For those concerned with implementing a court order, antibusing attitudes must be translated into feelings about compliance with the law on both a collective and individual level. The belief of many suburbanites that public action and public officials could stop busing resulted from misunderstandings about the constitutional basis of the busing order and what actions could stop busing, given our system of government.

In January 1975, I was one of several supposed experts facing some 800 irate citizens at a public meeting. Our task was to inform the people of the status of the case and the likely outcomes (see Chapter 6). It was one of the first times that the reopening of the *Evans* v. *Buchanan* case was discussed in public. As the panel tried to answer the questions, frustration on both sides increased. Finally, one of my fellow panel members realized the nature of our communications problem, and he began, "In the United States we have three branches of government, the executive, legislative, and judicial. . . ."

Two years later, in the spring 1977 poll, after many attempts to educate the public, a majority of suburbanites (60 percent) agreed with the statement, "If enough people show they are against it, busing can be stopped." The 1978 poll expanded upon this question. While few suburbanites (under 15 percent) thought that busing could be stopped if many people left the public schools, if many protest rallies were held, or if violence occurred during implementation, 39 percent agreed that "busing would stop if the Delaware General Assembly passed laws against busing" and 79 percent agreed that the "busing would stop if the U.S. Congress passed a law against court-ordered busing." In the 1978 poll only 37 percent of suburbanites (compared with 60 percent in 1977) thought that busing would stop if enough people showed they were against it. It is therefore likely that the percentage believing that local legislators or an act of Congress could stop busing had also declined since the beginning of the desegregation process.

Nevertheless, a large percentage of suburbanites clearly believed throughout the controversy that the actions of local and federal representatives could and should stop busing. In the winter 1978 poll, 46 percent of suburban parents, virtually all of whom then believed busing to be inevitable, preferred that public officials "resist" (46

Table 2-9
Racial Attitudes

Question	Agree	
	Whites	Blacks
The amount of prejudice against minority groups in this country is highly exaggerated.	56%	34%
Over the past few years, the government has paid too much attention to blacks and other minorities.	63%	13%
Do you think that in Wilmington or New Castle County MANY, SOME, only a FEW, or NO blacks miss out on jobs and promotions because of racial discrimination.	48%*	66%*
Do you think that in Wilmington or New Castle County MANY, SOME, only a FEW, or NO blacks miss out on good housing because white owners won't rent or sell to them.	46%*	63%*

*Agree = Many and Some.
Source: Spring 1977 poll.

percent) rather than "accept" (6 percent) or "work for" (40 percent) desegregation. (The people who felt that busing was inevitable but that it could be stopped if enough people showed their opposition evidently did not believe that "enough" people would show their opposition.) Eighty percent of suburbanites favored a constitutional amendmend to stop busing.

Not surprisingly, a large percentage of suburbanites expressed their willingness to pressure public officials to oppose busing. In the 1978 poll, for example, about three-quarters (72 percent) of those suburbanites against busing said they would work for a constitutional amendment to stop busing, over half (58 percent) said they would be willing to go to an antibusing meeting, and half reported that they would be willing to vote for a candidate whose main goal was to stop busing. The significance of these figures is not in the exact percentages but rather in the public's belief that political action could change the situation and its expressed willingness to take such action.

In the blue-collar school districts, a majority of respondents did not believe that the order should be obeyed in 1977 and a majority thought public officials should resist in 1978 (Table 2-10).

Table 2-10
Compliance Attitudes by School District

Type of School District	Percentage of Parents Saying Order Should Be Obeyed (spring 1977)	Percentage of Parents Saying Officials Should Resist (winter 1978)
Affluent (Alexis I, Alfred I, Mt. Pleasant)	73% (56)	49% (74)
Middle-class (Newark, Stanton, Marshallton-McKean	71% (118)	47% (151)
Blue-collar (New Castle–Gunning Bedford, Conrad, Claymont)	49% (91)	59% (101)
Black (Wilmington, De La Warr)	71% (312)	21% (192)

Source: Spring 1977 and winter 1978 polls.

Individual Compliance

A large proportion of parents reported that they not only wanted the order to be resisted but also planned to avoid its effects on an individual basis if possible. Suburban parents were asked if they would send their child to his or her current school if (1) it was desegregated but their child was not reassigned and (2) if the child was reassigned. Eighty-eight percent of the suburban parents reported that they would obey the court order by sending their child to his or her current school if no reassignment were involved. Only slightly over half were as agreeable in the second situation. As Table 2-11 indicates, a significant percentage of suburban parents reported that they would seek to avoid the busing of their child. Explained one, "I feel if we have the better system in the suburbs, we have an obligation to share our facilities but shouldn't send our children to a poor system. Black children should be bused to better schools; whites shouldn't be bused to worse schools." Thus, if their child were to be bused, 26 percent of suburban parents said they would send him or her to an existing private or parochial school.[38]

SUMMARY

The climate of opinion in the Wilmington metropolitan area created a dilemma for public officials faced with implementing the court's orders. Few strong advocates of busing were evident, even in the City of Wilmington. Opposition in the suburbs was almost unanimous,

Table 2-11
Suburban Parents' Reactions to
Two Desegregation Plan Conditions

	Child Not Bused				Child Bused			
Reaction	Yes	No	Maybe	NA*	Yes	No	Maybe	NA*
Send child to current school	88%	6%	6%		51%	29%	20%	
Keep child out of school to see what happens	5%	3%	4%	88%	21%	15%	13%	51%
Send child to a *new* private/parochial school set up to avoid busing	6%	4%	2%	88%	26%	12%	11%	51%
Send child to an *existing* private/parochial school	7%	2%	3%	88%	28%	12%	9%	51%
Move outside the desegregation area	3%	7%	2%	88%	12%	26%	11%	51%

*Those parents who said they would send their child to his/her current school (answering "yes" to the first option in this series) were not asked the succeeding options. Thus, the percent "yes" on the first option corresponds to the percent "not asked" in the following options.

Source: Winter 1978 poll.

feelings were strong, and predictions of dire consequences were predominant. A near majority in the suburban population thought that public officials could and should actively resist busing. In blue-collar areas, especially, feelings that the order should not be obeyed were very prevalent.

Suburban attitudes, however, did not rest on a firm base of knowledge or self-interest. Many suburbanites misunderstood the monetary costs of desegregation and the probability of their children becoming a minority in black majority schools. Feeling against busing seemed based on general attitudes about blacks and society. In the city, to the extent it could be explained, opposition to busing seemed to reflect information level. Those black parents least knowledgeable about desegregation were most opposed to busing.

This atmosphere strongly discouraged public and school official from advocating compliance with any federal court orders and hampered agreement among various constituencies on a particular desegregation plan. Busing was more than an issue on which people had differing views. In New Castle County, as in Louisville–Jefferson County, busing was a symbol. As McConahay and Hawley concluded there, "the debate is really over whose values will dominate public life and whose group will receive the concomitant public respect."[39]

3 / The Courts

As the percentage of black and minority students has increased in central cities and the flow of whites to the adjacent suburbs has continued, many policies to foster metropolitan desegregation have been considered.[1] However, the number of metropolitan areas undergoing school desegregation in any form is limited. A few have voluntary city-suburban plans (for example, METCO in Boston). A few have been ordered by the court to desegregate within a single school district (for example, Charlotte-Mecklenburg, N.C.; Louisville–Jefferson County, Ky.; Tampa–Hillsborough County, Fla.). Some are being encouraged to adopt some form of metropolitan desegregation by state officials (Illinois) or state law (Wisconsin). Only one metropolitan area, has been ordered to undergo city-suburban school district reorganization and school desegregation.[2] The Wilmington metropolitan area so far stands alone.

It is not yet clear whether the Wilmington situation is the first of many metropolitan court-ordered school desegregation situations or the last of the "busing" decisions.[3] Some civil rights lawyers argue that more busing is likely, since even under tighter U.S. Supreme Court rulings on desegregation, most communities could be shown to have had de jure school segregation.[4] Others argue that if the Supreme Court does not close the door on busing, Congress will. An analysis of the Wilmington situation may contribute to this discussion. Why did the court order the Wilmington metropolitan area and not others to reorganize and desegregate?

SEGREGATION IN DELAWARE

The origins of the metropolitan desegregation remedy that faced Delaware in the 1970s were in the historic *Brown* v. *Board of Educa-*

39

tion decisions of the 1950s.[5] The metropolitan remedy was ordered when the courts determined that despite *Brown*, the dual education system in Delaware had never been dismantled, state action having perpetuated separate school for blacks and whites in New Castle County. Knowing something of the history of race relations and schools in Delaware will help the reader to understand the court's decision.

Early History: Jim Crow

In *Simple Justice*, Richard Kluger wrote, "In spirit if not in law, Delaware was a Southern state, though it took the Union's side in the Civil War."[6] Only a small part of the state lies north of the Mason-Dixon line; Kent and Sussex Counties, once slaveholding territory, wielded major influence in the years before industrialization and reapportionment. It is not surprising that the Delaware Constitution, enacted in 1897, a year after the *Plessy* v. *Ferguson* Supreme Court decision perpetuated segregation, called for separate Negro and white school systems. In fact, in 1919 it was required that Moors and Indians also intended distinct schools.

In 1920, the quality of education for Negroes in Delaware was dismal. Negro schools were underfinanced because Negro property taxes amounted to very little. Whites could attend schools for twice as many months a year. Pierre S. duPont contributed $2.6 million for the construction of eighty-seven schoolhouses for Negroes, to be built between 1920 and 1930, but his gesture did not alter the picture to any great extent. The quality of Negro education remained abysmal as Delaware approached the decades of the Warren Court.

"Even the most liberal community in Delaware—Wilmington— remained a Jim Crow town in 1950," observes Kluger:

> All the public schools were segregated, not just the grammar schools. There were no black nurses in the white hospitals, and not nearly enough hospital beds were available to Negroes, who made up 14 percent of the state's population. There were no black clerks in the banks or retail stores. Restaurants and movie theaters and hotels in downtown Wilmington were strictly segregated, and no black man served in the Delaware National Guard. The state college for colored people at Dover was not nationally accredited, and nothing approaching equal protection of the laws was practiced in any walk of life throughout the state, which functioned as a fossilized racist encampment on the traditionally white-supremacist Eastern Shore Peninsula.[7]

Robert J. Taggart adds to the bleak picture:

> Despite the massive gains of the black schools, there were still two
> racially-separated systems of education in Delaware by 1950. In that
> year, there were over 50 black school districts, overwhelmingly one-
> room affairs. By 1950, a black could receive a twelfth grade education
> only at Wilmington's Howard High School and Dover's Delaware State
> College preparatory department. There was no four-year secondary
> school in Sussex County until 1952, when William Jason High School
> opened. As late as 1953, the state provided no funds for black transpor-
> tation, and blacks were not allowed to share white buses under any
> conditions.[8]

Delaware Joins the Landmark Brown Case

Despite the state's southern heritage, the Delaware Court of Chan-
cery was the scene of a number of landmark decisions.[9]

For example, Vice-Chancellor Collins Seitz ruled in 1950 that the
education of Negroes at Delaware State College was inferior to that of
whites at the University of Delaware. He ordered the admission of a
Negro plaintiff to the university, and "the University of Delaware
became the first southern coeducational institution of higher learning
to be integrated at the undergraduate level."[10]

As chancellor, Seitz continued to support Negro claims for equal
educational treatment.

> At the secondary level, *Belton* v. *Gebhart* concerned seven Howard
> High School students who lived in Claymont and believed that the
> Howard-Carter Vocational complex was so inferior to Claymont High
> School that they should be allowed to enter the much closer white
> Claymont school.
>
> The *Bulah* v. *Gebhart* case challenged segregation in elementary
> education in Hockessin. Originally, Mrs. Bulah wanted her daughter
> simply to gain a ride on the white-only school bus that drove nearby the
> black school. The bus driver refused, with the sanction of state law.
> Mrs. Bulah then sued the State Board of Education to have her daughter
> accepted into the white school on the grounds that the black school was
> notably inferior.
>
> After personally visiting the Hockessin, Claymont, and Wilmington
> schools, Chancellor Seitz agreed with Mrs. Bulah and the Claymont
> plaintiffs that the black facilities were clearly inferior to facilities
> available to whites. In both cases, the lack of state-financed pupil
> transportation for blacks was crucial. The Delaware Supreme Court
> upheld both cases with modifications and the state appealed them to

the U.S. Supreme Court. The Delaware cases were joined by cases from Kansas, Virginia, South Carolina, and the District of Columbia to form the famous *Brown* v. *Board of Education* of Topeka case of 1954 that destroyed *de jure* segregation supported by the U.S. Constitution.[11]

Delaware Desegregation: First Try

The desegregation process in Delaware in the late 1950s and early 1960s appears to have had all the trappings of current experiences with busing: success and failure, resistance and compliance, white flight and acceptance. The process varied tremendously across the communities in the state.

The City of Wilmington integrated smoothly and rapidly. According to historian Robert J. Taggart, "Wilmington was one of the first cities in the nation to plan for desegregation and to implement it."[12] By September 1956, all grades in the city were officially desegregated, but several schools remained racially identifiable.

In the university's home site, Newark, "integration has been relatively smooth and problem free . . . [due] to the small number of Negro students, penetration of the community by urban residents, and the growing autonomy of the local school districts."[13]

Southern Delaware experienced major resistance and conflict. Public opinion was decidedly "Southern." In a straw poll Kent and Sussex County residents were asked if they would accept black children into white schools; 68 voted yes; 5,605 voted no.[14] Southern towns joined forces to fight integration through the courts, and it took the 1964 Civil Rights Act to force the last fourteen districts to admit black students by 1967. It should be noted that this did make Delaware the first southern state to comply fully with the elimination of the dual system.

Delaware scored another first in Milford, located on the Kent and Sussex County line.

> Eleven black students asked to be admitted to Milford High school in September 1954. The school board, after consulting with a lawyer, let them into the previously white school. After ten quiet days, however, there was a large anti-integration citizens' rally held, and opposition became so intense with a successful white boycott of the schools that the Milford Board of Education was forced to ask for a ruling from the State Board of Education. The State Board declined to support the local board on the technically legal ground that the local board had failed to submit an integration plan prior to implementation. The Supreme Court validated the State Board position in November of 1964. For several days, the State Board ran the poorly attended Milford schools until a new board could be mustered to serve. The second board, reacting to overwhelming public pressure organized by a non-

Delaware racist crusader, Bryant Bowles and his White Peoples Party (NAAWP), quickly agreed to resegregate Milford High School and to send the black secondary students to a black Georgetown school. Milford was therefore the first example in the South of organized resistance to the *Brown* decision.[15]

Albert H. Young, the state attorney general at that time, has described some of the strategy of the antidesegregation leaders during this period:

> The meetings of the NAAWP were designed to incite anti-Negro feelings among citizens of the community, to advocate violation of the State school attendance laws in order to perpetuate segregation. The President of one of the local school districts closed the school in sympathetic boycott and permitted meetings to be held on his property. Crowds milled around the school. Some people took names of children who attended the school. Parents were threatened and intimidated. Merchants were asked or told where they stood.
>
> At public demonstrations, Bryant W. Bowles said: "As long as there is breath in my body and gunpowder to burn, my daughter will never go to school with a Negro."
>
> Charles West, a Vice President of the local chapter stated: "I don't want bloodshed. But if it comes to that I am all for it. The fire has not yet begun to burn. I believed God intended for us to have bloodshed before we see our race jumbled."
>
> The Chaplain of the organization, the so-called Reverend Manean Warrington announced: "You can destroy a school building easier than you can allow your own race to be destroyed. I personally will fight this thing through the entire State if it costs my life."
>
> A petition was presented to the local school board requesting it to rescind its action in admitting the 11 black children to the Milford High School. The members of the school board resigned and a new school board assumed office.[16]

According to Young, this incident, "as notorious as the Little Rock Affair," led the Delaware Supreme Court to "knuckle under to the threat of violence by a small segment of a local community headed by an outside instigator."[17]

The desegregation process went more smoothly upstate in the City of Wilmington.

Evans v. Buchanan

The Wilmington School Board in the period 1954–1957, following the *Brown* decision and acting under authority of the State Board, established a desegregation plan that created "racially neutral" geographic attendance areas. The Wilmington Board, however, continued to follow a free transfer policy by which students in a given attendance area could transfer to another school if space were available. Since many residential areas in Wilmington were differentiated by race, and particularly since there was a general white movement to the suburbs, the effect was that most city schools that were predominantly black before *Brown* remained so after three years of the initial desegregation plan.

In 1956, Mrs. Brenda Evans, a black parent who lived in the downstate Clayton School District, filed suit in the federal District Court charging that the Clayton district was not admitting students in a racially nondiscriminatory manner and that the district had not submitted a desegregation plan to the State Board of Education. This suit was filed naming the State Board of Education as defendants, for it was their responsibility to develop an effective desegregation plan in light of the *Brown* decision. Since Madelyn Buchanan was president of the State Board at that time, the lawsuit eventually became known as *Evans v. Buchanan.*[18]

In 1957 the federal District Court found that the State Board had made very little effort to provide nondiscriminatory school systems. The court enjoined all local school districts from refusing to enroll black students and ordered the State Board to develop a comprehensive plan for the desegregation of all public school districts for the fall 1957 term. This decision was subsequently affirmed by the U.S. Third Circuit Court of Appeals in 1958.

The plan submitted by the State Board called for desegregation on a grade-by-grade basis over a span of twelve years. This plan was rejected, and the board was required to develop a revised plan which would desegregate all grade levels of the public schools with the opening of schools in the fall 1961 term.

The modified plan eventually approved by the District Court included two stages. In the short run, any black student desiring admission to a white or integrated school would be allowed to transfer through normal administrative procedures. Looking to the future, the court instructed the State Board to plan for completely integrated, unitary school systems that would eliminate separate black school districts. The State Board was required to recommend to the General Assembly a new school code that would eliminate categorizations and enrollments in public schools based on race. Legislation was proposed but was not enacted by the General Assembly.

Resorting to administrative and agency prerogatives in the period 1965–1967, the State Board proceeded with a plan that closed many small school districts. This eliminated de jure segregated school districts, principally in rural Kent and Sussex Counties.

Reopening *Evans* v. *Buchanan*

In the summer of 1971, *Evans* was reopened in the U.S. district Court by five black parents who had children in the Wilmington public schools. These parents had been helped by the local ACLU and white liberals in Wilmington; the local NAACP did not support the suit at this time because it feared that blacks would bear the brunt of desegregation and would lose newly won power (reflecting the black clientele) in the city school district.[19] As noted previously, by the early 1970s the public school enrollments in Wilmington were about 70 percent black; many schools that were solely or predominantly black before *Brown* remained so over fifteen years later. Almost all suburban districts continued to be over 90 percent white in their public school enrollments. This court battle was to last another decade.

Throughout the litigation over the extent and nature of the constitutional violation, the basic arguments of the plaintiffs and defendants remained constant.

The plaintiffs argued that Delaware schools had been segregated by law and many schools in Wilmington had never been desegregated. They also contended that, because of this, the state still had the legal obligation to dismantle the vestiges of the dual system. This required the desegregation of the Wilmington schools through whatever means necessary. Because both state and county governments were responsible for perpetuating segregation in Wilmington schools, the remedy could include schools within their broader jurisdictions and did not have to be limited to the city.

The defendants claimed that the dual system had been dismantled and that the burden was on the plaintiffs to prove that any subsequent county or state actions were purposely intended to segregate. Furthermore, where segregation existed, the defendants argued that it was not because of state action but rather of choices made by individuals.

These legal arguments were not new. The plaintiffs were arguing that the schools were still segregated by law. The nature of some of the laws had changed, but if they no longer had an obvious racial nature, they still had an obvious racial impact. The defendants were arguing that segregation was by happenstance—de facto not de jure—and that state action was not the cause of racial segregation. While the arguments were familiar, some of their historical context was unique.

The 1968 Educational Advancement Act

When the case was reopened in 1971, the plaintiffs argued that in 1968 the General Assembly and State Board of Education knew or should have known that Wilmington and suburban school districts constituted a racially discriminatory dual public school system in violation of the U.S. constitution. The plaintiffs also maintained that state officials knew "there were reasonably available other methods of school district organization" that would not have segregated Wilmington.[20] The plaintiffs argued that despite the 1954 *Brown* decision requiring Delaware to dismantle its racially separate school districts, many Wilmington schools remained "black" or racially identifiable.

The plaintiffs' arguments were analogous to those made in single-district segregation cases, in which the school authority gerrymandered attendance boundaries, built schools to maintain or increase racial segregation, and adopted policies that left black schools black and white schools white. Thus Howard High School was serving only black children up to 1956 and never served more than 6 percent white students. But the plaintiffs also argued that "in suburban Wilmington the formerly all white schools remain identifiably white by any relevant measure."[21]

The plaintiffs claimed that the 1968 Educational Advancement Act "was designed to perpetuate and has in fact perpetuated the racially discriminatory dual public school system then and now existing in New Castle County."[22] In this act, the State Legislature gave the State Board of Education the authority to reorganize and consolidate school districts in Delaware for a period of a year. To state education officials, this act was part of the national movement toward improving the effectiveness and efficiency of local school districts, especially in rural areas, by making them large enough to support adequate educational programs. As a result of this act, the number of districts was reduced from 49 to 26, continuing the policy of consolidation begun in 1919, when there were 450 school districts in Delaware.

The plaintiffs also argued that the 1968 act was racially motivated. Two provisions in the act excluded Wilmington from the purview of the State Board. The act stated that the boundaries of the Wilmington schools must be coterminous with the boundaries of the City of Wilmington.[23] These lines had been coterminous since 1905. Furthermore the act limited the maximum size of any reorganized districts to 12,000 pupils. Only the Newark and Wilmington districts had an excess of 12,000 students when the act was passed. The plaintiffs claimed that the act was drawn in part to lock black children into the Wilmington city lines and schools. (At that time, in 1971, 72 percent of Wilmington's students were black.) The plaintiffs quoted a memo from the state superintendent of schools advising the State Board that the pupil limit "was inserted to avoid consolidating other districts with Wilmington."[24] The plaintiffs argued that these limiting provisions were the price that had to be paid for the support of suburban legislators in the Wilmington metropolitan area.

The plaintiffs contended that the act perpetuated the dual system not only despite the state's obligation to dismantle it under *Brown* and subsequent court orders but also despite a number of outside consultants' reports which suggested that the educational problems in Wilmington might be somewhat alleviated through a wedge or pie-shaped reorganization.

The defendant State Board argued that the actions and effects described by the plaintiffs were neither racially based nor the result of state action.[25] They claimed that blacks had not opposed the Educational Advancement Act in 1968. The exclusion of Wilmington from any future consolidation was based on historical fact (such as the city's boundaries having been drawn in 1919), and on principles of educational administration (that 12,000 was the upper limit for efficient school district size). Consequently, according to the defendants, the act was the result of nonracial considerations. The District Court, however, disagreed.

U.S. District Court Ruling

The members of the three-judge panel agreed that the Wilmington schools were segregated, in their July 12, 1974 decision on the reopening of the *Evans* v. *Buchanan* case.[26] The majority clearly delineated the facts:

> Despite the fact that the Wilmington Board adopted racially neutral geographic attendance zones, Wilmington continued to have many racially identifiable schools. Under the desegregation plan adopted by the Wilmington Board, all of the pre-*Brown* colored schools that remain open continued to operate as virtually all-black schools. . . . In the period from 1956 to 1973, no de jure black school had an enrollment of less than 91 percent in any year. . . . The presence of these schools is a clear indication that segregated schooling in Wilmington has never been eliminated and that there still exists a dual school system. . . . The desegregation plan for Wilmington has not been effective, and this Court must conclude that a unitary school system has never been established.[27]

The majority declined to select or specify a remedy at this point. They failed to decide whether an intra- or interdistrict plan was necessary, and also whether the 1968 Educational Advancement Act was unconstitutional, which had been a major contention of the plaintiffs. The court reaffirmed the State Board's responsibility to desegregate and ordered the Board to submit a Wilmington-only *and* a metropolitan-inclusive plan. However, the court left unsettled the key question facing most of the public: Would they order an interdistrict busing plan?

Judge John Gibbons, the dissenting judge on the panel (a U.S. Curcuit Court judge from New Jersey), argued that the 1968 Educational Advancement Act was unconstitutional and that the only possible remedy was a metropolitan remedy.

He declared that "states like Delaware have the affirmative duty to establish a unitary school system in which all vestiges of the formally legally required racial segregation have been eliminated, root and branch." Gibbons cited Justice Burger: "the measure of any desegregation plan is its effectiveness." Furthermore he contended that "restrictions imposed by state law were 'unconstitutional' to the extent that they interfere with the achievement of fully effective desegregation of formerly dual systems." Gibbons hung his hat and his opinion on his interpretation of the City of Emporia case, concluding that "the presence or absence of a benign legislative motive is not relevant to our inquiry." What is significant is the effect, not the motive, of the act alleviating de jure segregation. Gibbons decided that "the State Board of Education which had the affirmative obligation of carrying out the mandate of Brown II [that is, the remedy] was effectively prevented from doing so" by the act, and the act was therefore unconstitutional.[28]

Given the small percentage of white students remaining in Wilmington schools and the white majority in suburban schools, Gibbons concluded that the only practical remedy for segregation in Wilmington was an interdistrict plan, and that such a plan was appropriate given the role of the state in perpetuating the dual system. A few days later, however, the U.S. Supreme Court handed down the Milliken decision.[29] Was the door to a metropolitan plan now closed?

Evans v. Buchanan and Milliken v. Bradley

The U.S. Supreme Court's decision on July 25, 1974, in Milliken v. Bradley limited the conditions under which it would permit an interdistrict school desegregation remedy. Residents of suburban New Castle County breathed a sigh of relief. The U.S. District Court vacated its order for plans to be developed and invited the suburban districts to enter the case. (The Wilmington school district had entered the case as an intervening plaintiff in August 1972.) On January 15, 1975, the District Court called on the plaintiffs and the defendants to submit written and oral arguments concerning the applicability of the Detroit or Milliken case to Delaware. As expected, the suburban districts entered the case as intervening defendants and argued, with the previous defendants, that the Milliken case controlled the question of remedy in the Wilmington case. Specifically, they cited the Supreme Court's statements that "the scope of the remedy is determined by the nature and extent of the constitutional violation" and "before the boundaries of separate and autonomous school districts may be set aside by consolidating the separate units for remedial purposes or by imposing a cross-district remedy, it must first be shown that there has been a constitutional violation within one district that produces a significant effect in another district. Specifically, it must be shown that racially discriminatory acts of the state or local school districts, or of a single school district, have been a substantial cause of interdistrict segregation."[30] Since the plaintiffs had not argued that any suburban district had been guilty of unconstitutional acts, the defendants argued that no interdistrict remedy could be considered.

The plaintiffs sought to distinguish the Wilmington case from the Detroit case. The U.S. District Court accepted this contention in their decision of March 27, 1975.[31]

The court's interpretation of the Milliken decision was that "in light of the Milliken holding [this court] is authorized to consider desegregation relief embracing more than the Wilmington district only upon findings either that school districts in New Castle County are not meaningfully separate and autonomous, or that there have been racially discriminatory acts of the state or of local school districts causing inter-district segregation."[32]

The court began by noting the non-school discriminatory action of the state: "To a significant extent these demographic changes, i.e., the net migration of white population and increase of city black population in the last two decades, resulted not exclusively from individual residence choice and economics, but also from assistance, encouragement, and authorization of governmental policies."[33] The court cited the 1936 Federal Housing Administration mortgage underwriting manual, a history of racial discrimination in the housing market, racially restrictive covenants, the Delaware Real Estate Commission's reprint of the National Association's Code of Ethics (which called for maintaining neighborhood homogeneity), and public housing policies in New Castle County. The court also cited the familiar litany of school board policies, in this case enacted by the Wilmington School Board, which led to the fostering of school segregation.

Significantly, the court also noted two education-related acts of the state that increased school segregation. Delaware's General Assembly had enacted legislation in 1968 subsidizing the transportation of pupils enrolled in nonpublic, nonprofit elementary and secondary schools. This statute limited the subsidy to intradistrict transportation, but, according to the court, the State Board allowed the funding of interdistrict busing. After the attorney general issued an opinion condemning the violation of the statute, a revised statute, allowing interdistrict transportation, was passed by the General Assembly. Thus, the court noted, "the present total expenditure for nonpublic school student transportation is presently 7–800,000 dollars per year."[34] The effect of this subsidy was to help many white children in Wilmington to attend private or parochial school in the suburbs.

The court accepted the plaintiffs' argument that the 1968 Educational Advancement Act was unconstitutional. Judge Wright, writing the opinion for the majority (Gibbons and Wright), concluded that there was no racial motive behind the act, but, like Gibbons, he argued that the state had an obligation to consider the racial implications of the act. The majority was not convinced that keeping the Wilmington school district lines coterminous with the city lines was a compelling justification, for the lines were "historically permeable." For example, special students had been crossing city lines for years. The majority dismissed the defendant's contention that educational considerations of district size were a compelling justification for excluding Wilmington from reorganization under the act. After citing a number of those who testified at the hearings, the court's majority stated, "in short, there is substantial disagreement among professional educators as to the desirable maximum size for school districts."[35]

The court, therefore, concluded, "by the variety of federal, state, local conduct . . . , governmental authorities have elected to place their 'power, property, and prestige' behind the white exodus from Wilmington and the widespread housing discrimination patterns in New Castle County." Segregation *was* the result of government action spanning the city and suburbs.

The court also concluded that Wilmington and the suburban districts were not meaningfully "separate and autonomous." It recognized that since the 1950s the city and suburban districts had operated independently of each other, but it also noted that before *Brown*, *de jure* segregation was a "cooperative venture involving both city and suburbs."[36] This left the door open for an interdistrict desegregation order.

The state appealed the decision to the U.S. Supreme Court. Both sides hired appellate lawyers from among the nation's best-known legal names. To argue their case locally, the State Board defendants had called upon William Prickett, then president of Delaware's Bar Association. For the appeals, however, constitutional scholar Philip Kurland of the University of Chicago served as a consultant and the primary lawyer. The attorney representing the Wilmington School District plaintiffs was Louis Lucas of Memphis. He had been chosen as lead lawyer for his recognized leadership in the field of school desegregation law, including the Detroit and Louisville cases.

On November 27, 1975, the U.S. Supreme Court announced that "the judgment is affirmed."[37] On January 15, 1976, the Supreme Court denied the state's request for a rehearing.[38] Although subsequent appeals reargued the question of violation, no changes were made in the basic finding that a constitutional violation had occurred.

Thus the District Court, with the silent approbation of higher courts, accepted the plaintiffs' argument: local and state decisionmakers had continued to make decisions that had had a racial impact on school enrollments in New Castle County, thus unconstitutionally perpetuating school segregation in Wilmington. While the court did not find that the 1968 Educational Advancement Act was racially motivated, the court did conclude that its racial effects were substantial and significant, given Delaware's continuing obligation as a de jure state to desegregate its schools. The most significant conclusion of the court was that the remedy did not have to be limited to the city of Wilmington, for in its judgment the state government had played a significant role in hindering school desegregation.[39] A metropolitan remedy was thus left open as a possibility although the national significance of this case was unclear.

National Significance of Wilmington

The Evans v. Buchanan case has offered hope to those who feared that the Milliken decision had closed the door on metropolitan remedies. The U.S. Supreme Court let stand the decision of the three-judge panel to entertain metropolitan, as well as single-district, desegregation plans. The Delaware plaintiffs had satisfied the federal courts that an interdistrict violation had occurred by citing in part federal, state, and county government actions of national scope, such as the placement of public housing and the use of the 1936 federal underwriting manual.

Yet this hope for future metropolitan solutions to segregation must be tempered by the realization that the Wilmington case was based upon unique circumstances. The plaintiffs could not prove that the Educational Advancement Act was racially inspired, but, given all the court decisions to date, it appears they did not have to. Delaware's record of de jure segregation required only a finding of racial impact. Only the southern states have had a similar history. Furthermore, it is not known how many states have passed legislation, like the act and the transportation funding bill, that adversely affected the prospects for desegregation. Of course, those seeking court orders leading to metropolitan desegregation can challenge the constitutionality of other types of state governmental action.

The significance of the *Evans* v. *Buchanan* case is also unclear because the majority of the U.S. Supreme Court failed to write a substantive opinion. The majority at one point affirmed the decision, disclaimed jurisdiction at another, and denied certiorari at a third, but only a minority wrote an opinion.[40]

Thus it is not surprising that in Orfield's book advocating metropolitan desegregation he calls the Delaware case a "most important case" at one point and "not of decisive importance" at another.[41] The Court's allowing an interdistrict, metropolitan plan to be considered supports Orfield's first conclusiion, and the question whether other areas will be able to show similar interdistrict discriminatory governmental action supports his second. Only time will tell how the federal courts will treat pending metropolitan cases like Atlanta and Indianapolis. Nor is it clear how state courts will approach the metropolitan school desegregation issue. In California, where *de facto* as well as *de jure* desegregation has to be remedied, the judge in charge of the Los Angeles case, for example, appointed an advisory panel, which recommended development of a metropolitan remedy for the Los Angeles area.[42]

In the Delaware case, the court did not turn to an expert panel to fashion a remedy. Ironically, the court turned to the state, the architect of segregated schools, to remedy its violation.

STRUGGLE FOR A REMEDY

The remedy for the constitutional violation in Delaware emerged from a series of court decisions over a three-year period. The decisions of the U.S. District Court and the U.S. Court of Appeals placed the onus for determining the nature of the remedy on local and state officials—the very officials, as we have noted, whose actions were held to have violated the Constitution. The onus, however, eventually came back to the courts. The fragmentation of authority between city and suburban school officials was such that the courts ultimately had to step in and create new governmental structures to carry out the planning and implementation.

To understand the scope of the challenge to local and state officials, let us examine more closely the content and sequence of the courts' decisions that are summarized in the first section of Figure 1-1 (Chapter 1).

Phase 1: Free-for-All

The district court's first effort to develop a remedy was its request—to both parties of the suit and to anyone else who wished—for submission of both Wilmington-only and interdistrict plans. Parties of the suit were required to submit their plans to the State Board of Education, which would then review and pass them on to the court by August 1975.[43]

Five types of desegregation plans were submitted to the three-judge panel, which considered them in hearings held during October, November, and December 1975. The proposals were to: (1) establish a county school district, (2) divide the Wilmington School District into five sections to be recombined and reorganized with suburban districts, (3) exchange pupils across school district lines within clusters or groups of city and suburban schools, (4) establish magnet schools and freedom-of-choice plans within transfer zones defined as in (2), and (5) transfer students only within the Wilmington public schools.[44]

On May 19, 1976, the majority found none of the desegregation plans submitted to the panel to be "completely acceptable taking into consideration all practicalities of the situation."[45] The Wilmington-only plan was rejected because, given the few white pupils in the city schools, it would not lead to the desegregation of the Wilmington schools. The magnet plan was rejected primarily because it would not certainly result in desegregation. The pupil exchange plan was judged to be too complex administratively. Consideration by the court of the other two plans led to a new alternative.

Phase 2: Interim Board and Ratio Constraint

The court constructed a plan that combined elements of the five-district reorganization and county plans and called for the establishment of a single reorganized school district for most of New Castle County (omitting Appoquinimink, the small, rural, desegregated district farthest from the city). The court determined that all intermediate and high schools in the desegregated area would have from 10 to 35 percent black students at each grade level by September 1977. All elementary schools had to be desegregated in the same ratio by September 1978.

Following Delaware state law on the reorganization of school districts, the court left the responsibility for determining assignment plans, faculty salaries, tax rates, and other key decisions to a five-person interim school board to be appointed by the State Board from the current local school boards involved. The Interim Board was appointed on July 6, 1976, and charged by the court with the task of planning and preparation. Funding and staff for the Interim Board were to come from the State Department of Public Instruction and the affected local districts. Finally, the State Board was told to set a date for the interim board to take full authority and responsibility for the public schools in the desegregation area.

The majority decision gave the State Legislature the right to devise different plans that would reach the racial assignment ratios by the dates specified.[46] If it so desired, the legislature could divide the large district into several districts. If the legislature did not take action in line with the court's guidelines, the court's own one-district plan would serve as the framework for desegregation.

In June 1976 the Delaware State Legislature enacted legislation that established a thirteen-member Interim School Board, composed of two representatives from each of the two largest school districts in New Castle County (the Wilmington and Newark School Districts) and one representative from each of the nine other districts in the desegregation area. (See Chapters 4 and 5.) The Interim Board was sworn in during July 1976. By September, this board began planning for desegregation.

The defendants appealed the March 1975 decision to the U.S. Supreme Court. The U.S. Department of Justice then intervened, claiming that the case should be remanded, along with the Indianapolis case, to the U.S. Court of Appeals.[47] The Justice Department also held that, although an interdistrict remedy was required, the three-judge panel had gone too far in specifying the percentage of black students. (The U.S. Supreme Court had affirmed an earlier three-judge panel decision that an interdistrict remedy was permissable because of state action in maintaining desegregation.) After the Supreme Court refused to hear the case for want of jurisdiction, the case was then appealed to the U.S. Court of Appeals for the Third Circuit. The entire Third Circuit heard the case on March 30, 1977. Its decision was announced on June 15, 1977.[48]

Phase 3: The "But For" Standard

The Third Circuit majority acknowledged that "in cases of summary adjudication, of course, it is not always crystal clear what exactly was adjudicated by the Supreme Court." It concluded that, in this case, "the Supreme Court affirmed the finding of one or more interdistrict constitutional violations."[49] The circuit court then restated several supreme court guidelines on remedial school desegregation orders:

- to eliminate unconstitutional racial discrimination "root and branch"
- to return the school system and its students as nearly as possible "to the position they would have been in but for the constitutional violations that have been found"
- to promise "realistically to work in overcoming the effects of discrimination . . . to achieve the greatest possible degree of actual desegregation, taking into account the practicalities of the situation."

The circuit court restated the "limitations by which a trial court must abide"—specifically, not to order "that every school in every community must always reflect the racial composition of the school system as a whole."[50]

While the circuit court found no misuse of discretion on the part of the three-judge panel, the majority dismissed the racial guidelines with the following language: "Although we find no misuse of discretion in the basic concept of the remedy, we are disturbed by language in the district court's opinion which can be interpreted as requiring an enrollment of 10–35 percent black students in each grade."[51] While the District Court had stated that this was not a racial quota, the Court of Appeals feared that it would be interpreted as such and removed the constraint. One dissenting judge described the dilemma thus presented to the Delaware authorities seeking a remedy: "Neither the modified order nor the majority opinion reveals what desegregation means in this case. . . . I must confess that if I were a Delaware official charged with desegregating the schools . . . I would not know where to begin."[52]

The Court of Appeals decision inspired a new search for a remedy. The 10–35 percent black criterion was forgotten and "but for" became the new standard. That is, the desegregation plan was supposed to restore the situation to what it would have been "but for" the constitutional violations.

Both the legislative committee on desegregation and the State Board of Education developed "but for" plans. The State Board plan called for busing all black children living in public housing in the City of Wilmington (about 1,800 students) to suburban schools. The State Board was reacting to the court's claim that if public housing had been built in the suburbs, more blacks would be living and going to school in the suburbs. The State Board plan also called for an additional 3,650 students from the city to be assigned to suburban districts, bringing the total of reassignments to 5,450 out of 11,960 Wilmington students. This plan was intended as a remedy for the other violations that the board judged to have had significant interdistrict effects—such as racial segregation in public and private housing and transportation subsidies for non-public school students. They assumed that even if the 1968 Educational Advancement Act had permitted Wilmington to be consolidated, the city school district lines would not have been altered.

The Legislative Committee, also seeking to develop a "but for" plan that would minimize the impact on the suburban school districts, proposed a plan based on the concept of "reverse volunteerism." Wilmington students would be assigned to suburban school districts, and, if the parents decided to volunteer them to remain in Wilmington, they would stay in the city schools.

Hearings were held by the U.S. District Court Judge Murray M. Schwartz in July 1977. (Schwartz was given jurisdiction of the remedy phase of the case after the May 1977 Court of Appeals ruling.) There the State Board presented a plan that combined its own with the Legislative Committee's plan. In its report to the court, the State Board argued:

> There is no basis in the record of this case that justifies any Federal Court's using its power to issue a sweeping remedial order that will, among other things, eliminate nine Delaware school districts and create a "super district" in their place which will be immediately responsible for the education of more than sixty percent of all Delaware school children. To put it another way, there is nothing in the record that even faintly suggests that "but for" the alleged constitutional violations the educational system in New Castle County would have in any way been the system that the order of the Circuit Court is imposing on the people of Delaware.[53]

The state presented its plan on a take-it-or-leave-it basis. Judge Schwartz seemed to be in the position of having to choose between two unsatisfactory alternatives—one, too limited and inequitable, and the other, too broad and sweeping. The State Board hoped its request for a stay would offer a way out, for "it is this court's duty to order a stay rather than enforce an order which the court knows is contrary to law."[54]

Phase 4: New Board and Single School District
On August 5, 1977, Judge Schwartz accepted the State Board of Education's request to delay the implementation of any school desegregation plan until the U.S. Supreme Court had ruled on the State Board's appeal.[55] The Supreme Court was expected to decide in October at the earliest whether or not to hear the case.

ew Board majority voted to submit a "10–2" plan, that is, a
re students in the city and De La Warr school districts would
ed to the white suburban districts for ten years while the
in the white suburban districts would attend schools in these
for two years. The Wilmington representative on the New
bmitted a plan based on an 8–4 concept. The court ordered
assignment committee of the New Board to develop a 9–3
ich the court placed at the center of its final order on January
(See Chapter 4.)

ase 5: Final Order

he Court of Appeals and the District Court had placed the
f fashioning a remedy on local and state officials. Not only
orders specifically assign to state and local officials the task
ping and reviewing plans, but the District Court also rejected
res that would free that court from its dependence on state
l officials. The court rejected a request for a monitoring
ion similar to the one established in the Denver case.[60] This
ve opened up the process to citizens without official govern-
. The court did not appoint outside experts to advise it of
e plans, as had been done in Boston and Milwaukee.[61] (In
n the court required expert advice on the pupil assignment
lied on a committee of the school board that it had created.)
t went even further and rejected demands that it should
good educational plan:

were urged throughout the hearings in the case to be concerned
h the quality of education offered by the area schools. That is much
e properly the concern of local officials and the parents of children
he schools. Our duty here is not to impose quality education even if
could define that term. . . . We do not find there is a mandate for
rict courts to concern themselves with how well the educative
ction is being performed.[62]

depending on local and state officials to fashion a remedy,
did want the remedy forged by negotiations with all parties
d—black and white, state and local, educational and gov-
l. The State Legislature was invited and encouraged to de-
acceptable remedy. The court established the Interim Board
lew Board. In fact, as fall 1978 approached, Judge Schwartz
ough in vain, to persuade plaintiffs and defendants to bar-
ctly to reach a mutual settlement.[63]

d of uncertainty rising from decisions of the U.S. Supreme
ng over these attempts at compromise. In July 1976, the
Court ruled in *Washington* v. *Davis*, a police applicant

Judge Schwartz ordered the State Bo
New Castle County Planning Board, kı
replace the Interim Board; he ordered t
desegregation of the schools within a si
ber 1978. The judge reserved the righ
earlier than September 1978 if the U.S.
the case or otherwise turned down th

The State Board plan, which feature
volunteerism, was rejected by Judge Sc
State Legislature did not enact this plaı
only if the court ordered it. He felt th
placed "the entire burden of the reme
been violated," that is, on black child:
"promise realistically to work now,"
than a twenty-year delay in dismantl
tem.[56] In other words, if all black childi
would become all white, and if no b
would remain black.

Judge Schwartz mentioned four ot
the stay. First, harm would occur if the
decision after the single district had b
dents who had been reassigned to new
tion plan would have to be reassigned
Second, the case raised "difficult an
although he did not believe that the l
(such as Dayton) affected the rulings i
implementation of a mandatory deseg
be not too harmful to the plaintiffs (blɛ
tary transfer plan was available to the
would "increase public uncertainty a
than dealing with the final result, no
to be."[57]

Reports from the New Board were
Schwartz every two weeks. In the ca:
Board disagreed, the judge ordered
reasons and nature of their differenc

Judge Schwartz ordered the plan to
ty assignments. The New Board plan
tion of students in grades 1–11 for S

The "dismantling [of] the dual s
accomplished by vigorous pursuit of
Judge Schwartz, and he ordered an

The N
plan wh
be assig
student
districts
Board s
the pup
plan, wl
9, 1978.

P
Both
burden
did thei
of devel
alternati
and loci
commis:
would h
ment tie
alternati
fact, wh
plan, it r
The cou
define a

W
wi
mc
in
we
di:
fu

While
the cour
concern
ernment
velop an
and the
tried, al
gain dir

A clo
Court h
Supreme

selection case alleging discrimination against blacks in hiring, that if there were no discerned acts of intentional discrimination—that is, no motivation or intent to discriminate—that any adverse impacts along racial lines would not be a sufficient showing to invoke a court-ordered remedy to alleviate racial disparities in employment or, more generally, to undo the effects of adverse impact alleged by minority plaintiffs.[64] This added additional fuel to the "desegregation-fighting" fire in new Castle County. The State Board had consistently argued that neither it nor the state had engaged in discriminatory actions. The suburban boards for the most part adopted this view, especially since each local district was currently operating in unitary fashion—there were no dual, segregated systems of education operating in any suburban district; school assignments and enrollments, it was argued, were done in a context of a "unitary" system for each suburban district.

The defendants also took hope from the test of "intention," referred to by the Supreme Court in *Washington* v. *Davis* and in the school desegregation cases of Austin, Indianapolis, and Dayton. The District Court's March 1975 ruling indicated that the court did not find that the Educational Advancement Act of 1968 was racially motivated, or, said another way, that it had an intentionally discriminatory purpose. This was a keystone of many subsesquent arguments by state and suburban defendants before the courts. The District Court had ruled, and in fact had stated in its March 1975 decision, that the EAA was not intentionally discriminatory. This was one of the factors that influenced the court to order an interdistrict remedy. In many quarters, therefore, it was concluded that it was only a matter of time before the decision would be overturned, and thus planning efforts were kept to a minimum. The District and Appeals Courts added to the uncertainty by failing to give precise and lasting guidelines to what they would consider adequate desegregation plans. Their most ambiguous guideline was the "but for" criterion when the Appeals Court rejected the 10–35 percent minority standard.

Thus it was amid increasing uncertainty about the outcomes of future appeals and the legal meaning of desegregation that the District Court was looking to the black and white school and governmental officials of Delaware to reach a compromise on a plan. Because the District Court's reliance on state and local officials was so important in shaping the desegregation implementation process in Delaware, it may be useful to consider the reasons for this dependence.

It would appear that in relying so greatly on local officials and local bargaining and in supplying only vague guidelines, the judges were illustrating the model of judicial restraint proposed by Tyll Van

Geel.[65] According to Van Geel, the restraint model assumes that the demands of interest groups are normally met through the workings of the political process.

Opposed to the restraint model is that of judicial activism, which is concerned less with social peace and stability and more with neglected rights and values. This model wishes to correct the inability of powerless minorities to influence the policies of legislatures that are discriminating against them. Judicial activists have little faith in local decisionmakers, seeing them as part of the problem to be overcome.

Decisions rendered within the model of restraint may have uncertain impact since carrying them out is left to local officials. Activist decisions may wreck conventionally negotiated plans of the legislative or executive branches. Judicial decisions of any kind, coming as they do from outside the political bargaining process, may cause resentment and lead to difficulty in implementation. According to Van Geel, judicial intervention, particularly on the activist model, can discourage people from using the regular political process.

It appears local ties as well as political philosophy led the District Court judges in the Delaware case to depend on local officials. Of the four judges who defined the remedy at the District Court level, only Judge Gibbons was not from Delaware. From Newark, New Jersey, he was the strongest and earliest advocate of a metropolitan plan. Judges Caleb Layton and Caleb Wright shared an old Delaware name as well as Delaware ties.[66] Judge Schwartz, also a Delawarean, lived in the Alexis I. duPont School District and sent his three children to its schools. All three Delaware judges would have been rejecting their local ties if they had rejected the local authority of school and state officials. This is not to say that the Delaware judges always were sympathetic to local officials. The first hint of displeasure came from Judge Schwartz. He charged local school officials with playing the role of lawyer instead of school administrator and accused the State Legislature of dragging its heels.[67] Even while making these accusations, however, Judge Schwartz maintained a strong dependence on the local school decisionmakers.

Antibusing leaders suspected another reason for the court's reliance on local authorities. Having someone else propose the actual desegregation plan would allow the judges to avoid the passions sure to be aroused. As it happened, the local authorities were unable to submit a fully acceptable plan. This forced the court into a more directive role, and the judges did become lightning rods for the inevitable storm of blame.

SUMMARY

The federal courts had ruled that the segregation of schools in New Castle County was more than the result of normal demographic trends and individual decisions. Delaware's dual system of schools had never been dismantled, and the black schools in Wilmington remained as vestiges of the legally segregated system of decades before. Through actions capped by the Educational Advancement Act in 1968, Delaware's government officials had perpetuated the black schools in the city. Given the high percentage of black children in the Wilmington schools, a metropolitan remedy was the only conceivable one.

Declining to fashion its own remedy, the District Court referred for advice and action to those very institutions that had violated the Constitution. The court hoped that state and local officials could negotiate an acceptable desegregation plan. The federal courts, however, provided no consistent set of signals and constraints to Delaware's officials. When the District Court had first ordered school and state officials to develop a desegregation plan, it did not specify what sort of plan would be acceptable. When the District Court did establish what it considered an acceptable percentage of black students for each school, the Court of Appeals disallowed the ratio because it smacked of a quota. Meanwhile, the U.S. Supreme Court continued to make decisions that muddied the water and increased uncertainty. These ambiguities were perceived by state and local officials as increasing their options and, therefore, as the chapters ahead will show, the pressure to compromise was lessened.

The difficulties for state and local officials were heightened by actions of the courts at all three levels.[68] On the one hand these officials were beholden to a public deeply opposed to any action that would lead to busing. On the other hand they faced court orders to develop an acceptable plan that would inevitably include busing. The court had presented a considerable challenge, if not an insolvable dilemma, to the school and governmental officials of Delaware.

4 / School Officials

The U.S. District Court directed school officials at the state and local level to develop a constitutionally valid school desegregation plan. The court established a number of procedures in a locally based bargaining process. School officials in the city and suburban districts were unable to reach agreement on an acceptable plan. The suit was reopened in 1971. It took seven more years and the final federal order for the city and suburban school officials to move together toward the first day of a desegregated school system.

This chapter describes the various pressures that shaped the actions of school officials and hindered city-suburban agreement and early preparation for implementation. School officials continually faced serious dilemmas. Should they prepare to comply with the court order or be attentive to the strong antibusing sentiment in their school districts? Should they work for agreement on an acceptable desegregation plan or continue to try to forstall desegregation in the courts? Proponents of compliance and defiance both established their positions early and held fast throughout the process.

While the Wilmington School Board did not originate the desegregation suit, it quickly supported the suit with words and actions. With an integrationist majority, the board joined the suit as an intervening plaintiff in 1972 and hired Louis Lucas to serve as counsel.[1] Although controversies arose over the features of a desirable desegregation plan, the Wilmington Board never publicly wavered in its support for desegregation, even if that meant mandatory reassignment of pupils and dissolution of the Wilmington School District.

The defendants at the state and county school level never wavered in their determination to oppose busing and school district reorganization, but neither did they fail to state their willingness and responsibility to carry out whatever the court ordered.[2] The defendants appealed to higher courts as each decision went against them, maintaining that they were not at fault for any racial segregation found in the Wilmington Public Schools.

From these divergent stances the parties approached the development of reorganization and desegregation plans.

DESIGNING A REORGANIZATION AND DESEGREGATION PLAN

Two questions involving the content of a school desegregation plan took precedence:

First, Delaware officials faced the basic issue of structural reorganization. If the eleven school districts in the desegregation area had to be reorganized, what new governance structure should be created?[3] Among the obvious options were creation of a large single school district, combination of the school districts into a new set of local districts, and establishment of a two-tiered structure of governance with the power shared by local districts and a central school board. These alternatives raised basic issues, like efficiency (is a large school district more or less efficient than a small one?), responsiveness (can a large school district be as responsive to parents as a small district?), and equity (was equity of tax rates worth the loss of local control of school spending?).[4]

One of the thorniest issues involved "leveling-up" personnel costs. (This ultimately led to a teachers' strike, described in Chapter 8.) Studies have found that the cost of busing is modest when measured only by additional transportation costs.[5] In the Wilmington case, a potentially larger economic issue was that an interdistrict remedy could easily cost ten times more than just the added cost of transportation. Wilmington teachers had the highest pay scale in the state. If the schools of Wilmington were desegregated with some suburban districts, the teaching staffs would presumably also be desegregated by exchanging Wilmington teachers (over 60 percent black) for primarily suburban teachers (over 95 percent white). If salary equalizations were not enacted, teachers working next door to each other, with the same education and years of experience, would have large salary differentials. The average annual salary difference was about $2,200. As a matter of fact, the Delaware Code called for salary equalization in reorganization situations. If all New Castle County districts raised their salary schedules to equal the Wilmington scale, the estimated added annual personnel cost would be 22 million.[6] This cost could double the property tax rate in many suburban districts.

If leveling-up did not take place, suburban teachers could attempt to force equalization through the courts or political means or collective bargaining. Teachers in Delaware had locked horns with the public several times already in recent years. There had been a state-wide teacher strike in 1975 and a twenty-seven–day strike in Wilmington in 1975.[7] Both the Delaware Federation of Teachers (representing the city) and the Delaware State Education Association (an NEA affiliate representing the suburban districts) advocated leveling-up.

Thus one of the explosive questions that plagued school officials trying to devise a desegregation plan was: Should salaries of educational personnel be equalized to the highest salary schedule (Wilmington scale), or could this expenditure be avoided?

A second basic issue was the thorny one of pupil assignment. Among the specific options were voluntary plans (such as magnet schools, voluntary transfer plans, tuition voucher plans) and a variety of mandatory plans (such as clustering schools, grade centers).[8]

Also at issue during the early decision making was the scope of the desegregation plan—that is, how many districts or schools should be covered? Should only the districts adjacent to Wilmington be included? Should the desegregated districts of adjacent De La Warr and rural Appoquinimink be included? Should the large and more distant Newark School District be part of the plan? Finally, on what basis should students be reassigned to schools if a mandatory plan were adopted—by grade level? by random procedure? by neighborhood?

Positions on Plans

The position of the defendants—State Board and suburban districts—was based upon their overall goal of maintaining white support and participation in the public schools. Operationally, this meant that the defendant boards sought to procure a plan that would minimize the concern of whites and maximize the stability of suburban white schools. This meant that the defendant boards sought plans that would:

- minimize changes in white school districts (maintain school district lines and personnel, keep white schools open, maintain the system of local school districts)
- minimize increased taxes (avoid leveling-up, keep desegregation expenditures limited)
- minimize busing of whites, that is, involuntary assignment of white students (use voluntary means, minimize number of years or time that whites would be bused)

• minimize busing inequities among whites if busing had to be mandatory (that is, treat all whites in the suburbs the same).

This position was tempered at times, primarily in deference to the particular interests of various school districts. One conflict among suburban districts, for example, was over the inclusion or exclusion of the Newark District.[9]

The Wilmington School District was chiefly interested in maintaining control over the city schools and treating all parties to the suit equally. Its representatives opposed plans that would divide the district, especially if no other district was dismantled. They favored plans that would leave a large percentage of Wilmington children in desegregated schools in the city. For a better understanding of these issues, let us look again at the sequence of court decisions, this time in terms of the school officials' responses to them (summarized in Figure 1-1, Chapter 1).

Phase 1: Free-for-all

In its March 1975 decision, the three-judge panel had invited everyone to submit a plan but had offered no formula, guidelines, or requirements. The three major school decision-making groups offered quite different plans. (A list of all of the plans submitted to the court during the desegregation process is presented in Appendix 1.)

The State Board of Education favored a multidistrict plan in which the Wilmington School District would be divided and recombined with suburban districts. (At various times the State Board suggested a three-, four-, five-, and six-district plan.) No student assignments were specified; these would be the prerogative of the new boards.

The State Board thus wanted the New Castle County districts reorganized along the lines envisioned in the 1968 reorganization act, the Educational Advancement Act, but this time with the division of the city district. They contended that this would retain certain advantages of small districts, like responsiveness to students and parents. In addition, the State Board was concerned about the effect of an upstate reorganization on small downstate school districts. A move to a county-wide school district in the north was considered by some to be a threat to small districts in the south.

Under pressure from local districts and antibusing forces, the State Board also submitted a zone transfer plan. Under this plan magnet schools would be created within each of five transfer zones, analogous to the five districts.

At this time, the suburban districts were not ready to submit plans calling for mandatory assignments. Some districts argued that they should not be included in the remedy. Some of the suggested plans called for voluntary transfers or mandatory reassignments for only a few weeks per year or hours per day. (The De La Warr District—serving about half whites and half blacks and financially starved—pushed for a countywide school district throughout the process.)

The Wilmington Board submitted a mandatory pupil reassignment plan. The submission, however, was not unanimous. Two black members of the board, both active in politics and potential mayoral candidates, voted against submitting it. One of them, Wendell Howell, then the vice-president of the board and later president, made an "impassioned protest" blasting the plan and its emphasis on mixing bodies. He called desegregation "an illusive dream" and called for improvement of educational standards in city and suburban schools.[10] Howell later submitted a voucher magnet-school plan to the State Board. Soon, several black activists had filed a friend-of-the-court brief arguing that blacks opposed busing.[11]

Since the time that the Wilmington School Board had intervened on the side of the plaintiffs in the *Evans v. Buchanan* case, membership on the board had changed. It was becoming obvious that the Wilmington Board's desire for desegregated education was in direct conflict with a strong black interest in maintaining the Wilmington School District. As in many other places in the country, desegregation was a threat to the black establishment. The Wilmington school system was the only power base that local black leadership possessed.[12]

The twelve-member Wilmington City Council had only two black members. There was a white mayor and white majorities among state representatives, on the County Council, and in business and community organizations. But the school board had a black majority and had employed a black superintendent for nearly a decade. A majority of school principals were black and a large percentage of posts in the school administration were filled by blacks.

Pupil enrollment in Wilmington was almost entirely minority. To achieve desegregation would require a metropolitan area pupil assignment plan and a related reorganization plan. Either of the two obvious metropolitan remedies would dissolve the Wilmington district—one into a county district, the other into pie-shaped wedges. Somehow, to satisfy public pressure and to maintain the power of blacks, the Wilmington Board had to come up with a plan that would preserve its school district. Their first plan called for interdistrict exchanges of students without a new governing body to oversee these exchanges. Since this plan would put most Wilmington students under suburban district authority for the majority of their school years, questions were raised about who would be responsible for city students in the suburbs and vice versa. In response, the Wilmington Board offered the concept of a "superboard" to oversee the exchanges. This plan was rejected by the three-judge panel because of its administrative difficulties. There seemed no way that Wilmington could have both desegregation and black influence as before: a "victory" in the suit would almost certainly mean the "loss" of the school district.

The State Board presented all of the various plans to the three-judge panel, but, as described in Chapter 3, the panel rejected all of the plans and established a mechanism that, after the State Legislature's intervention, became the thirteen-member Interim Board of Education in the summer of 1976. The Interim Board, composed of two members from both the Wilmington and Newark School Districts and one for each of the other nine districts under court order, struggled for a year to develop an acceptable plan.

Phase 2: Interim Board

Initially the Interim Board of Education attempted to reach decisions through a rational process of choosing specific objectives and examining alternative ways of reaching them.

As Figure 4-1 indicates, about half of the Interim Board held jobs in Delaware's chemical industry, a circumstance that may explain the Board's early technical view of the tasks before them. Early in its existence, the Board established criteria on which to evaluate alternative desegregation plans. The criteria included establishing the lowest possible citizen-to-board ratio, ensuring access to the Board and administrative structure for parents and children, achieving basic equality of funding, moving a minimum number of students, and meeting the court-set racial ratios in each grade in each school.[13]

As the Board was confronted with the political realities of making decisions, however, it quickly abandoned the formal criteria. It found that plans that rated high on one scale failed miserably on another.[14] For example, a single school district would bring financial equity at the cost of a high citizen-to-board ratio. And while one member might be most concerned about the citizen-to-board ratio, another would be most concerned with moving a minimum number of students. To complicate matters, several members of the Board focused only on satisfying their highest priority concerns; items low on their lists could just wait. For example, several members opposed mandatory busing above all else, thus greatly limiting their choices. Such single-mindedness made it impossible to deal with the wide range of issues

Figure 4-1
Members of Interim Board of Education

School District	Board Member	Occupation/(Employer)	Race
Alexis I. duPont	Bruce Kirk	Engineer (DuPont)	White
Alfred I. duPont	Gilbert Scarborough, Jr.	Businessman (insurance co. owner)	White
Claymont	James Elder	Mail clerk	White
Conrad	Clifford M. Steele	Engineering designer (DuPont)	White
De La Warr	Alberta Torrence	Homemaker	Black
	David Green*	Accountant	White
Marshallton-McKean	Mary DiVirgilio	Homemaker	White
Mt. Pleasant	Aaron Hamburger	Marketing specialist (DuPont)	White
Newark	Priscilla Crowder	Homemaker	White
	William Clark	Chemist (Hercules)	White
New Castle– Gunning Bedford	George Rosentreter	Sales rep. and district manager (Oxford Chemicals)	White
Stanton	Joesph Reardon	Chemist (DuPont)	White
Wilmington	William Lewis	Personnel specialist (retired, DuPont)	Black
	Benjamin Amos*	Director (Wilmington Housing Authority)	Black
	Wendell Howell	Counselor (Delaware Technical and Community College)	Black

*Appointed after resignation of school district's first representative.

involved in achieving desegregation. As choices had to be made, rational criteria faded into the background.

The Interim Board attempted to build an organizational structure that could serve as the basis of organizational decision making. But instead of developing a unifying structure, the Board recreated its own divisions. Rather than appoint a superintendent, the Board kept the Superintendents' Council that had been established a few months before to meet the need for communications across school district lines. All school district superintendents in New Castle County were members.

To develop a comprehensive plan for decision making and management, the Board and Council utilized the federal educational laboratory, Research for Better Schools (RBS). An RBS report recommended establishment of sixteen task forces to accomplish more than seven hundred tasks and meet one hundred objectives in the following areas: communications, administration, curriculum, instruction, inservice training, desegregation plan(s), buildings and grounds, transportation finances, professional personnel, support personnel, reorganization plans, pupil personnel, intergovernmental and court relations, legal relationships, and governance.[15] The Superintendent's Council was given the responsibility of reviewing all task force work and making recommendations to the Interim Board.

Rather than hiring an acting superintendent, the Interim Board voted to hire an administrative director. It thus placed great power in the hands of all the superintendents in the county, and, by giving the administrative director very limited powers and recruiting him from within county school organizations, it effectively locked itself into local school district organizational values, routines, and interests.

Parochialism thus took precedence. There were several reasons for this. The Interim Board was not a school board. It was a planning body, not an operating structure (that is, it had no authority over the schools), and so board members felt that the typical school district organization was not appropriate. In establishing the Interim Board, the State Legislature emphasized that the members were intended to represent local school boards, not the general public.[16] This assured that no individual or school district would have too much decision-power. Appointing even an acting superintendent from one district would threaten other districts. Appointing an acting superintendent from outside would threaten everyone.[17]

The superintendents were under varying pressures from their own school boards and their instructions differed. Some wanted to take action; others did not, or felt they could not. Some still did not believe that desegregation would take place; others thought that it was inevitable. Some people feared losing their position in any school district reorganization; others saw scope for their ambitions. The jockeying for leadership and the conflicts across districts and among personalities worked against a unitary structure. Besides the overriding city-suburban split, there were legal battles between districts adjacent to and those further from the city. Old rivalries among school districts reinforced the divisions. No governmental unit had existed to bring district representatives together. The county had no educational arm. The state Department of Public Instruction (DPI) was not aggressive and had no history of positive leadership if it had wished to press for cooperative planning. The court order not only did not overcome localism in setting up the Interim Board; localism and parochialism were built right into the Board's structure.

Conflict sometimes threatened to reach the physical level. As will be described more fully in Chapter 6, a group of staff and community leaders met in secret over breakfast approximately twice a month to discuss the progress of desegregation planning and implementation. Because he was chairman of the county superintendents' organization, Dr. Carroll Biggs, Alfred I.'s superintendent, was invited to breakfast in spring 1975. Thomas Minter, then superintendent of the Wilmington schools, was also invited. Minter mentioned the Breakfast Group and Biggs and his attendance within the hearing of Dr. George Kirk, superintendent of the Newark Schools and vice-chairman of the county superintendents. A rival of Biggs, Kirk grew very angry. He wanted to know why Dr. Biggs had been chosen to represent the suburban superintendents and why Dr. Biggs had not told the other superintendents of the meeting. To oil the troubled waters, organizers of the breakfast invited all three officers of the county superintendents' organization to the next breakfast: Biggs, Kirk, and Alexis I. Superintendent Dr. James Pugh. Unfortunately, Pugh and Biggs had been at odds over a number of issues. They got into a row that observers described as almost a fist fight. Pugh never came again.

Such conflicts were only partly sparked by personal rivalries and ambitions to the possible county superintendency. They also represented conflicts over leadership style, school district interests, and professional views of how best to prepare for school desegregation. For example, Biggs seemed more comfortable working with the community to mobilize a supportive constituency. Kirk was recognized for his ability to attract and work with high quality teachers and administrators. Biggs appeared suave and cool in public; Kirk let his emotions show more easily. Their strengths could be described as those of a "Dr. Inside" and a "Dr. Outside."

The process and content of Interim Board decisions were affected by all of the above factors. The Interim Board found it difficult to reach decisions, especially ones that threatened local interests. In fact, some associated with the Board saw delaying decisions as a "politic" way to avoid dilemmas. Said Board member Mary DiVirgilio, "I can't find the words to tell you how I disagree with [a particular] plan. We're just passing the buck. We are more political than the General Assembly. We just don't want to face the issue."[18] A News Journal reporter concluded that the board had been "putting off the most significant—

and difficult—long-term educational and administrative decisions."[19] Even Carroll Biggs said, "The pure raw politics of the situation has inhibited any decision. It's very difficult for any district to give up its own position and protect its own interests."[20] U.S. District Judge Murray M. Schwartz also charged the Interim Board with playing politics. "From what I read in the newspapers . . . I am afraid that those responsible for the education function have in part played lawyer and in part played politics."[21]

It is not surprising that the Board's decisions were parochial. A *News Journal* editorial concluded that "the members of the Interim Board . . . still are thinking more . . . of their own home districts than of the new integrated school district they have been asked to construct. Their outlook continues narrow."[22] The editorial noted that no matter what plan was discussed, the Board members were concerned primarily with the issue of schools closing in "their" district. When considering reorganizing plans, the Board also insisted on recombining rather than dividing suburban districts. Near the end of the Board's existence, even its president, Gilbert Scarborough, Jr., criticized the Board's parochialism. "I think we failed miserably," he said, citing the various local outlooks that "outweighed our commitment to the pupils. We've had three years to study plans. We ought to get our heads together somehow."[23]

Given the Interim Board's task, some decisions had to be made. Ultimate decisions reflected not only the interests of the old school districts but a deeper underlying division between the representatives of districts that were mostly black and those that were overwhelmingly white. With only one exception, the white school district representatives voted for plans that not only limited the impact on their districts but also placed a higher burden on the two majority black districts. First, the Interim Board recommended that current school districts be maintained for two years with an Intermediate School Authority (analogous to the Interim Board of Education) created to oversee pupil assignments. This would allow the Interim Board to oversee desegregation in all grades while appeals to higher courts continued. The State Board rejected this plan because it did not meet the court's directive to reorganize the districts. Then, the Interim Board voted to establish six reorganized districts immediately rather than wait for the final appeal decision. They had great difficulty deciding what area the districts should encompass. (That had been one of the attractions of the Intermediate School Authority concept; it would have deferred the decision on how to divide the districts.) The reorganized districts would divide Wilmington but recombine (not divide) some suburban districts. Thus the Board continually opted to maintain the traditional white suburban districts. The single-district plan was seen only as the last resort if the State Legislature refused to accept this multidistrict plan.

Pupil assignment then had to be decided by the Interim Board. The majority decided to make the Wilmington and De La Warr schools into fifth- and ninth-grade centers. In a meeting, representatives of these districts objected, saying that this would "emasculate" their districts and that busing only black children (with few exceptions) for ten to twelve years and whites for two of twelve was inequitable.

Wilmington Board president and Interim Board member Wendell Howell charged that the center concept would be discriminatory because it would alter only Wilmington's and De La Warr's high schools:

> A desegregation process which closes high schools in the black areas only, and one in particular which closes all black schools, will be correctly perceived by the students, black and white, as racially motivated. Black students attending schools in the white high schools will come there with extreme resentment about the systematic closing of secondary education in the black community. White students in the same schools will perceive themselves automatically as "the winners, because they are white" and view the black students as intruders. If, on the other hand, changes were occurring in both areas, i.e., white secondary students coming into the Wilmington secondary schools and black students going into suburban high schools, neither group would perceive itself as either victor or vanquished, but hopefully, would view themselves as having a responsibility to make both communities proud of them by the way in which they conducted themselves.
>
> The racially discriminatory elimination of all Wilmington secondary faculty, with their continued employment a matter of suffrage at the hands of the suburban suburban districts who will continue to operate secondary programs, will be destructive to teacher, pupil and parental relations. Those black faculty employed in the suburbs who resent keenly their supplicant status, *they* will experience the same reception problem from white faculty and students in the suburban secondary schools. Again, if it were a two-way process, faculty and staff, as professionals, staff on both sides would be stimulated to work creatively, share experiences, and act in a manner which would stimulate the educational growth of children.
>
> In short, a plan which eliminates the secondary schools in Wilmington is morally wrong because it hurts children directly, and through effect, on faculty and staff. It is constitutionally wrong because it is that kind of racially disparate treatment, obviously rooted in racial motivation, which caused the litigation in the first place; and, it is most likely to lead to litigation by boards, pupils and teachers.[24]

The Board's concern was with equity within the white community and the threat of white flight. The Wilmington pupil assignment plan would have meant the busing of some suburban children for only two or three years and the busing of others for seven or eight. The majority adopted the center plan instead chiefly because it called for the busing of *all* suburban children for only *two* years. The center plan was passed despite the objections of many educators, members of the public, and two of the task forces, who felt that single grade centers were educationally unwise.

Given goals such as stability of white suburbs, conservation of the school district status quo, and cost minimization, it is clear that so-called "educational" goals were secondary. The actions of the Interim Board did not indicate concern with maximizing educational choices for students, furnishing the best educational facilities, or maintaining a continuum of curriculum. Many vocal members of the public and educational leaders criticized the Interim Board for being too political and not being concerned about education.

Wendell Howell lamented, for example, that "once the court has made its decision on desegregation, the rest of the decisions are political. They should be educational, but they are political."[25] At a Delaware Humanities Forum, an audience member asked Superintendent of the Stanton School District George Glynn to comment on the central theme of the program, "Where are the values?" Glynn missed the educational mark by answering, "Yes, I wanted to say something about property values."[26] After hearing a task force report on the political advantages of one plan, Wilmington representative Benjamin Amos said, "I'm interested in educational reasons, not political reasons."[27] A *News Journal* editorial lambasted the Board for its reactions to yet another plan: "Little was said about educational goals, continuity in the education process, or about the all-important question of governance."[28]

Many viewed the Interim Board as a failure. The District Court had established the Interim Board to design an acceptable plan, but the Board was unable to. Perhaps the court expected the representatives from the various school districts to develop a typical school-district organizational structure. If it had been given a single professional leader and a centralized structure, the Board might more easily have narrowed its options and focused on an acceptable plan. Perhaps the court had hoped that the representatives of the districts would reach consensus on the definition of a good plan and find a common basis on which to evaluate alternative plans. Instead, the Board found that its members brought with them very different evaluative criteria and saw different relationships between plans and outcomes.

Even failing to develop a unifying structure or a unifying decision-making process, the Interim Board still might have reached agreement by identifying the different interests and views of its members and seeking a compromise. But the suburban white majority did not bargain successfully with the De La Warr and Wilmington minority, and even had difficulty reaching agreement among themselves. Why was bargaining so difficult?

The first reason was the underlying ideological disagreements among the board members. The racial division was, of course, the most severe and manifested itself in various ways. Wendell Howell, who became the Wilmington spokesman on the Board, antagonized several white members. They thought that he was overly aggressive, too political, and not trustworthy; they saw him in many ways as a stereotypical black.[29]

Another ideological disagreement was the differing views of whites and blacks on equity in planning. To blacks, equity meant a 6–6 plan (both whites and blacks bused for six years.) To whites equity meant treating all suburban children the same as each other and treating all Wilmington and De La Warr children the same as each other but not necessarily treating the two groups equally. White leaders saw treating whites equally as a necessity in order to minimize white flight and to preserve the public school system; black leaders saw this concern as racist. White leaders failed to see why blacks thought them racist. In any event, whites did not need black votes to maintain a majority on the Board and so felt no pressure to compromise with the black representatives.

It may be that the resistance to compromise was built into the Interim Board by the terms of its establishment. Board decisions were only advisory to the court. To give up more in the Interim Board bargaining than they might well win in the next round in court looked to both sides unnecessary and perhaps unwise.[30] In fact, both sides were convinced that they would eventually win. Explaining a loss in court to constituents would be easier than explaining why a point was bargained away. Further, the Interim Board lacked the mechanisms that usually help overcome major ideological and parochial divisions in large decision-making bodies. The Board lacked norms to encourage cooperation and logrolling; there were no votes to be traded on issues of disapproportionate interest; and there was no superintendent or staff to facilitate bargaining.[31]

Finally, the great public interest in the issue and the new sunshine law that opened almost all Board meetings to the public made bargaining more difficult. Any sign of compromise in public was seen as a sell-out. Suspicion-dominated relationships among the superintendents kept them from leading the public with a united purpose. Carroll Biggs, head of the Superintendents' Council inspired caution rather than consent because of his reputation as a wheeler-dealer. [32] The Superintendents' Council served to veto ideas to protect interests rather than to compromise or develop new approaches.

Thus, in one sense, the Interim Board was too political, in being closely tied to parochial interests; in another sense it was not political enough, in being unable to bargain internally. Racial conflict hampered the Interim Board, but not so much as did parochial interests so strong that they blocked every impulse to compromise.

Phase 3: The "But For" Plan
When the U.S. Court of Appeals in May 1977 disallowed the District Court's instruction to achieve a 10–35 percent minority ratio in each classroom and suggested instead that the criterion should be the racial composition as it would have been "but for" the constitutional violations, the Interim Board became important. Attention shifted to the state level as the State Board of Education and the Delaware legislature attempted to develop "but for" plans that would avoid busing white suburban students (see Chapter 5).

Phase 4: New Castle County Planning Board of Education
On August 5, 1977, U.S. District Court Judge Murray Schwartz rejected the state's "but for" plan and ordered the appointment of a new five-person board to plan for a desegregated single district for September 1978. The State Board immediately received nominations from the local districts and appointed four members of the old Interim Board (Scarborough, Clark, DiVirgilio, and Howell); the new member was Earl Reed, Jr., vice-president of the Gracelawn Memorial Park, a cemetery in New Castle. The court gave the New Board until September 30, 1977, to develop plans.

The New Board shared many of the characteristics and difficulties of the Interim Board. It continued to keep the public at arm's length, and at least one member felt excluded as well; the one female Board member claimed that decisions were being made in the men's room.[33] Among its accomplishments was appointment of a five-member Superintendents' Council composed of the superintendents of their own five districts. This Council did appoint an acting superintendent, George Kirk. The New Board was unable, however, to reach agreement on a pupil assignment plan. A white majority dictated a 10–2 plan that blacks considered too favorable to whites. The minority Board member submitted a plan loosely based on the 8–4 concept, but the white majority feared the variability of its treatment of the suburbs. On January 9, 1978, Judge Schwartz called the majority white plan inequitable to blacks because they were to be bused for ten years and the black plan inequitable to whites because of the range of years they would be bused. He rejected both plans.

Phase 5: Final Order

When Judge Schwartz rejected both the majority and minority plans on January 9, 1978, he ordered the Board's Pupil Assignment Committee to assign Wilmington and De La Warr students to suburban schools for nine years, and suburban students to the city or De La Warr schools for three consecutive years. At least one high school would remain in Wilmington or De La Warr, and Wilmington would serve students in grades K–12. Details of the pupil assignment plan, such as school closing and method of assignment, were left to the New Board. The judge did accept the NCCPBE's proposal that four pie-shaped areas within the single district be organized for administration and pupil assignment.

Judge Schwartz's order was not limited to technical matters. The NCCPBE had joined the plaintiffs in arguing for ancillary relief, that is, for remedial educational programs designed to advance the victims of school segregation to the educational level they would have achieved but for segregation. The State Board argued that such action was the responsibility of the NCCPBE and should not be a matter of judicial judgment. Quoting extensively from the recent U.S. Supreme Court decision supporting ancillary relief in the Detroit case, Judge Schwartz specified eight guidelines for ancillary relief in his January 1978 order. Specifically, he ordered the New Board to

> formulate and implement a comprehensive in-service training program for teachers, administrators, and other staff, institute an affirmative reading and communication skills program which does not resegregate pupils, provide curriculum offerings and programs which emphasize and reflect the cultural pluralism of the students, institute an effective and nondiscriminatory counseling and guidance program, establish and enforce nondiscriminatory guidelines for new construction, review of building needs, and the appropriateness of each proposed building project or school closing, provide an appropriate human relations program throughout the unitary school system, develop a code of rights and responsibilities regarding such issues as student conduct and suspension and expulsion, and reassign faculty, administrative, and other staff personnel . . . in order to insure that schools do

not retain their former racial identity through racially identifiable faculty and staff assignments.[34]

The means of fulfilling these eight tasks were left to the New Board but the means of paying for them was specified in the court order.

Judge Schwartz set a maximum tax rate of $1.91 per $100 of assessed valuation for operating expenses for the county school district. This rate was below Wilmington's. He refused to order personnel salaries and benefits leveled-up to those of the highest school district, leaving that issue to local authorities. He also ordered the state to pay a proportion of ancillary program costs for five years. In response, the State Legislature passed a "taxcap" that limited the property tax rate for the county school district for operating expenses to 1.595. Judge Schwartz disallowed this action, but the July 1978 Court of Appeals decision reversed Judge Schwartz and reinstated the cap.

Local and state school authorities had trouble not only with internal problems in developing an acceptable plan but also with the external problem of preparing people to accept and carry out a plan. In dealing with constituents, employees, and governmental officials to prepare for desegregation, school officials again faced major political obstacles.

PREPARATION FOR IMPLEMENTATION

The strong political opposition to busing in Delaware presented school superintendents with a basic dilemma: they had to choose between accommodating their constituency's adamant desire to avoid busing—and serving their constituency's actual interests and their own professionalism by preparing for a likely busing order.

Smith, Downs, and Lachman's analysis of over 1,100 studies of school desegregation implies that superintendents must play a number of roles to achieve effective desegregation.[35] Superintendents are advised, for example, to plan comprehensively before the implementation of desegregation, to orient their students and staff and increase communications with the community.

Pre–Final Order Preparation

Among the eleven school districts in the desegregation area, there was a great range of preparations. Early in the court suit, the Alfred I. duPont School Board established a citizen's task force which, among other activities, held meetings and distributed newsletters about the status of the suit. In the Newark School District only public pressure forced school officials to reach out to the general public, distributing a newsletter about the suit and establishing a special communications group of community members.

In the blue-collar districts of New Castle–Gunning Bedford, Conrad, and Claymont, no organized attempt was made to prepare the public for desegregation. Feelings against busing were so intense that no superintendent, even assuming he believed it would help, dared to bring up the subject of preparing for busing. The three affluent districts—Alfred I., Alexis I., and Mt. Pleasant—organized groups which did take some part in informing the public. These districts had no choice because their publics demanded information on busing. Among the middle-class districts, one would have an active program, another would have an active parent group and an inactive school group, and still another would have no activity at all. Here, where opinions were more varied and less intense, the operating styles of the superintendents played a large role in determining the nature of preparations. The two districts with black majorities also varied in their preparations. De La Warr officials did not feel as strong a need to prepare for desegregation because the district was already desegregated. Wilmington's response was to establish an elaborate orientation program primarily for staff.

Throughout the preparation period, the role of the State Board in moving districts toward adequate preparation was minimal. The task of preparation was seen as a local responsibility. The DPI human relations staff was on a fixed annual appropriation of federal money and, moreover, suffered from high turnover. Neither state nor local school officials viewed human relations as a priority area.

School district preparation's thus reflected what had to be done (under public pressure) not what should be done (professionally). School officials continued to treat the public's input as insignificant. Legal and educational expenditures had to be made; emotional outbursts could be dispensed with. Suburban school officials were reluctant to feed white anxiety. One suburban school superintendent said to me privately, "The desegregation plan will bus about 20 percent of the children; if we discuss alternative plans in public then everyone will think that their child will be bused, so everyone will be upset."

Political considerations prevented most school superintendents from moving openly toward preparation, for they could be charged with "giving up." Many of their constituents considered treasonable any action or word that allowed the plaintiffs to claim that busing was possible or inevitable. One superintendent told me that a friend had lost his job over this issue. Willingness to begin preparation might be hazardous to a superintendent's employment, or render him unavailable for elevation to county superintendent when and if reorganization occurred. Finally, many of the superintendents themselves did not accurately perceive the probability of their losing the suit. In late fall 1977, a key superintendent in the planning process said to me at cocktail party, "Even I think it might really happen," as if, before that point, there had been little chance of the court order being upheld.

Post–Final Order Preparation

With the judge's order in hand, however, the New Board moved assertively to implement the school desegregation order. The Board first had to appoint a superintendent-designate for the county district-to-be. With the appointment of Thomas Minter as deputy commissioner for elementary and secondary education in the U.S. office of Education in Washington, Carroll Biggs and George Kirk became the obvious top two contestants for the part.

Right after New Year's Day 1978, Carroll Biggs received the nod. Immediately a local newspaper columnist, Ralph Moyed, wrote that a deal had been struck with Wendell Howell.[36] Biggs had secured Howell's vote and thus a majority of the Board, Moyed charged, by agreeing to appoint Howell's friends (like Superintendent Joseph P. Johnson and Finance Director Russell B. Dineen) to high county posts. These charges fitted Bigg's reputation as a "politician," while Kirk's supposed refusal to deal matched his reputation as a "professional." Biggs then engineered a three-year contract for himself, although the board was reported to have agreed in private to limit the first superintendent's contract to one year. It came as no surprise that Alexis I. Superintendent Pugh was not given a choice assignment, but Biggs' chief rival, Dr. Kirk, was named to the number two slot.

Dr. Biggs and the Board moved ahead on reassigning students, restructuring the organization, and redeploying personnel. Positions were found for all former administrative personnel in the new hierarchy. Within a month of his appointment, Biggs was being criticized for being too strong a leader.[37]

A pupil assignment plan was developed, passed by the Board, and accepted by the court; the plan established pupil assignments in each of four attendance areas. (To deal with declining enrollments, the plan also closed fourteen schools.) For example, the schools in the Newark district were linked to over a dozen schools in the city to form Area 3. Newark and city students were assigned to Wilmington schools for grades 4–6. All students in this new attendance area were assigned to Newark schools for grades 1–3 and 7–12. In the other three areas similar plans were developed. In Area 1, Alfred I. and Mt.

Pleasant students were assigned to the city for grades 4–6, but Claymont students were assigned to Wilmington for grades 7–9. In Area 2, Stanton and Marshallton-McKean students went to city schools for grades 4–6. Conrad's students were assigned to Wilmington High School. With the exception of two rural schools in the New Castle–Gunning Bedford district, students were assigned to De La Warr schools for grades 4–6. A total of 23,000 students were reassigned, 14,000 from the city and 9,000 from the suburbs.

Next, personnel were shifted among suburban and city schools and offices. Personnel from the component districts were assigned to curriculum coordination and development. In spring 1978 the New Castle County Education Association, a National Education Association (NEA) affiliate, by a vote of 2,825 to 1,263, won the right to be the teachers' bargaining agent, defeating the Wilmington-based American Federation of Teachers (AFT) affiliate. The NCCEA had about 2,400 members, primarily from the suburban districts, while the AFT had begun with a base of mostly city teachers (400). Other personnel (such as custodians and teacher aides) voted to have an AFT-affiliated union represent them. By the opening of school in September 1978, however, no contracts had been signed. Nevertheless, all personnel agreed to participate in preparation and the first weeks of implementation. As we will see in Chapter 8, however, the failure to reach a settlement with the teachers resulted in the school district's first major crisis, in October 1978.

With a court order to inspire and protect them, the Board and administration took comprehensive steps to prepare the staff for desegregation. Superintendent Biggs named the former superintendent of Marshallton-McKean, Dr. Richard Linett, deputy superintendent for human relations. Ninety-eight teachers were hired and trained as human relations specialists to work in this area. Linett then appointed a Human Relations Advisory Council. This group consisted of representatives of twenty-five major community organizations in the county, including many leaders of supportive community groups (see Chapter 6). By school's opening, this council had begun a monitoring procedure to ensure that principals were prepared to implement desegregation.

District personnel were involved in extensive preparations. Out of some 3,900 teachers in the county district, 470 were paid to participate in a four-week summer in-service institute. The first week of school was delayed so that all teachers could participate in four days of in-service training before the opening of school. Nonprofessional and administrative personnel also participated in workshops.

Finally, an essential step could be put off no longer. The NCCPBE had to deal with the long-neglected parents and students.

Parent and Community Involvement

The public was kept at arm's length by school officials throughout desegregation planning before the final court order of January 1978.

For example, in fall 1976 the Interim Board was under pressure to involve the public, but most of the superintendents and board members resisted it. Many Interim Board members accepted the superintendents' attitude that public participation would be an obstacle, rather than a help. To paraphrase one board member's comment about public meetings, "We should have public input now, and then we must get on with our real work."

The Board saw dealing with the public not as an opportunity to build acceptance but as a threat. They feared being hamstrung by the large antibusing organization, the Positive Action Committee (PAC). To them the public meant only disruption and delay. However, community groups urged that lay people be added to the task forces.[38]

On the day after election day, with few in the audience, the Interim Board took action. It decided to appoint advisory committees of twenty-six members each to every one of the sixteen task forces. Each of the thirteen Interim Board members selected a "lay person" and a student for each of the sixteen advisory committees, and then each advisory committee selected one representative to serve on the original task force. Thus, the Board "lowered" its technically oriented standards and allowed parents and students to join the educators in the decision making. The process, however, remained dominantly technical. The "lay persons" were appointed to committees on building and grounds, legal relationships, and transportation, but there were no task forces in areas of public concern such as extracurricular activities or child safety.

The Interim Board task forces did have to deal with specific and vexing issues such as how and to what extent the eleven districts with their differing personnel policies, curricula, student record system, and the like were to be combined into one with a consistent set of regulations, policies, and procedures. How the teachers, students, and staff should be prepared for desegregation was another perplexing challenge. The task forces produced piles of reports, which generally received high grades from knowledgeable members of the community and educators, but little immediately came of them. Parents, teachers, and students charged that they were placed on committees that were not dealing with issues of major importance to them and that administrators were not concerned about their views.

The Interim Board did not treat the public warmly. Statements by citizens were limited to three minutes at the end of meetings. Of course, overall public sentiment did affect preparations fundamentally by creating a "go slow" imperative, but few efforts were made to reach out into the community. It was charged that the Interim Board and Superintendents' Council made their decisions outside the public's purview. Someone said to me very aptly, "they built a moat around themselves."

Even the traditional PTA school support groups took little part in the planning. The parents, at most, played an advisory role, and many complained that their advice changed no decisions. Parent-based organizations were torn by a number of conflicts. They chafed at the reluctance of school officials to involve them in the planning process. Many members were torn between their desire to support public schools and their strong opposition to the busing plan.

Major confrontations over busing occurred at annual conventions of the State Congress of PTAs in the early 1970s. John Trager, a white Wilmington bachelor, won the vice-presidency of the state PTA on a strong antibusing platform. He and his supporters tried to use the PTA as a platform from which to attack busing. They were somewhat successful; the PTA supported a constitutional amendment to prohibit forced busing for the desegregation of public schools. At the same time, others (led by its president, Betty Lewis) directed the PTA's programs toward a smooth transition. The state PTA also held informational meetings, urged the creation of an information center, sponsored hearings on alternative desegregation plans, and, in general, gave much constructive support to those trying to "protect and prepare ourselves, our children, and our community for the awesome prospect of desegregating our public schools under court order."[39]

Since black members were in the majority on the Wilmington School Board, its entry as an intervening plaintiff in 1972 made it the preeminent black organization taking part in the desegregation process. Wilmington School Board representatives presented a minority perspective on the court-established planning boards and in the courtroom itself. Other black organizations contributed from time to time but none so consistently as the school board.

The Wilmington branch of the NAACP had refused to become involved in the case when it was reopened in 1971. Under the new leadership of James H. Sills (who in the summer of 1978 became a member of the county school board), the branch offered to support the case and enter the suit in 1974. The plaintiffs' lawyer advised the group not to do so at that time to avoid further delaying the resolution of the suit. In the end, participation of the Wilmington NAACP was largely limited to its later leaders' occasional complaints about inequities in the desegregation process.

The Wilmington Home and School Council, independent of the PTA since 1968, worked closely with parents (primarily through the federally funded Parent Educational Resource Center). Workshops and newsletters helped to bring needed information to parents. In spite of these efforts, however, Wilmington parents remained nearly uninformed throughout the process (Chapter 2).

The Committee for the Improvement of Education (CIE) was formed because of much strong opposition among blacks to busing and out of concern for the effects of desegregation on black children. CIE was accepted as a friend of the court. The committee argued against racial balance, for improving the Wilmington School District, and for the desegregation of county housing. It claimed that desegregation through busing had not led to better black pupil performance elsewhere.

After the 1976 court decision, a municipal judge, a city councilman, the president of the Wilmington Home and School Council, and other prominent city blacks organized to promote the Wilmington black interest in desegregation. The judge was named chairman. This group of black community leaders tried in several meetings to form a black political force focusing on school desegregation that would carry on after the expected dissolution of the Wilmington School Board. The group developed a proposal to seek local foundation funds to hire staff for monitoring the desegregation process; however, the foundations were never approached. In October 1977, this group sponsored a black solidarity rally against the 10–2 plan. About 250 people attended. As an ongoing organization, however, the group never got off the ground. During the making of the significant decisions about desegregation in the courts and on the court-directed boards, the chief minority spokesman remained the Wilmington School Board president, Wendell Howell. But in May 1978, Howell was accused of having improvements made to his home by public school employees, and he was forced to resign his school board positions.

Citizens' groups were formed in a number of suburban school districts with names like "Let's Make It Work" and acronyms like "CARE." These groups tried to prepare the public for desegregation and to pressure the school boards to begin preparation by holding coffees and public meetings. The groups joined forces with the few groups established by local school boards. With the exception of the group in the Alfred I. duPont district, district-based activity in the suburbs was modest to nonexistent. All citizen groups faced severe obstacles, including public apathy and opposition, a reluctance of the school boards to act, and uncertainty about their goals. In white blue-collar school districts like Conrad and Claymont, it was difficult to get school officials even to mention desegregation in school newsletters. Finding people willing even to express an inclination to help, much less to sit at a round table to work for peaceful implementation, was very difficult.

Post–Final Order

Once the final court order was in place, county school officials moved to inform the public. In spring 1978, countywide newsletters were distributed describing the desegregation order. These were supplemented with special reports called "School Business," which were sent to county business leaders. An elaborate system of citizens' advisory councils (CAC's) was planned. A representative council was to be selected by the principal at each school. These school councils were then to select representatives for councils at each school level (such as high school) in each of the four school district attendance areas. These councils in turn were to select representatives to serve on area-wide steering committees. Although only a few school level CAC's were operating before the first week of school, their impact was already being felt.[40] To supplement this structure and to improve communications with black parents, the superintendent met regularly with a group of black leaders from the city.

Student leaders were also involved in training workshops, the largest of which enrolled eight hundred students in late August. A summary of the Student Rights and Responsibilities Code was distributed to all secondary school students after editing to meet criticisms of its readability.

Although all of this activity sparked protests in March 1978 (three thousand students, from schools in almost all of the county's school districts, boycotted classes; one thousand were suspended), the New Board left no doubt that it would implement the law to the best of its ability.

The highlights of the New Board's communications were two open house days, one in April and one on September 10, the day before the opening of school. Over ten thousand people attended the city schools during the spring open house. The schools were also full for the preopening day, and the governor and mayor showed their interest by touring schools in Wilmington. Their appearance overshadowed the difficulties between school and governmental officials during the desegregation process.

Relations with Governmental Officials

Throughout the school desegregation process, relations between school officials and governmental officials had been strained. The conflict arose as increasing costs as well as public criticism of the schools began to break into their historical isolation. As Dolan and Soles point out:

> There has been a steady movement to bring the schools within the governor's purview so that full budgetary analysis of school expenditures can be achieved; this in spite of the strong opposition to changing the independent status of the Department of Public Instruction.[41]

They note that state educational expenses increased from about 4 million in 1935 to 165 million in 1975. Further, the increase in state expenses outdistanced pupil enrollments. When Governor duPont was struggling to avert the "bankruptcy" of the state in 1977, he aimed his budget axe at the public schools. Although the Finance Committee reversed the bulk of the cuts at the urging of local school supporters, it was clear that the struggle to pare school expenses would continue. The school government conflict erupted over desegregation on several occasions. In 1974, Melvin A. Slawik, county executive, appointed a group to advise him on how to achieve a peaceful reaction to the court order. This group's activities, and even its existence, angered a number of school superintendents. They saw the county executive's action as an attempt to take over the public schools and incorporate them into the county government. For their part, the county executive's appointees were chiefly concerned with the reluctance of school authorities to share information about the desegregation case with the public. Disregarding the preference of the school authorities for keeping out of the critical eye of everyone, the group continued to encourage them to act and then aggravated them further by consistently monitoring their behavior (see Chapter 6).

Statements against busing and the courts made by state legislators and statewide executives and representatives constantly added to the school authorities' difficulties. While politicians could talk about defying, delaying, or overturning a court order (see Chapter 5), school officials could not avoid the obligation to implement that order. Relations with the legislature were strained particularly over the legislature's voluntary desegregation plan.

Suburban school authorities had flirted with the idea of magnet schools throughout the county molded on those in cities like Houston, Dallas, and Milwaukee. They abandoned the magnet idea for at least two reasons. The plan began to look very expensive, and the court demanded proof that it would desegregate schools. The state Legislative Committee on Desegregation, however, took up the idea of magnet schools as a way out of the desegregation dilemma and hired an outside consultant to investigate the plan's feasibility. The consultant agreed with the school authorities about the planning time and cost involved in a full magnet plan, and the legislators backed away in time to avoid a battle with the educators.

In summer 1977, the executive staff task force appointed to enhance and smooth the desegregation process began work. Again, a number of superintendents were annoyed at public officials entering the fray at the last minute with their customary inadequacy. The educators' discontent focused on the establishment of a countywide Information Center. A quickly arranged meeting between the director of the Information Center and the Superintendents' Council served to dissipate some of the tension. By September 1978, governmental and school officials had successfully cooperated on crisis intervention plans as well as on media and information centers.

Relations were not always harmonious. After the "but for" decision, Governor duPont aroused fears of state intrusion into educational matters by persuading the State Board of Education to accept the one-way busing plan. Probably not by accident, soon after this conflict the governor appointed a commission to consider whether DPI should be brought into his cabinet. Similarly, the governor met legislative criticism that the State Board was too compliant toward the court by including in his multidistrict authorization legislation a special citizens' panel (with a majority appointed by legislative leaders) that would review the State Board plan.

Thus, despite the need for school and government cooperation, the two groups held to different perspectives on the case and clashed several times during the desegregation process.

Putting It Together

As the opening of the 1978 school year approached, the New Castle County School District had an operating board of education ready to implement a reorganization and school desegregation plan. Fortieth largest among school districts in the nation, its budget was $155 million.

Most of the old suburban school boards were still busy with legal dickering on the last Saturday before schools were to open. This last-minute legal manuevering led U.S. Supreme Court Justice William Rehnquist to consider a stay. Wanting to have its cake and eat it too, the County Board authorized Superintendent Biggs to file an affadavit detailing all the steps taken by the school district to prepare for the opening of school.[42] Unwilling to formally oppose the stay, the Board informed the court of its preparedness for desegregation. The affadavit listed fifty-three actions that had been taken to prepare for school opening. The stay was denied and busing began on September 11, 1978.

During the Phase 1 free-for-all, preparations had been few and far between. During Phase 2, the Interim Board's task forces planned activities but did very little to prepare students or teachers (only one in-service day was held for teachers). During the "but for" phase (3), activity came to a halt. The New Board saw itself as developer of desegregation plans, not implementor of the plan. School officials were spurred to the real task of preparation by the Supreme Court refusal to grant certiorori in October 1977, and serious efforts began after the final desegregation order on January 9, 1978.

SUMMARY

The courts had given state and local school district officials the opportunity to negotiate a desegregation arrangement agreeable to them, but they had difficulty bargaining. They were hampered by their conflicting ideological views and divided by their varying organizational interests and values. The antibusing sentiment among their constitutents was very strong, and any who were perhaps probusing were quiet about it. The white majority, which dominated decision making, openly espoused local white school district interests. The plans they generated placed a disproportionate burden on blacks and seemed unlikely to work; consequently, they were rejected by the court.

In a sense the courts had established the Interim Board and its successor gambling that the legal adversary process could be turned into bargaining; the gamble did not work, for the political forces that had kept the city and suburban districts segregated and separated for years were continued to operate.

Suburban and state school officials acknowledged their responsibility to implement whatever plan the court ordered, but they steadfastly maintained their position against busing. Because many voters were wary of the impact of desegregation, Wilmington representatives did not argue for busing but concentrated on stating the interests of their constituents.

Local and state school authorities were reluctant to involve the public and to begin desegregation preparation before the final court order. They were no more able to work smoothly with political officials. If desegregation had come in September 1977 as ordered, Delaware might have faced major problems. The stay issued in August 1977 gave time for a more congenial atmosphere for desegregation to develop. It seemed that little could be done until the final legal disposition of the Wilmington case had removed the uncertainty and allowed public officials to confront the situation without seeming to betray their constituency.[43]

5 / Governmental Officials

The court challenge to state and local government was substantial. It was no less than to change the pattern of racial segregation in the Wilmington metropolitan area and to help a hostile public accept a reorganization of the school districts and the busing of thousands of students. Let us first look at the actions of the State Legislature, for it was the legislature that was explicitly invited by the federal courts to remedy school segregation.

THE STATE LEGISLATURE: SYMBOLIC ACTION

Legislatures are supposed to be the heart of the political bargaining process.[1] The U.S. District Court had invited the Delaware State Legislature to redress the constitutional violation committed by its 1968 Educational Advancement Act. Highly exposed to the great public opposition to busing, how could the Delaware State Legislature respond to public pressure to oppose busing as well as to court pressure to develop a constitutionally acceptable plan?

The legislature did respond to the various court decisions, but never decisively enough to develop a constitutionally acceptable plan. Formulated with an eye on public hostility, the plans they proposed fell short of guaranteeing the desegregation of the schools.

The State Legislature offered no positive leadership in preparing for the implementation of school desegregation. Instead, its actions tended to inflame the general situation, increasing rather than reducing anxiety. Those actions reflected both the effectiveness of strongly organized opposition to busing and the beliefs of the legislators themselves. Virtually all legislators were themselves ideologically opposed to busing and were sympathetic to those who hoped to resist the court's directive.

Because the legislature was concerned with the legal propriety of its actions, its activities are best examined within the phases diagrammed in Figure 1-1 (Chapter 1).

Phase 1: Free-for-All

When the three-judge panel declared the Wilmington schools segregated, it indicated that the Supreme Court decision on Detroit limiting busing across district lines (see Chapter 3) was not applicable in this case, and invited any interested party to submit a desegregation plan. Many interested parties, however, wanted nothing to do with desegregation if it meant busing, and instead turned to putting pressure on the State Legislature to "do something." The Positive Action Committee (PAC), the major antibusing organization described in Chapter 7, urged New Castle County legislators to take a stand against busing. Several lawmakers did so by attending and even addressing strong antibusing rhetoric to well-attended PAC meetings. In response to specific PAC demands and general public sentiment, the State Legislature established a joint committee in July 1975 to study the impact of proposed remedies ordered by the U.S. District Court. Committee objectives were to obtain a stay, to review proposed desegregation plans, and to acquire legal advice.[2]

The committee asked the judges to delay the date on which plans were to be submitted in order to allow the legislature to act. When the judges responded that the legislature could find ways to participate without the delay, angry lawmakers demanded that the judges appear in the legislature to explain their actions.[3] With feelings running high, the State Legislature seemed ready to pass a variety of obstructive legislation. But the legal consultant to the defendants, Philip Kurland, noted that an explicit legislative act aimed at halting desegregation would add weight to the plaintiffs' basic contention, that state action was furthering school segregation. He advised the legislature to "be like Caesar's wife; be beyond reproach."[4]

The legislature saw that they faced a dilemma. If they pleased their constituents by acting against forced busing, they would prove the plaintiffs' contention that state action was responsible for the segregation in city schools. Taking any antibusing action would hurt the state's appeal. Consequently, the joint committee was dissolved in September 1975. Its final report recommended that the "General Assembly avoid entering the case at this time," and emphasized the need for the legislature to adhere to the law.[5]

The state legislators spoke out vehemently during this period. In discussing a state constitutional amendment to prohibit changing school district lines without voter approval, Senator Dean Steele, a suburban Republican, said that he didn't "give a damm what the courts do,... we've got to at least try this." The president *pro tem* of the Senate, J. Donald Isaacs, a Democrat from the Appoquinimink district, called the bill a "waste of time," but he voted for it.[6] State Representative Winifred Spence, a Republican also from the Appoquinimink district, probably spoke for many when she said the busing is a "form of child abuse" but the General Assembily could do nothing about it but speak out.[7] Some legislators were willing to go further. Suburban Republican representative John Arnold said that he was not afraid to face contempt of court charges, if necessary, to assert what he viewed as legislative prerogatives.[8]

While the most conservative members of the Assembly were offering such radical antibusing rhetoric, the few more liberal members of the State Legislature were certainly not advocating desegregation. At most they were working behind the scenes to tone down the emotional responses of the legislature. Such legislative asctions ranged from supoenaing a federal judge to passing ligislation that would "fine not less than $20,000 nor more than $40,000 or imprision for not more than five years or both" any federal judges who, in the legislature's opinion, exceeded their authority.[9]

The primary restraining force on the State Legislature was its members' fear of jeopardizing future appeals. Legal advice came mostly from two sources.[10] The first was Professor Philip B. Kurland of the University of Chicago Law School. Not all of his advice was heeded, as is shown in the following exchange between Kurland and Senator Thomas Sharp before a special session on March 15, 1976—a session set up specifically to discuss the legislature's options with Kurland.

> *Senator Sharp*: Thank you, Mr. Chairman. Professor Kurland, what would the result be if the state were to fail to implement a court-ordered plan?
>
> *Professor Kurland*: I assume that there would be a hearing on contempt of court initiated, presumably by the plaintiffs in this lawsuit and those who have authority to expend money or to secure the buses or whatever it is that has been ordered and have not done so, will be asked to show why they should not do so, and in the event of failure to show cause, why they should not be punished appropriately for not doing so, that punishment usually involving a daily fine and/or imprisonment until such time as conformity is secured.
>
> *Sen Sharp*: Are you saying then that the state officials would probably go to jail?
>
> *Prof. Kurland*: No, I expect the state officials would probably comply.

Representative Sincock questioned whether enforcement of a court order would affect members of the legislature.

> *Representative Sincock:* Thank you, Mr. Chairman. Professor Kurland, following along the lines of an earlier question from the vice chairman, Senator Sharp, the point raised is what happens if a state authority ignores the orders of the court. I believe that you pointed out some rather grim alternatives, but I believe from this morning's discussion that these alternatives would in effect be applied to other than the legislative part of government. Is that correct?
>
> *Prof. Kurland:* I know of no instance in which the legislature has been held in contempt for enacting legislation which would be limiting, or attempting to be limiting, on the district court order. The courts chose instead simply to say that the legislation is invalid, ineffective and not controlling on the state officials.
>
> *Rep. Sincock:* These again being administrative officials, correct?
>
> *Prof. Kurland:* Executive Department.

Although Kurland held out little hope for a voluntary plan being acceptable, the legislature later passed such a plan.

Kurland informed the legislature about the problems with other paths of resistance:

> *Senator Berndt:* Suppose we dissolve the Board of Education.
>
> *Prof. Kurland:* I expect they may find or look for other sources of revenue from within your state bonds.
>
> *Sen. Berndt:* Well, can they force our Treasurer to sign a check? Is that where it comes from?
>
> *Prof. Kurland:* Oh, yes.
>
> *Sen. Berndt:* Just go to the Treasurer and say just sign the check or we're carting you off to Leavenworth or some other unpleasant place?
>
> *Prof. Kurland:* It is not likely to be quite so unpleasant, but it will be a jail, yes.
>
> *Sen. Berndt:* Suppose we dissolve the office of Treasurer?
>
> *Prof. Kurland:* The one thing I think you probably can do within the terms of the decisions that heretofore have been reached is to abolish public education in the entire state.
>
> *Sen. Berndt:* They could do that?
>
> *Prof. Kurland:* The entire state. You.
>
> *Sen. Berndt:* I didn't get the implication.
>
> *Prof. Kurland:* I think that under the existing decisions, and I won't guarantee this is a prediction, that you can end public education in the state of Delaware. You have to get your own constitution amended first, but I don't think that would be inconsistent with the equality doctrine of the Supreme Court in Brown and in the cases that followed. Short of that, we're going to have to, if you are going to provide education, you

are going to have to provide desegregated education in accordance with the terms of the United States Court's order.

Sen. Berndt: Okay, we'll keep education in the state of Delaware. Suppose when the buses are delivered, we tell the bus company, the manufacturers, we're going to pay you $1 a year and you'll get paid off in 350,000 years or something like that.

Prof. Kurland: If you get the bus companies to deliver the buses under those circumstances, I'm quite sure that will satisfy the court.

Sen. Berndt: Suppose we come up with a plan and say we'll accept busing in the seventh, eighth grades and ninth grades. We don't want it in elementary or high school. It will have no bearing on it.

Prof. Kurland: It's been tried and failed.

Sen. Berndt: It's all or nothing at all.

Prof. Kurland: It's what the trial court now suggests as a necessity for desegregation. The time for phased desegregation, which was immediately after the Supreme Court decree in 1954, is no longer acceptable and the court has said so. They say that the time for desegregation is now. It is total. It must be accomplished as soon as they, the trial court, assumes within its bounds the discretion as it should be.

Sen. Berndt: Let me go back to this other point about shutting down all education. You mean they can close our schools.

Prof. Kurland: They can't; you can, so long as you close all of them.

Sen. Berndt: We don't want to do that, or course.

Prof. Kurland: I should expect not.

Sen. Berndt: So, we send the children to school. Are they going to stand in front of the school door, arms bared, and say, you shall not enter?

Representative Arnold: Senator, let's not debate with the professor.

Sen. Berndt: I'm trying to find out what is that power they have over us, and I'm just trying to propose other things. Can they do this or can't they do it.

The warning voiced by Kurland that most impressed the lawmakers was the chance that passing discriminatory legislation would harm future appeals:

> *Representative Byrd:* Mr. Kurland, we discussed briefly, your opinion of changing the mandatory attendance laws. We also talked about different legislation that might come before this body as far as affecting an appeal before the Supreme Court. I wish you would address yourself to that for a few minutes, please.
>
> *Prof. Kurland:* Let me address myself to the general question and then to the specifics. The trial court held and the Supreme Court did not reverse the decision that Legislation by this body, the Educational Advancement Act, which the trial court found was not ill-motivated, but only had segregatory effect. They found that statute a basis for

holding that the state was in violation of the Fourteenth Amendment because that was a segregatory act. Any action by this body which in effect, not in purpose, not in intent, but in effect can be read as a segregatory act, the way the Educational Advancement Act was read as a segregatory act, would be a basis for the court imposing interdistrict remedy totally apart from the order already existing. My answer to you then is, could it be read in effect, your proposed legislation, could it be read in effect as a cause of continuation of existing segregation in the schools. With respect to your particular statute, I would say that danger is quite clear. But I want to emphasize that it is not only in terms of that particular proposition, but in terms, generally, of any action taken by this body at this time. You have to be concerned that you have a court which finds effect, frankly, segregatory effect, where I find it very difficult to see segregatory effect. But then they are there and I am here.[11]

The second major constraining force was the counsel to the Special Legislative Committee on Desegregation. All legislation that might affect a possible appeal was sent to this committee and was reviewed by counsel. Several bills were successfully stopped by this procedure.

It is sobering to realize that Kurland's substantial contribution in bringing an aura of reason to the State Legislature came about almost by accident. A legislator happened to overhear one side of a critical conversation between Kurland and another legislator, and, realizing that Kurland was providing helpful wisdom, urged that Kurland's views be given wide publicity.

When I first asked a state lawyer how well known Kurland was, the lawyer replied, "He is the second best constitutional lawyer in the United States, and the best one, Alexander Bickel, has been dead for months." Since he brought bad news, however, Kurland's views were resisted throughout by many legislators. It took time for Kurland's national reputation to be appreciated in Delaware.

Phase 2: Interim Board and Ratio Constraint

The May 19, 1976, majority decision of the three-judge panel had moved the State Legislature into a second and critical phase. The court established a framework for desegregation by ordering that a new district be created from eleven of the twelve existing districts in the county. But the court also acknowledged the legislature's power even under the federal order. First, it left some key issues unresolved (such as equalization of personnel policies) and at the discretion of the legislature; second, it invited the legislature to alter the court-proposed plan as long as the basic criteria were met. The critical question then became: What role would the legislature play? It could totally support the State Board of Education and the Interim Board, working with them for full and nondisruptive compliance. At the other extreme, it could totally support the PAC antibusing position and pass legislation unacceptable to the court and harmful to the transition. Or it could simply refuse to deal with the State Board's recommendations.

Responding to pressures to "do something," the legislature took two major steps. It expanded the Interim Board from five to thirteen members. The court had ordered the State Board to appoint a five-person board from among groups of current board members because Delaware had a tradition of five-person boards and because working relationships were likely to be better in a small body rather than a large one. The legislature gave all districts one representative, except for the largest districts (Wilmington and Newark), which were given two apiece. This move was received with mixed feelings. Some were pleased that each district would have direct representation but others thought that parochial interests would be harder to sidestep in the expanded Board and that organizational problems would hinder action.

In response to pressure from PAC, the legislature also passed legislation establishing a "freedom of choice plan" among the eleven school districts.[12] Under the legislation, parents wishing to enroll their children in other school districts could apply during July 1976 for transfers, subject to acceptance by the requested district. PAC called on groups working for peaceful implementation to transfer their children and to encourage others to do so. More than a thousand students applied, a large majority of them white students seeking to transfer from majority black to white schools.[13] Faced with the threat of increasing segregation, all but one school district disallowed such minority-to-majority transfers. Fewer than three hundred blacks transferred from the Wilmington School District to suburban districts. Thus, the freedom of choice plan had little effect on the racial makeup of the county schools.

The following year another voluntary plan was enacted. Participation by all school districts was mandatory as was publicizing of the plan by the state superintendent.[14] With the threat of mandatory assignments looming large, 317 blacks from Wilmington and De La Warr opted to attend white suburban schools. Very few whites crossed school district lines in the opposite direction.

As it became clear that the voluntary plan was attracting no more than a handful of whites into the city schools and insufficient numbers of blacks into the suburban schools, the Legislative Committee explored the concept of magnet schools. However, the Committee worked primarily in a vacuum, with little communication and cooperation with school officials, community groups (except for some members' close ties to PAC), or even its own advisory committee. The Committee was so opposed to busing that they did not wish to deal with advocates of peaceful implementation—not even those on its own advisory committee. Breaks in this self-imposed isolation were few and accidental. On September 13, 1976, for example, there was a meeting of Marshallton-McKean parents working toward peaceful implementation. Speakers included representatives of the legislative committee on desegregation and Mary DiVirgilio, the Interim Board member from Marshallton-McKean. Planned as informational, the meeting turned into a dramatic confrontation between the Board and the Committee.[15] This meeting exposed the serious differences among the Board, the legislature, and the public on how to respond to the court order.

I have mentioned before how the Legislative Committee's isolation led to an impractical flirtation with a magnet school plan. This concept came to a quiet end despite months of discussion for several reasons.

First, the Committee members seemed never to consider magnet schools as a serious educational alternative. As one legislator told me in private, "Most legislators are not interested in education; they're just against busing." Magnet schools seemed a handy device to avoid busing whites against their wills.

Second, the Committee's study of magnet school plans was hamstrung by a lack of professional educational assistance. Not trusting outsiders and fearing that their work might be damaging to future appeals, the Committee relied heavily on their counsel. After months of consideration, the Committee finally hired Allen H. Zelon in late 1976 to develop a magnet school plan for New Castle County. Zelon was a former president of a community school board in New York which had established a magnet school for the gifted. His plan for Delaware called for schools for the gifted in Wilmington and De La Warr at the secondary level, with programs to be developed through community input.[16] When the report was completed, almost as an afterthought the chairman of the Committee asked a few people (I was one of them) to review it. That was about the extent of public consultation.

The Committee did speak with a representative from Dallas, where magnet schools had been developed through a serious bargaining process.[17] There, the executive director of an education group, the Dallas Alliance, had visited more than forty cities to investigate their desegregation activities. The Delaware Committee only contemplated a trip (I am tempted to write "a bus ride") to Zelon's school at Coney Island. Lacking the staff and expertise to develop its own magnet plan and being unwilling to mount a full-scale hearing, the Committee opened itself to charges that it was not conducting itself as a professional body.[18]

A third obstacle to successful adoption of a magnet plan was the probable cost of a program of sufficient scope to satisfy the courts. The expense was significant in a state that had been declared by its governor to be on the verge of bankrupcy in 1976. The governor may have exaggerated, but fiscal crises were indeed common in Delaware. In view of the possible high costs of leveling-up countywide school expenditures, legislators could not seriously consider a costly magnet school plan.

The final and most important failing of the magnet school concept was the general lack of enthusiasm for it. Wilmington school officials did not see it as a real possibility. Suburban and state officials considered it disruptive and expensive and of doubtful legality. The legislature itself did not favor it on its educational merits. The only substantial support came from members of a small association of parents of gifted children. Critics dismissed them as elitists. In the end, deserted by its proponents and damned by its enemies, the plan simply died.

Phase 3: The "But For" Plan

You will recall that in spring 1977, the U.S. Court of Appeals gave a new criterion for desegregating the New Castle County schools—the objective was now to be the restoration of segregation's victims to the status they would have achieved "but for" the effects of the constitutional violations (see Chapter 3). The Legislative Committee reacted by proposing a plan based on the principle of "reverse volunteerism." Their plan called for assigning all children in Wilmington to suburban schools and allowing those who opted out of the arrangement to remain in the city.[19] The plan was rejected by Judge Schwartz. Once again the State Legislature had shown itself unwilling to develop a plan that would mean mandatory busing of whites or even blacks.

Phases 4 and 5: New Board and Final Order

In December 1977, with the final order imminent, Governor du Pont (along with the Democratic attorney general, Richard Wier) asked the legislature to authorize a multidistrict reorganization of the school districts in the desegregation area. He called a special session for December 16, 1977. Two nights before, he talked with legislators and discovered that many had not received copies of the proposed legislation. A secretary had mailed them with too little postage.[20] It could be said that for want of a stamp, the war was lost; in reality, from the start, the army lacked more than a stamp. This was a battle that few soldiers were willing to fight.

Most upstate legislators opposed the plan because they saw it—or thought their constituents would see it—as a referendum on busing. They were afraid that favoring such a plan would prevent a successful appeal of the court decision. One suburban senator said, "It's a busing bill. My constituents aren't guilty, and I'm not going to plead them guilty by voting for this bill."[21] Wilmington's legislators opposed it because they supported the city school board in proposing a county district. Democrats throughout the state were wary of supporting a Republican governor's bill on a major issue. (Only one upstate Democrat voted for it.) At least one legislator was accused of being a beneficiary; the failure of the bill resulted in the creation of a single district, and it was asserted that the legislator would obtain a better position in the new district.[22]

After a day of heavy lobbying against the bill by PAC and for the bill by suburban and state school authorities, only sixteen of the forty voting house members supported it. Most of the positive votes came from downstate legislators who feared the impact of a county district on their schools.[23]

On January 27, 1978, after Judge Schwartz had set an operating tax rate of no higher than $1.91, the State Senate passed a "tax cap" bill. S.B. 435 established a formula based on the average local funding in the existing eleven districts, adjusted for inflation, with an increase of 10 percent for desegregation costs.[24] Within two weeks both houses had passed a four-district reorganization bill as well as the tax cap bill.[25] Judge Schwartz immediately asserted that his January 9, 1978, order took precedence over these bills: "Unless and until the court order is changed, this legislation means nothing."[26] The appeals let stand Schwartz's decisions on the four-district plan, but it did uphold the legislature's tax cap. The court ruled that Schwartz did not extend "the requisite deference to which legislative judgments in the field of taxation are entitled."[27] This decision established a tax rate lower than the Board rate by 9.5 cents; it would mean $2.5 million less for the proposed county district.

During the life of the New Board the legislature continued to deal in symbolic bills. In fall 1977 the legislature passed resolutions disavowing the New Board and urging President Carter to remove Judge Schwartz from the bench.

Summary of Legislative Activity

The Delaware General Assembly did not accept the court's invitations to enact a constitutionally acceptable school district reorganization and desegregation plan. The legislature was ideologically opposed to and politically wary of desegregation. Within the legislature, there were no advocates of desegregation or of any form of involuntary student transfer. The legislature's voluntary transfer and "but for" plans placed the burden of desegregation almost entirely on blacks, because they were the only ones who chose to be transferred. Consequently, with no other direction to go, the legislature focused its energies on symbolic rather than substantive activity. It passed resolutions against busing and against those thought to be responsible for bringing busing to Delaware instead of enacting desegregation plans likely to be accepted by the courts. Only after the final order did enabling legislation for a state reorganization plan pass—narrowly. But by then the court's plan was already being implemented and the legislature's plan was summarily dismissed by the federal courts.

It must be noted, however, that the State Legislature did not accept antibusing organization demands to pass obstructionist legislation. While a major confrontation between states' rights and federal authority loomed, the legislature never went over the brink to obstructionism.

Also on the positive side, the legislature offered an environment for a limited kind of public involvement. As the legislature became more engaged with the issue of desegregation, a forum for public discussion developed. Many state legislators welcomed the opportunity to demonstrate their opposition to busing and what they were doing to stop busing. PAC leaders at first, and representatives of groups more supportive of desegregation later, tried to influence legislators as the contest wore on. The peak of the interaction was the debate over the governor's four-district plan in December 1977.

Public involvement in the legislative process must be placed in perspective. The legislature, especially as represented by the Special Legislative Committee on Desegregation, was primarily interested in hearing from those who agreed with them. The Legislative Committee never met with the advisory committee it had set up, probably because the advisory committee was dominated by individuals much more open to the possibility of desegregation and supportive of public schools. The Legislative Committee refused to meet with the Delaware Committee on the School Decision (DCSD) or other community groups with a different stand on the issue. In fact, the Committee refused to hold its meetings in public even after the State Legislature passed a sunshine law. Nor did it hold hearings on any of its desegregation plans. The legislature was eager for the rewards of opposing busing but it was not open to genuine public discussion of its role.

Consequently it is not surprising that the legislature played no direct role in preparing for implementation. In fact, the legislature tended to be left out of coordination efforts such as the Information Center and the Breakfast Group. Some were wary of the way that the law makers exploited the issue; and the legislators really were not very interested.

Thus, rather than offer positive leadership to meet the realities of the court's actions, the legislature limited itself to criticism of the court's role. In short, the legislature, almost unanimously, exploited the passions around the issue and avoided the substance. The State Legislature's behavior stood in marked contrast to the actions of Delaware's state executives.

STATE AND LOCAL GOVERNMENTAL EXECUTIVES: SUBSTANTIVE ACTION

While in other communities the mayor of the central city has been the focus of demands for governmental leadership on the issue of desegregation, in this metropolitan case, where the state was the primary defendant, the county executive and the governor were on the spot as well.[28] During the period covered by this volume, there were two sets of these three executives. Governor Sherman W. Tribbitt, Mayor Thomas C. Maloney, and County Executive Melvin A. Slawik were in office before the first Wilmington metropolitan decision in July 1974. During the life of the Interim Board, Governor Pierre S. (Pete) du Pont IV, Mayor William T. McLaughlin, and County Executive Mary D. Jornlin took office. We have looked at the behavior of the State Legislature in relation to the various court decisions, but the actions of the governmental executives may be evaluated more usefully by their individual styles and political goals. Thus, their response to the federal court challenge is described by individual below.

County Executive Melvin A. Slawik

The first political executive to take action was County Executive Melvin A. Slawik, a Democrat. A former social worker and state legislator, Slawik was elected in 1972 on a platform of increasing county services.[29] About two-thirds of the New Castle County population live in unincorporated areas and are serviced by the county rather than municipalities. Slawik was an activist executive with strong social commitments coupled with working-class sympathies.

In May 1974, in response to a community group's initiative (see Chapter 6) and before any court decision on the Wilmington metropolitan case, Slawik appointed a Committee of Twelve to advise the county government on how to prepare for the impending court decision whatever its content. Slawik's committee was very diverse; it included the most vocal prointegration and antibusing advocates as well as representatives of more establishment groups like the American Association of University Women. The work of this group, later called the Delaware Committee on the School Decision (DCSD), is described in Chapter 6, for it functioned more as a community group than as a governmental one.[30] It is remarkable that Slawik, at considerable political risk and with no official responsibility in education, took the initiative very early to prepare the way for the desegregation process. Until he was removed from office after his conviction for lying to a federal grand jury in spring 1976, Slawik supported the DCSD with staff and an open door. He stated his position early in 1975: "While we may be against busing . . . we're for upholding the law and making sure everything works out as best as possible. Unless we prepare, we might have another Boston, We're hoping to generate a climate of obeying the law, whatever the court decision."[31]

As this statement makes clear, not even Slawik approved of forced busing. In January 1976, for example, he called on the DCSD to ask the court for a year's delay in implementation of the latest court order.

Governor Sherman W. Tribbitt

Governor Sherman W. Tribbitt, the state's chief executive from January 1972 to December 1976, also supported the DCSD. He agreed to make the committee a statewide group by executive order on January 21, 1975. A year later the Positive Action Committee (PAC), an antibusing organization claiming more than 10,000 members in New Castle County (see Chapter 7), called on the governor to dissolve the DCSD. The president of PAC demanded that "the DCSD cease this politically inspired infiltration of the educational system . . . with biased, politically inspired, and racist notions" and threatened that "should this form of brainwashing continue to take place within our public schools . . . PAC would investigate the possibility of taking legal action." Governor Tribbitt responded by saying that he had "absolutely no intention of disbanding" the DCSD and charged that the PAC message's allegations were divisive.[32]

Although opposed to busing, the governor took the position that he would not "stand in the schoolhouse door" and would implement the court's order with the resources at his disposal, preferably without disruption or violence. His antibusing position was widely advertised twice—once when he attacked the presiding judge of the three-judge panel for predetermining the merits of the case and again when he urged the National Governor's Conference to support an antibusing constitutional amendment.[33]

Although Governor Tribbitt had a reputation as a very cautious politician and slow-moving executive, in spring 1976 he was quick to accept the recommendation of the state police, the Department of Public Instruction, and the attorney general's office that he establish a county wide rumor control and desegregation Information Center. Committing some members of his staff and a few thousand dollars in contingency funds, he appointed a highly respected administrator as director of the Center—Clifford E. Hall, the secretary of highways and transportation. The Center received few calls after it opened on the day of the May 19 court decision but establishing it had some symbolic value. The governor received credit for acting responsibly and not giving in to the antibusing pressures.[34]

Governor Tribbitt assigned the state police jurisdiction over desegregation-related law enforcement. Before the governor took his step, responsibilities were ambiguous. Outside the City of Wilmington, where city police had jurisdiction, either county or state police would have authority, depending on who reached the scene of a problem first. State police accepted this responsibility in a totally professional manner, although the governor resisted their requests for funds and personnel for large-scale desegregation planning and equipment. For example, the officer in charge of the planning effort, Lt. Norman Cochran, took my course at the University of Delaware on desegregation, travelled to a number of communities (Boston, Louisville, Prince Georges County) that had already faced the problem, and worked with a large number of community and other resource people. Cooperative workshops with clergy, school officials, and police were held to establish crisis management teams. The state police played a major role in the establishment of the Information Center and directed the effort that led to the spring 1977 training of state, city, and county police for desegregation duty. (In August 1978, Cochran became the acting superintendent of the state police, an appointment testifying to the importance of his work.)

Despite Governor Tribbitt's strong position against busing, he also spoke out for peaceful implementation, even though this position brought him considerable political heat.

Mayor Thomas C. Maloney

As a young, attractive, activist politician, Thomas C. Maloney was caught between his responsibilities as mayor and his ambition to become a U.S. senator. As mayor of Wilmington he recognized some potential advantages of a metropolitan desegregation plan. After the July 1974 decision, Maloney was reported to be pleased, saying, "The benefits to the city in terms of education and property values are clear."[35] But as a candidate for the U.S. Senate against Senator William V. Roth, who had solid antibusing credentials, Maloney had to appeal to a predominantly white antibusing constituency outside of the city. Within a year and a half of approving the initial court decision, Maloney was calling busing "our national nightmare."[36] He chose not to reappoint one white advocate of metropolitan desegregation to the Wilmington School Board and declared in a newspaper advertisement, "I have always been against forced busing."[37] (Critics of the mayor called him Mayor "Baloney" and labelled such behavior as characteristic.)[38] On the positive side, Mayor Maloney adopted the DSCD when Governor Tribbitt extended it statewide in January 1975. One of his staff people helped the committee, and another served mainly as a conduit to the mayor. In summer 1977, Mayor Maloney failed in an attempt to induce a negotiated settlement of the suit (the details of which have not been revealed).

In January 1977 the guard changed. In the November 1976 election, Maloney was soundly defeated by incumbent Senator Roth. William McLaughlin succeeded Maloney as mayor, Tribbitt lost in a landslide to his Republican opponent, Congressman Pierre S. du Pont IV, and (with Slawik out of office) Mary Jornlin, a Republican, was elected county executive.[39] The busing issue appears to have played a minor role in these elections (Chapter 7). PAC endorsed Roth and the losing county executive candidate. In fact, Mary Jornlin, a city resident, had said that she would, as a symbolic gesture, consider riding a school bus on the first day of the implementation of any court-ordered desegregation plan. Congressman du Pont made it clear that his opposition to busing would not keep him from implementing a federal court order. Nevertheless, the three new personalities brought with them three different approaches toward busing.

Mayor William T. McLaughlin

Mayor William T. McLaughlin not only favored planning for desegregation but on at least one occasion stated his support for interdistrict desegregation on television. McLaughlin showed interest and support by regularly attending the Breakfast Group (see Chapter 6), speaking out for peaceful implementation, working to help the county executive and governor take more positive stands, and reappointing to the Wilmington Board the advocate of desegregation who had not been reappointed by Maloney.

In his inaugural speech, McLaughlin called on politicians to take a responsible position on busing:

> Another way we can continue to make progress is to work for peaceful and effective implementation of whatever school desegregation plan is ultimately adopted. We can no longer be concerned about philosophical positions on forced busing. I respect the positions of both sides. But what we shall be required to do will be dictated by the courts and be legally binding. . . . I call on all public officials, national, state, and local to put aside the rhetoric which was so prevalent before the elections.[40]

After the U.S. Court of Appeals decision, which others were calling outrageous and preposterous, the mayor said:

> People on both sides of this issue must come to the realization that without mutual cooperation, our community will be faced with destructive civic disorder and turmoil. The political leaders, especially, must realize this. It is time for all of us in positions of political leadership to begin to lead and not to follow. We are responsible for bringing the people together, not dividing them.[41]

In the summer of 1978, McLaughlin wrote a letter to all city employees asking them to support a smooth transition.

McLaughlin's style contrasted strongly with that of his predecessor. Far from having political ambitions, McLaughlin announced that he was not interested in running for reelection. Where Maloney had been a flamboyant and aggressive mayor, McLaughlin was low key, relaxed, and more attuned to intimate personal relations. If Maloney would work as a garbageman for a day to to dramatize a point and get press coverage, McLaughlin would work as a garbageman to gain a better understanding of the job and the people who filled it.

County Executive Mary D. Jornlin

Mary D. Jornlin took office as county executive with no obligations to the antibusing constituency. During the campaign, she had stated her determination to do what was necessary to ease implementation. She was also from the city, and she had been opposed by PAC. In addition, she was relatively uniformed on desegregation when she was elected. Her key advisors had not previously been involved in the problems. Community leaders worked with Jornlin and her top aides to bring them up to date on the issue. Within a few months, Jornlin's policy coordinator became a regular breakfast attender, participating in preparations for implementation. But as the day of implementation approached, Jornlin became involved in two hassles over school taxes. In both cases her actions increased public anxiety over busing. First, an alarming message was sent on the tax statements mailed to county taxpayers in the middle of July. According to a *News Journal* article, Governor du Pont "tracked down Jornlin at a conference she was attending in Atlanta" and persuaded her to tone down the wording.[42] Later, Jornlin declared that it was not the county's responsibility to pay for the mailing of the revised tax bills necessitated by the Circuit Court of Appeals ruling, again inviting public resentment.

Governor Pierre S. du Pont IV

Whereas Democratic Governor Tribbitt had been a Mayor Daley type of traditional politician—slow and methodical, working on an ad hoc basis, emphasizing personal relationships—Republican Governor du Pont was oriented more toward planning, expertise, and management.[43] Du Pont's election seemed part of a cyclical pattern in Delawate state politics, for Tribbitt had defeated Governor Russell Peterson, a forceful management-oriented Republican.

Du Pont took an active role in the desegregation process from the start of his administration. His aides attended the breakfast meetings immediately and offered help to all participants. His counsel, David Swayze, agreed to chair a Delaware Association for Public Administration conference, "The Impact of School Desegregation on State and Local Government in Delaware," which I arranged in March 1977.[44] The governor set a deadline for the State Board to complete a "but for" plan after the Court of Appeals decision. All this is not to say that the governor favored busing. For example, he called the Circuit Court of Appeals opinion "a stunning example of judicial craft at its worst . . . unclear, confusing and contradictory . . . [and] murky."[45]

Despite his opposition to busing, Governor du Pont was willing to lead. On June 24, 1977, he chose a black tie affair at a black church in Dover, the state capital, to deal dramatically with desegregation:

> One of the most serious and far reaching public questions facing us in the next few weeks is that of the State's approach to resolving the long-standing desegregation issue in New Castle County. As you know, the State firmly believes that there was not purposeful wrongdoing that led to the alleged segregation of minority school children in New Castle County. But in the decision handed down by the Circuit Court of Appeals on May 19th, the court held that some segregatory acts had occurred, and that a desegregation plan must be adopted for the coming school year. The State must be prepared to comply with that decision.
>
> While the opportunity certainly exists to reverse this decision on appeal, it is the opinion of Legal Counsel and the Attorney General that the chances of successfully obtaining an immediate stay of the Court's order are very small, and that any appeal of the Court's order cannot be heard until after the beginning of the next school year in September. Further, since the courts have consistently disagreed with the State's viewpoint over the past several years, it seems unlikely that a sudden change of direction will occur in the next two months. Therefore, it seems certain that the Court will impose some desegregation plan to be in place when school begins in September. . . .
>
> But the crux of the issue at hand is not which plan may be approved by the Courts. What we must understand is the near certainty that some plan will be in effect when two-thirds of Delaware's children go back to school in September. As Governor, I am acutely aware that there is no issue more sensitive among our people than this one. Continued rhetoric denying the existence of the Court's action is counterproductive. Such talk will seriously hurt the chances of our children to get the education they deserve in the environment they need to utilize that education. The reality is that the Court will require some plan to be in effect on the first of September, and we must begin taking appropriate steps to see that whatever plan is decided upon by the Court is promptly, properly, and fairly implemented.
>
> Therefore, the affected school districts and agencies of local government will have my personal support in the efforts they must make to implement whatever plan is finally ordered by the Court. Whatever the plan, the people of Delaware must know that responsible State elected officials are prepared to act in the best interest of all our citizens and to work with them in complying with the changes dictated by the Courts order as easily and as harmoniously as possible. After all, we are dealing with our children, and we have no greater responsibility, and the State has no greater investment, than in securing the continuity of their education for the future. I certainly hope that I can count on your support in helping us to meet this challenge.[46]

The governor was persuaded to establish a mechanism for involving his staff and the staff of New Castle County, the cities of Wilmington and Newark, and the U.S. Department of Justice to work together to plan for desegregation. A number of factors were pushing in the direction of such cooperation, including Mayor McLaughlin's willingness to lead and move on the issue, County Executive Jornlin's feelings of responsibility, and requests from community leaders through forums like the Breakfast Group.

The actual formation of the task force resulted from a fortuitous circumstance—all three executives were to appear jointly and discuss desegregation with business, religious, and professional leaders at a July 1977 meeting of the local National Conference of Christians and Jews (NCCJ). Pressures on the executives rose as this prominent event approached. Jon Chace, of the Community Relations Service of the U.S. Department of Justice, met with the executives beforehand and helped them concur on an agreement to establish a staff task force. At the NCCJ meeting, they announced their joint action. The governor also disclosed his plans to replace the DCSD with a more authoritative blue-ribbon group comprised of influential individuals in the state.

The staff task force was composed of members of the city, county, federal, and state governments. (Representation from Newark and the local superintendents was added later.) The task force divided its tasks into five areas: the Information Center, human relations, press and public relations, crisis intervention, and contingency planning. The governor's counsel served as the chairperson.[47] Their major accomplishment before Judge Schwartz issued the August stay was to establish an Information Center in the city-county Public Building in Wilmington with a director, staff, and equipment.

The director of the Information Center, Petey Funk, later said to me, "We thought we were prepared [in August 1977], but we had no idea of what was involved!" Intergovernmental preparation for September 1977 implementation had begun in earnest only two months before, when the task force was established. A few minutes after Judge Schwartz ordered a stay on August 5, 1977, David Swayze, the head of the intergovernmental desegregation task force, ordered the Information Center closed. The governmental and community leaders who had gathered at the center to read Schwartz' decision were relieved that they now had time for adequate preparation, but they also feared that the efforts of the governmental executives would wane as the crisis atmosphere passed. Fortunately, this near miss had a positive effect. Time was used wisely. By September 1978, elaborate plans and a great coordination of effort had indeed come about.

The most exciting and comprehensive preparations were the set of simulated desegregation crises held to test the readiness of the new mechanisms. One participant described the simulation as follows:

> Beginning at 8:30 a.m. on Wednesday, September 6, a full-blown surprise simulation involving nine school incidents, two problems with buses and four governmental action contacts were carried out over a two-hour period. Four schools (one per area) were beset by rumors with parents converging on the school, four then had racial incidents, and finally one had a serious incident that escalated well outside the school. In each case, callers simulating the principal called for some kind of police action and notified his area (and/or district) officials. The test was how well information got to the proper authority, action was initiated and then a report got back to the School Information Center. In the meantime, on a 45-minute lag basis, five people placed over 400 calls to the Information Center, school and governmental offices about the incidents to test for proper and knowledgeable responses. On paper, even the National Guard, the Governor-County Executive-Mayor and the Intergovernmental Desegregation Coordinating Group (IDCG) were mobilized.
>
> In a top-level debriefing at 2:30 p.m., each jurisdiction related its problems. Deficiencies noted were largely related to an inadequate number of phones, availability of phones, jammed switchboards and radio channels and inability to cope rapidly enough with reports for the large number of incidents. The Information Center had to cope with 160 extra calls over 2 hours on top of its regular load.
>
> All 17 jurisdictions/groups involved expressed their appreciation for the chance to test their readiness in a very realistic manner. All reported plans to try and remedy the deficiencies in communication uncovered.[48]

The Information Center proved to be a great aid, not only at the expected time—the first week of busing—but also at unexpected crisis times, such as after the tax rate changes and during the teachers' strike. From the reopening of the center on April 1, 1978, until November 30, 1978, over 34,000 calls, an average of 200 per working day, were received. On one day, the first day of the teachers' strike, over 2,900 calls were answered. During the first week of school 900 calls came in.

On September 5, 1978, a media center was established to supplement the Information Center. The new media center provided a site for press conferences with school and governmental officials during the first week of school. General information and daily bulletins were distributed to all media representatives. Over 200 newspeople were served—from Delaware and across the nation. In fact, another 300 had requested security credentials but did not join the ringside crowd when there was no fight.

The governor's blue-ribbon group was finally appointed on August 22, 1978, and named the Effective Transition Committee (ETC). Its tardy appearance could have been construed as too little, too late, but the ETC was in fact of some assistance. It reinforced Governor du Pont's commitment to see that the law was implemented peacefully and effectively.

The following people were appointed to the ETC:

J. Caleb Boggs, former Delaware U.S. senator and governor
Beatrice Ross (Bebe) Coker, black Wilmington community leader
Priscilla Crowder, former president of the Newark Board of
    Education and member of the Interim Board
Dave Nelson, athletic director and former football coach of the
    University of Delaware
William T. Quillen, Vice-president of the Wilmington Trust Co. and
    former Delaware chancellor
Theodore (Toby) Ryan, executive secretary of the Building and
    Construction Trades Council of Delaware
James Stewart, president of the Greater Wilmington Development
    Council (see Chapter 6)
Arthur (Skinny) Wilson, vice-president of the International
    Longshoreman's Association
Bill Bergey, all-pro linebacker, Philadelphia Eagles football team

An enterprising reporter telephoned Bill Bergey about his accepting the ETC appointment. Bergey, a Pennsylvania resident who had to fill the sports-star position in the absence of any professional athletes living in Delaware, told him, "I haven't accepted anything."[49] The mixup was later straightened out, but it revealed the symbolic rather than substantive nature of the ETC.

The ETC helped in at least two other ways. First, chairman, Robert H. McBride, served as a full-time staff person during the transition. McBride was a DuPont executive and a former state school board member (he had been the defendant next in line after Madeline Buchanan of *Evans* v. *Buchanan*). He worked directly with groups like the school district's Human Relations Advisory Committee and Information Center. Second, primarily through comprehensive reports written by its chairman, the ETC served to channel information from the community to governmental officials.

By the Friday before the opening of school, in part because executive cooperation had finally led to adequate preparation for desegregation, state officials refused to join the last-ditch effort to gain a stay from Justice Rehnquist.

ALTERNATIVE ROLES OF GOVERNMENTAL OFFICIALS IN SCHOOL DESEGREGATION

Why does one governmental executive call busing a "national nightmare" and another urge the state's citizens to comply with the court order "as harmoniously as possible"? Perhaps we can by understand these differing responses of Delaware executives by constructing a table (Figure 5–1).

Figure 5-1
Types of Public Official Desegregation Leadership

Stance	Activity Level	
	Proactive	Reactive
Positive	*Positive Leader* Governor du Pont County Executive Slawik Mayor McLaughlin	*Helper* County Executive Jornlin Governor Tribbitt
Negative	*Obstructionist*	*Issue Exploiter* Mayor Maloney

Some public officials have taken a proactive and others a reactive role when faced with desegregation. Reactive officials let events overtake them. Proactive officials act to affect the events. This is the first dimension of desegregation leadership. Further, officials may take either a positive or negative stand, supporting or opposing the content of an order and the efforts to implement it. This is the second dimension. Combinations of these two dimensions define four categories of public officials.

The *positive leader* initiates actions to achieve effective school desegregation. County Executive Slawik, Mayor McLaughlin, and Governor du Pont were positive leaders.[50]

Helpers, in this context, respond to desegregation problems but tend to act at the last minute or only under great pressure. County Executive Jornlin and Governor Tribbitt were such helpers.

Obstructionists actively work to subvert compliance with the court order. Cataldo described this type of behavior:

> Ten years after *Brown I* and *Brown II* . . . schools in the deep South remained almost totally segregated. State and local policymaking elites—governors, state legislators, school boards—refused to comply meaningfully with the *Brown* decisions and with subsequent lower federal court decisions, responding instead with defiance or tactics of evasion and delay.[51]

Although the obstructionist role was popular elsewhere, none of the Delaware executives fit into that category.

The *issue exploiter* tries to use events to benefit from the opposition to desegregation. Orfield has described many public officials faced with desegregation who held out false hopes and denounced busing even when it was inevitable.[52] Mayor Maloney's words and actions placed him in this category.

Why then did the government figures choose the roles they played? Dunaway's California study of the parts played by mayors in school desegregation is helpful here.[53] He concludes that "the mayor's actions on busing are more likely to reflect political self-interest than personal philosophy or administration of the law: mayors tend to act pragmatically rather than idealistically."[54] To understand the extent to which political self-interest determined the role of executives in Delaware, we must define self-interest for each individual. Otherwise, it is a vacuous concept.[55] After the event it is possible to see any factor as having been in the positive or negative self-interest of a politician. For example, if a politician's constituency is opposed to busing, his being opposed to court-ordered busing can be seen as representing his constituents' views. But one can explain a politician's taking a more positive position by asserting that the constituency would not favor opposition to the law. To be a useful concept, political self-interest has to be defined either *a priori*, by means of its causes, or at least in a way specific enough to allow predictions. For Delaware executives, the nature of their constituency—and thus presumably their political self-interest—accounted very little for their choice of roles in the desegregation process. The two occupants of each of the three executive positions played different parts. Since the individuals in the same position acted differently, constituency alone cannot explain their behavior.

There is a way, however, to explain how constituency and political self-interest affect executive behavior. It is to consider that executives' political self-interest is related most closely to their future constituency, rather than to their present one. Mayor McLaughlin declared his intention to serve only one term, so presumably he was not working for future votes during that term. Mayor Maloney, on the other hand, ran for the U.S. Senate and so needed to appeal to suburban antibusing voters during his term in city office. McLaughlin's concern remained with city residents, those who might benefit from metropolitan desegregation through access to suburban schools and a reduced tax rate. As for Governor du Pont, he was frequently mentioned as a possible 1980 vice-presidential candidate. This may have given him a perspective different from Governor Tribbitt's in dealing with desegregation. A possible national constituency may have balanced du Pont's concerns about antibusing sentiment in Delaware. (I know that I brought the national implications to du Pont's attention. In a meeting with candidate du Pont immediately before his election in 1976, I mentioned the national attention he was receiving and asked him to support the DCSD's activities to avoid being blamed for the failure of desegregation. I pointed out that some political analysts believed that Boston Mayor Kevin White failed to receive the Democratic Party's second spot in 1976 because he did not work to see the court order in Boston peacefully implemented.)

Dunaway claims that mayoral action becomes more visible as the threat of racial conflict increases.[56] In Delaware, fears of racial conflict mounted as opening day approached. People did not worry about *more* violence, they just worried more *about* violence. Executives thus felt increasing pressure to initiate constructive measures to calm and defuse the situation. It is important to note that all three of the second set of executives did play a positive, although in one case a reactive, role.

If "political self-interest" as it relates to a future constituency explains some of the words and actions of Delaware's executives in the desegregation situation, it does not explain them all. Other factors must be sought to explain County Executive Slawik's early formation of the DCSD and his support of its work; Mayor McLaughlin's tireless efforts to prepare the public for desegregation; and the scope of Governor du Pont's preparations for implementation. As Dunaway suggests, the personal style of executives can also affect their role in the desegregation process.[57]

Governor du Pont's managerial and planning approach to government contrasted starkly to Governor Tribbitt's more *ad hoc* approach. Du Pont—suave, articulate, a graduate of Harvard Law School—approaches all subjects, including desegregation, from a perspective different from that of Tribbitt—down-home, hardware store owner, essentially a small-town politician. Whereas Mayor Maloney and County Executive Jornlin have seemed more comfortable on television than behind a desk, Mayor McLaughlin and County Executive

Slawik pursued their goals by means of personal relations and coalition building. Each executive, in short, approached desegregation in the same fashion that he or she had approached previous issues.

While both political self-interest and personal style were important in determining executive behavior in Delaware, the relation between the two factors was not simple. Executives did not simply try to further their political self-interest on the busing issue. Rather, executives followed their usual style while trying to minimize their political losses. In other words, the executives worked hard to avoid losing political ground because of their positions and actions on busing. Except for McLaughlin, they continually assured the public that they were against busing. But some executives were personally motivated to move well beyond public necessities to address the problems of implementation. Political self-interest was a factor that kept them from moving as far toward preparing for implementation as Christine Rossell and others have advocated.

Administrative and Political Tasks

Rossell's division of mayoral roles in preparing for desegregation into two categories—political and administrative—helps us to understand the impact of Delaware's executives. Under political roles she includes: legitimizing the court order, coopting resistant groups, and mediating disputes. Under administrative roles she includes: aiding in designing the school desegregation plan, coordinating the dissemination of information, coordinating safety plans, and coordinating community participation.[58] To a large extent, the Delaware executives avoided political roles when they could, because they had trouble in playing them successfully. Certainly the political tasks that they were not able to avoid gave them great difficulty.

Only one executive, Mayor McLaughlin, appeared eager to legitimize the court order. Mayor Maloney and Governors Tribbitt and du Pont vehemently criticized the courts, the judges, the desegregation orders, and the process. The county executives avoided such potshots. Everyone but Mayor McLaughlin maintained a strong antibusing position, often proclaiming the rightness of the antibusing cause. However, when pressed, all the executives maintained steadily that they would fully implement the law. When the time came, the executives put the implementation of the law first and urged the public to do the same.

No executive was successful in coopting resistant groups or mediating disputes. The most significant attempt at involving resistant groups was Governor du Pont's proposal that the State Legislature pass a four-district reorganization plan in the winter of 1977–1978. This effort to encourage political bargaining leading to a desegregation plan was not successful. Executive efforts to involve antibusing leaders in a broad based committee foundered as the issue became more and more heated. Mayor Maloney, looking for a compromise plan, and Governor du Pont, looking for an acceptable plan, both failed.

Given the nature of the Delaware situation, the problem of developing the desegregation plan was basically political rather than administrative, as Rossell's categorization would suggest. When executives did attempt to play a political role, they ran into an ideological wall each time. The antibusing leaders and the legislature did not cooperate. The most positive aspect of the executives' political role was their expressed willingness to fully implement the court order.

In contrast to their inability to fulfill political functions, the governmental executives were very successful in accomplishing administrative tasks. By school opening, September 1978, the executives had achieved the following: a countywide desegregation Information Center; an active intergovernmental task force on desegregation planning; a desegregation-trained state police working cooperatively with school officials and clergy; a regular breakfast meeting at which school officials, top governmental administrators, and community leaders discussed desegregation problems; and a formal alliance of supportive community groups.

The executives' success in filling the administrative roles was due to a number of factors. Most of these activities were outside public view. Some took place at bureaucratic meetings; others like the breakfast were totally secret. Furthermore, many of the activities were at least one step removed from the executives. Thus, the actions of the DCSD could help in the preparation and at the same time draw the criticism of antibusing leaders to a group that was outside the executives' direct control and responsibility. In this way, political criticism could be kept at arm's length while necessary tasks were accomplished.

The success of the administrative function was also attributable to professional aid that helped to identify problems and solutions as well as resolve differences across agencies and governments. When I began planning for a desegregation Information Center in spring 1975 as part of my DCSD responsibilities (see Chapter 6), it was a major accomplishment just to get representatives from the various school districts, state and local government agencies, and community groups together to talk about anything. It took a political broker independent of the various executives to obtain from each of them a commitment to work together. The broker and consultant functions were both successfully carried out, in part, by a representative of the federal executive, Jon Chace. His effectiveness in the role of Washington's representative in Delaware, however, stood in marked contrast to the way in which Delaware's representatives played their roles in Washington.

DELAWARE'S U.S. SENATORS AND REPRESENTATIVES: SYMBOLS AND SUBSTANCE

Although they were not in a position to affect the desegregation plan directly, Delaware's federal representatives did not ignore the busing issue. On the contrary, their rhetoric and actions closely paralleled those of the State Legislature. Delaware's U.S. senators differed greatly in personal style and ideology, but both were strong antibusing activists in Washington. Both introduced constitutional amendments and legislation to limit busing.

Senator William V. Roth, a conservative Republican with ties to the wealthy segment of Delaware's population, kept up a verbal and legislative barrage against busing. Roth introduced legislation to give state courts remedial jurisdiction over desegregation, to establish a national commission appointed by the president to study busing while implementation of all cases was delayed, and to amend the constitution to prohibit the assignment of pupils according to race.[59] Roth's actions were consistent with his general conservative prosuburban, middle-class approach. At last, immediately before busing began on September 9, 1978, Senator Roth did urge lawful implementation, but he did so in a letter that was more a reflection of the mood in the county than a cause of it.[60]

Senator Joseph R. Biden, Jr., felt the political heat on the busing issue. He had won a surprising victory in the 1972 election, defeating incumbent J. Caleb Boggs, a conservative former governor. Biden, a Democratic county councilman not yet thirty years old on election day, waged a vigorous campaign, appealing not only to the old Democratic coalition of blacks, ethnic groups, and labor but also to many middle-class suburbanites who were attracted by his youth, vigor, and candor. In Washington, these qualities earned him immediate national attention. He often voted with the Senate's liberal Democratic wing. In June 1974 Senator Biden voted with a one-vote majority to kill an antibusing amendment that he considered unconstitutional.[61] This vote earned him severe PAC criticism.

In September 1975, Biden said in a speech in the Senate that "because of talks with constituents and reading the accounts of busing troubles in Boston and other cities," he was leaning more and more "to an anti-busing position."[62] That same month, he introduced an amendment to limit the power of the U.S. Department of Health, Education and Welfare to withhold federal funds from localities that would not agree to busing. The amendment had no effect on the Delaware situation, but it served notice that Biden had decided to be a leader in the antibusing camp. Biden went on to call busing a "bankrupt concept" that violated the "cardinal rule of common sense." Busing was the "domestic Vietnam."[63] Biden later claimed, "No one has done more to stop forced busing than Joe Biden."[64]

During the 1976 presidential campaign, Biden became the first senator to back Jimmy Carter. This seemed somewhat ironic, since his antibusing stand seemed more in tune with that of President Ford, who in June 1976 attempted to have antibusing legislation introduced in Congress.[65] Carter expressed opposition to busing, but he also sent his daughter to a majority black school, opposed constitutional amendments against busing, and called the 1964 Civil Rights Act the "best thing that ever happened to the South."[66] (This act gave the federal government the power to force school desegregation.)

Biden was named Carter's national campaign cochairman, but he continued to disagree with Carter after the inauguration. In February 1977, he opposed Carter's appointment of Wade McCree as solicitor general because McCree refused to oppose busing.[67] In April 1977, the Carter administration entered the Delaware case to argue for busing (but against the 10–35 percentage ratio).[68] When Biden cosponsored a bill to limit busing, President Carter called it "unnecessary" and "arguably unconstitutional."[69] On the positive side, Biden helped to change federal regulations for granting school desegregation funds. At Biden's urging, the Carter administration allowed Emergency School Aid Act [ESAA] funds to help pay for court-ordered activities. Under the previous regulations, federal funds could not be used for this purpose. The receipt of the ESAA grant saved the Delaware state government millions of dollars.[70]

While Biden struggled with the busing issue, he was failing to please PAC President James Venema. Venema constantly attacked Biden's position and threatened to run for his Senate seat. On February 23, 1978, Venema, a registered Independent, announced that he would not challenge Biden for the Democratic nomination but would run against him in the general election as a Republican.[71]

Delaware's representatives in Washington thus exploited the busing issue. Congressmen du Pont and Thomas Evans were also vocal in their opposition, the strident voices of Senators Roth and Biden received the greatest publicity. Their failure to discuss the alternatives realistically put great strain on the bargaining process. It was left to representatives of the executive branch of the federal government in Delaware to make the constructive approaches that furthered the give-and-take necessary for implementation.

Federal Executive Officials

Jon Chace, Community Relations Specialist for the Community Relations Service (CRS) of the U.S. Department of Justice, could be awarded the title, "Most Helpful Individual in Delaware's Desegregation Process." He is the kind of person who would never seek such recognition, however, and that is the secret of much of his success.

Jon Chace had the knack of putting people at ease, and in a tense situation like that surrounding desegregation, that was an important quality. In addition, he was young, good-looking, gentle in manner, and humorous. A newspaper profile said he had "the skills of a diplomat, social worker and counselor."[72] Using them he worked behind the scenes to have a significant effect on the implementation process.

The Justice Department's CRS arm is empowered, under the 1964 Civil Rights Act, to enter a situation where "peaceful relations among citizens of the community are threatened." CRS has already spent over a third of its budget on "resolving disputes associated with racial conflicts and tensions in educational systems."[73] Chace, stationed at CRS's Philadelphia office, had these organizational resources behind his efforts. He had the national ties to link local leaders facing desegregation for the first time with the sources of information that they needed. Chace helped to establish and develop the desegregation Information Center and through it put local people in touch with data and experience in Boston. Chace supplied the DCSD with information on monitoring commissions for a court brief; he gave the police descriptions of how law enforcement officials in other communities had handled similar situations. Chace arranged for community leaders to go to Boston and Louisville and for police officers to visit other communities. He found speakers for the DAPA conference on desegregation.

Political skills were vital to Chace's effectiveness. He helped to deal with personal conflicts among superintendents, governmental officials, and community leaders. He offered advice, ideas, and alternatives to leaders whether they were planning something like the DAPA conference or forming a new organization. He helped to plan the Effective Transition Committee (ETC) and named it as well. This required unusual problem-solving sense. He helped to form coalitions of governmental executives and their staffs (the intergovernmental staff task force) as well as community groups (see Chapter 6), showing great skill as a mediator. Somehow he was able to be calm and helpful amid strong public feelings against busing and to work for peaceful implementation despite the widespread conviction that busing would somehow be avoided. He was a support and a resource from the very beginning of his involvement, which began with the DCSD's official request to the Justice Department in 1975.

Perhaps it seems strange that, during the implementation period, the primary help from a federal source in Delaware was attached to the Department of Justice rather than the Office of Education. The reason was that the Office of Education had limited leverage in the situation. Because only two of eleven school districts in the desegregation area were eligible for Emergency School Aid Act (ESAA) funds before actual implementation of the court order, federal funds were few and their use did not influence events. Examples of federal funding are the following: The Wilmington District utilized Title IV funds and the services of a federal general assistance center—the Center for Desegregation and Conflict at the University of Pittsburgh—for many desegregation-related activities. The Center also helped the State Department of Public Instruction to hold two conferences a year primarily for educators, as well as two others for students. Two DPI human relations specialists were also funded through Title IV, but they served the whole state and turnover in these positions was high. Before the final order, the nine suburban—primarily white—school districts received little help from the Office of Education.[74] On the day before school opened in September 1978, it was announced that $6,614 million in ESAA funds would be awarded to the county school district to pay for the remedial relief specified in the final order.[75] Thus, the funds relieved the state's taxpayers but did not determine what actions were to be taken.

In sum, the technical aid from the federal government was of little use in implementation, but the politically based help of Jon Chace from the CRS was invaluable.

SUMMARY

Delaware's governmental officials were not united in their attitudes toward desegregation. Some were positive leaders, some were helpers, some were exploiters of the issue. Only a very few tried to obstruct the court order.

To many New Castle County state legislators, busing was an opportunity to score points with the public. Much symbolic antibusing legislation was offered and some was passed. There was a general avoidance of serious consideration of desegregation plans or of preparation for implementation.

To Delaware's representatives in Washington busing was an issue ripe for exploitation.[76]

For Delaware's state government executives, busing was an issue on which they were forced to be defensive, given the feelings of their constituents. At the same time, the executives felt the weight of their responsibility to implement the law. Several of them played the role of positive leader, and as a group, they dealt constructively with the issue.

Delaware's executives tried to lead the State Legislature toward the passage of an acceptable plan but they could not overcome the ideology and political self-interest that pulled the legislators in another direction. The plans that the legislature did develop tended to be unfavorable to black interests, and all of them were unacceptable to the court. The court order alone did not change the political and social forces in Delaware.

While the executives did not succeed in obtaining a poltical resolution to the court's challenge, they did accomplish much in the way of preparation for desegregation through administrative means. Those activities came both very early and very late in a long process. In between, community groups filled the void. It is to their role that I now turn.

6 / Supportive Community Organizations

If a Martian had landed in New Castle and said, "Take me to your leaders," on at least two mornings each month almost every leader in Delaware responsible for implementing the school desegregation order could have been found at a secret breakfast meeting in Howard Johnsons restaurant. There—all together, in one place—the Martian could have found the mayor of Wilmington, the Governor's counsel and his education assistant, the county executive's policy coordinator, the president of the school board and the deputy superintendent of the county school district, and the presidents or chairpersons of nearly every parent and community group in the country, and me. Rather than Martians, the Breakfast Group met with representatives from communities anxious to learn how the positive aspects of Delaware's implementation could be duplicated elsewhere. For there were many positive things in the Delaware situation—widespread community involvement, much cooperation among leaders, and effective community group efforts. This chapter describes and analyzes the community's response to the court orders.

Community involvement has been named by a number of desegregation analysts as a key to peaceful desegregation.[1] The Wilmington metropolitan area benefited from the participation of many active religious, business, educational, and civic organizations in the desegregation process. The participation of these groups was primarily concerned with preparing the community for desegregation and with lobbying officials to take supportive actions; they were not called on to contribute to developing acceptable desegregation plans. Their most effective involvement was in coalitions that bridged gaps between sectors of the community. A comparison of the desegregation activities of two important sectors of the community—religious and business—will illustrate community group involvement and set the stage for an examination of the coalitions that came to play a significant role in dealing with the problems of implementation.

RELIGIOUS ORGANIZATIONS

Moral commitment impelled Delaware's religious communities to become extensively involved in the process of desegregation. Religious leaders not only disseminated information and exhorted their people to keep the peace, they also pressured public and school officials to make adequate preparations for desegregation, and they took part directly in those activities. The religious community was never static in its approach; it continually reorganized and redirected its efforts to match each situation. Among the groups chiefly involved were the National Conference of Christians and Jews (NCCJ), the Delmarva Ecumenical Agency (DEA), the Delaware Equal Educational Process Committee (DEEP), and the Interfaith Task Force (ITF).

The Delaware Equal Educational Process Committee

DEEP was formed early in the desegregation process as the outgrowth of the Urban Coalition task force on desegregation. The leaders were generally linked with religious and city groups and interests. DEEP declared that it would support desegregation even if busing was required. A suburban Methodist minister, the Rev. F. David Weber, chaired the committee. He became the chief spokesman for DEEP and received much publicity in that role.

DEEP had only four hundred members where its opposite number, PAC, had ten thousand. Nevertheless, its uncompromising stand in favor of implementing the court order made it the chief counterweight to PAC. When the media wanted to balance a PAC antibusing blast, it could always turn to DEEP, nearly the only group willing to speak for busing. This had a curious effect. DEEP won few converts and indeed was eventually shunned by most other groups—but its very extremism gave those other groups more room in which to manuever. Without DEEP the choice might have been between compliance never and compliance when hell froze over. With DEEP far out ahead, a group like DCSD (the Delaware Committee on the School Decision) that was reluctantly willing to consider making the best of an unpopular judgment could appear neutral rather than dangerously out of touch with the public. But DEEP did more than extend the continuum of choices. Its boldness spurred neutral or hesitant groups to work more actively for peaceful implementation; and it also offered practical help with activities such as an all-day conference in which Gary Orfield presented his desegregation research.

The impact of DEEP was made largely by of its chairman, Dave Weber. He cajoled, advised, argued, and helped others to work for desegregation. It was not unusual for someone active in a supportive community group to receive an early morning telephone call from Dave Weber, for his moral commitment, exuberance, energy, and creativity led him to push others to implement what DEEP and he could not accomplish alone. Weber's probusing zeal made him and his ideas unpopular. Yet his ideas were always the most exciting ones in circulation, even though their great volume occasionally included some that were impractical. Probably Dave Weber's most important suggestion was the establishment of a group that would meet informally and privately to discuss desegregation. Without using his name, I took up his idea in forming the Breakfast Group described below. Weber's probusing position forestalled his being named to the DCSD and other formal positions. Yet he was behind virtually all of the activities in the religious sector.

In October 1976, DEEP decided to stop holding programs, since others were now working toward peaceful implementation and the issue of busing/desegregation had been settled by the court order. What was clear if unspoken was that public feeling was running so high against busing that an explicitly probusing group like DEEP could no longer work directly with others. It continued for awhile, holding executive committee meetings out of the public eye. By the date of DEEP's demise, supporting coalitions had been formed and longstanding groups had shifted energies to deal with desegregation.

The National Conference of Christians and Jews

The Delaware Region National Conference of Christians and Jews asked state and then county political officials early in 1974 to establish a committee to help ease the desegregation process.[2] As reported in Chapter 5, County Executive Slawik responded by appointing what became the DCSD. On March 24, 1976, the NCCJ then attempted to involve the business, professional, and religious leadership of Delaware by holding a conference on desegregation at picturesque Longwood Gardens. SANE, a business group described below, emerged soon after, although the seeds had been planted long before. In July 1977, an NCCJ sponsored meeting of a few top business, religious, and governmental officials precipitated the decision by governmental executives to form an intergovernmental staff task force (see Chapter 5). As these examples indicate, the NCCJ's main role was to encourage the formation of new organizations of high-level community leaders to deal directly with desegregation.

NCCJ supplemented their organizational efforts with direct human relations activities in the schools. In January 1977, NCCJ hired a new regional director, Helen Foss, to plan and coordinate human relations programs for schools and community groups. Foss, a former teacher, had been the director of the Green Circle program, a human relations program for children in the public elementary schools. Her talents in this area allowed her and the NCCJ in turn to play a major role in desegregation coalitions. By September 1978, the NCCJ had institutionalized these human relations programs and had received $27,000 in Emergency School Aid Act (ESAA) funds. The NCCJ saw the Green Circle human relations program expanded to the high school level and applied to workshops on desegregation for school officials, police, and clergy.

The Delmarva Ecumenical Agency

In cooperation with the NCCJ and with leadership from Dave Weber, the Delmarva Ecumenical Agency—an organization of Christian churches in Delaware, Maryland, and Virginia—kept over four hundred members of the clergy informed through mailings and meetings. The DEA developed police and clergy relationships through discussion meetings, planned a series of joint ecumenical worship services for city and suburban churches, and sponsored conferences on desegregation for clergy in the county. Leaders of fifteen denominations in Delaware (such as AME, Baptist, Catholic, Methodist, Presbyterian, Episcopal, Lutheran) issued joint statements throughout the desegregation process calling for peaceful implementation. For example, one week after the May 19 court decision they released a statement that stressed the need for peaceful reaction: "We call for compliance with the decision of the court. We hope that Wilmington and New Castle County can be an example to the nation of orderly compliance with the law. . . . We, as religious leaders, are opposed to the use of violence, disruption, or the spreading of rumors. We need an atmosphere of calm and understanding. We must preserve our schools and community and protect our children."[3] The DEA also worked within individual congregations and religious bodies.[4]

The Interfaith Task Force

In fall 1978, the Interfaith Task Force (ITF) was established by the religious community to pursue desegregation activities and to draw the criticism that the DEA and NCCJ were taking on this issue. The first formal meeting of the ITF was a well-orchestrated luncheon attended by the governor, business leaders, representatives of political executives and leaders of all major religious groups. The governor, who was pressing the legislature to enact multidistrict enabling legislation, also stressed his desire for the community to unite to implement the law, whatever it might be. ITF sponsored an interfaith religious rally in June 1978 and four ecumenial services in which school district officials participated the night before schools opened.

The religious community put to use national resources and consultants, local funds and leaders, and inkind services (such as providing places for desegregation groups to meet) in its work to achieve smooth implementation. Key religious leaders were given free time to work and study in this area, to become better informed, and more able to provide leadership. In mobilizing efforts for desegregation, the religious community had several advantages over other local groups. Some of their people who were strongly committed to desegregation, could take professional working time for study, detail work, and leadership; and they had organizations already established to deal with the issue (NCCJ and DEA on the county level and church and society committees at the congregational levels).

The religious community was hampered by a number of factors. Because of their religious and social beliefs, several key leaders were advocates of desegregation even if it entailed busing. Their moral fervor did not gain wide support among the public—or even among their members. DEEP was greatly distrusted because of its probusing reputation. Ultimately the religious community built new organizations and turned to a theme of reconciliation instead of conversion. In contrast to those pastors and church executives who supported desegregation by whatever means, many ministers did not wish to clash with their congregations on this issue, especially in areas where resistance was the greatest. In any event, much of the public dismissed the clergy's position as being one they were professionally obligated to take ("They *have* to be in favor") and naîve ("They don't know how the schools and children will suffer"). Over a period of time, however, steady witness was effective. They turned to coalition building and participation. They worked with police to establish practical crisis teams. The new executive director of the NCCJ brought expertise in human relations. In the end the religious leaders were a major force in soothing the community and smoothing the way to implementation.

THE ROLE OF BUSINESS

Delaware is a favorite location for studies of the influence of business on public affairs. The many studies have not yet led to agreement on the nature of the relationship. To understand the Delaware corporate community's response to desegregation, it will be helpful to compare the views of three well-known academics, Bauer, Pool, and Dexter, with two of Nader's Raiders, Phelan and Pozen.[5] Then we will look at other studies of the role of business in Delaware.

Elephant or Chicken?

Delaware is "where the elephant takes cares not to dance among the chickens," according to Bauer, Pool, and Dexter. They analysed the role of the DuPont Corporation in the debate over the extension of the Repiprocal Trade Act in the early 1950's. In essence, their argument is that in some areas DuPont was too big to be effective politically. Despite the DuPont Company's protectionist position, Delaware's senators and representative voted for reciprocal trade legislation.

These authors blamed "a certain local suspicion of the DuPonts" for the failure of Francis V. DuPont, a leading politician in the state, to occupy a U.S. Senate seat. They found that the company had "so many irons in the fire" that the company's real interests were not clear. Disagreeing with a charge by the liberal weekly *The Nation* that Delaware was "the ward of a feudal family," they acknowledged that "the cynical reader may believe that we have been taken in," but concluded, "Delaware congressmen and senators appeared to be free to choose for themselves, without much pressure, on foreign economic policy issues."[6]

Another interpretation was advanced less than a decade later by two of Ralph Nader's associates:

> Dupont dominates Delaware as does no single company in any other state. The scope and mechanisms of its influence are studied and assessed in this report. Virtually every major aspect of Delaware life—industry, commerce, finance, government, politics, education, health, transportation, media, charitable institutions, environment, land, recreation, public works, community improvement groups, and taxation—is pervasively and decisively affected by DuPont Company, the DuPont family, or their agents.[7]

The different conclusions of those studies may have several causes. First, they may reflect changes over a period of time. In 1971, Delaware's congressman was Pierre S. du Pont IV; its governor, Russell

Peterson, was a former DuPont executive; and the mayor of Wilmington, Hal Haskell, was a wealthy scion of the corporation and family. Second, the different conclusions may have resulted from different starting points: the academics searched for direct influence. The Nader study found that "DuPont's techniques in using its power are, by and large, not as crude or roughshod" as the methods of sway used by other powers in other towns: "Dupont's deployment of direct and derivative power in the state is complex, subtle, and far reaching."[8] Third, they may have resulted from differences in scope, since the academic study considered only foreign trade policy. Finally, and I think predominately, the difference in conclusions reflected differences in ideology. One is from the perspective favorable to a pluralist view of political life and the other from one skeptical of corporate concentrations of power.[9]

Greater Wilmington Development Council

The Greater Wilmington Development Corporation (GWDC) was formed in 1960. It is an example of the many business organizations formed to work for urban redevelopment during the years 1954–1965. The DuPont family and company were instrumental in the formation and development of GWDC. Phelan and Pozen, in their analysis of the GWDC, suggest that business responses to a major problem are likely to be shaped by the organization through which they are made. The analysts make the following points, which apply as well to the GWDC as it approached the process of desegregation.

1. GWDC is an elite institution, representing those who dominate the corporate scene. "GWDC is in no way representative of the city's population; corporate dominance was not avoided and has continued to the present, especially among the officers and in the executive committees."

2. GWDC's financial base is corporate and selective. "GWDC has always outmuscled other community groups"; it is much richer than other groups, since it "levees an informal tax" to raise funds for each project.

3. GWDC is expertise oriented and does not seek community consensus. "GWDC tends to go outside the community, hiring consultants who come to Wilmington for short times, rely on already gathered data, and talk mainly to city officials or corporate executives. . . . It does not make serious efforts to canvass other community groups before bringing its resources to bear on a public decision. . . . GWDC has also arranged trips to see how other cities handled problems."

4. GWDC is a private government without public accountability. "Practically every new urban concept in Wilmington originated in GWDC and was then carried out by public planners. . . . Since GWDC is the only funding source available for most studies, it can manipulate consultants without fear. . . . In sum, GWDC so overwhelmed competing private interests and became so influential in traditionally public spheres that in many ways it served as a parallel city government."

5. GWDC is reform oriented in education. Education has been a major priority of GWDC. An employee of GWDC worked with a GWDC group in formulating three goals, one of which was to "promote racial integration of city and county schools."[10]

In another study of GWDC and other development councils, Barnekov and Rich concluded that attempting to deal with social concerns and programs often places business organizations in a difficult position.[11] "Businessmen have . . . discovered that social programs bring them into direct contact, and sometimes confrontation, with community groups. The elite composition of the councils, combined with a lack of public sanction for social programs, has made the councils vulnerable to external criticism and to demands for public accountability."[12] Some business development councils have become involved in social issues because of a belief that only a mobilization of the private sector can confront local community issues successfully. They have also acted out of self-interest, to protect assets and influence and to enhance their public image. These various studies help to explain the corporate reaction to desegregation when it became a major social issue.

The potential financial effect of desegregation obviously had a great deal to do with the corporate community's interest in the issue. The DuPont Company alone in the City of Wilmington held over $200 million in property in 1973, according to Phelan and Pozen.[13] The choice of reorganization plan could affect the metropolitan tax structure (see Chapter 8). Further, company hiring and executive recruitment would be affected by the quality and stability of the schools in the county.

The business community thus had many reasons to be interested in the outcome of the desegregation process. It also had the resources to play a significant role. Business people, however, faced the same dilemma as school and public officials; any stance supporting the desegregation order would run counter to the intense public opposition to busing. Determining the corporate position was a very delicate decision. It is for this reason that, although business help can be of critical importance in smoothing the way to desegregation, it often has not been given.[14]

SANE of Delaware

The business community decided to deal with the Delaware desegregation case by setting up a separate organization. The first step was made by the DuPont Company, which loaned a public affairs executive, Dr. Joseph Rule, to the GWDC. He was to analyze how other communities had desegregated without turmoil and to advise the business interests on possible actions. Rule followed the GWDC approach described by Phelan and Pozen in point 3 above. He traveled to more than a dozen communities that had undergone court-ordered desegregation and talked to their key governmental and business leaders. Rule identified Greenville, South Carolina; Detroit, Michigan; and Memphis, Tennessee, as model situations from which Wilmington could learn.

In Memphis, formation of an organization called formation of IMPACT—Involved Memphis Parents Assisting Children and Teachers—was spearheaded by the Chamber of Commerce. IMPACT's plan of action included "newspaper and television advertisements, fact sheets, a telephone rumor control system, neighborhood meetings, a speakers' bureau, church and organizational support, research, and troubleshooting." IMPACT ran a very effective advertisement that depicted one of the city's biggest high schools with a For Sale sign in front. The ad said in part: "This is what can happen to our entire public school system if we don't get together and work things out." One television ad ended with a catchy slogan: "IMPACT— not the pros, not the cons, just the facts." The ads, supplemented by various personal contacts, helped to put IMPACT at the center of the peaceful implementation drive in Memphis.[15]

In Greenville, South Carolina, the Chamber of Commerce also led reactions to a federal court order to desegregate the schools within two weeks. The Chamber held a meeting for civic and business leaders and quickly helped to organize a small army of volunteers to move books and school equipment. In cooperation with the Mayor's Human Relations Committee and local advertising groups, a public information plan was quickly set up.[16]

Detroit's business efforts were channeled into a large coalition. PRO-Detroit (People and Responsible Organizations for Detroit) was formed through early efforts by Detroit's Urban Coalition (New Detroit, Inc.). At first, its honorary cochairpersons were the current and the former mayors and its three actual cochairpersons were a UAW official, the executive director of a civic group, and the former president of the city PTA. Kathleen Straus, former president of the Detroit League of Women Voters, was hired as staff. The organization raised funds and developed two media campaigns. One had the message, "Just be cool," and the second, "Detroit's Kids . . . Love 'em." PRO-Detroit helped city council members and state legislators to join in supporting resolutions for peaceful implementation.[17]

A third approach studied by Rule but not offered as a model was the one taken in Dallas. There the Chamber of Commerce had helped to establish a committee of fifteen persons—five black, five brown, and five white—who actually designed Dallas' desegregation plan. He also considered where business had taken a very active role, albeit late in the process. Going a step further than in most other communities, Boston businesses became directly involved with the development of several educational programs. These included a human relations program, a skills assessment program, a partnership program in which business firms contributed staff time, money, and equipment to high schools, a pool of business executives that acted as resources for the school committee, and a group to write funding proposals.[18]

After visiting fifteen communities in all, Rule recommended the formation of SANE of Delaware, Inc., a body that seemed to be most like Memphis' IMPACT. SANE was incorporated in April 1976.

The board was clearly an elite group. Named chairman was Rodney Layton, a wealthy partner in the Wilmington corporate law firm of Richards, Layton, and Finger, and a former chairman of the Urban Coalition. His residence was an estate in Pennsylvania; he was reported by Phelan and Pozen to have sent his children to Tatnall, a local private school.[19] Among the other members were William Copeland, president of the Continental American Life Insurance Company and, like Layton, a member of various boards of directors; Arva Jackson—the only black member—at one time a board member of the United Way, GWDC, and the University of Delaware trustees, and an executive with HEW; and Francis West, director of the Division of Consumer Affairs in the state and member of local boards like Blue Cross–Blue Shield.

With members like Layton and Copeland, the SANE board did not represent the total Wilmington metropolitan community. Further, its less elite representatives, West and Jackson, reportedly did not exercise as much influence on the board as did Chairman Layton. Rule was named the agent of the SANE corporation, essentially a paper title; he held no other formal post with SANE. There was no formal connection between SANE and the DuPont company.

SANE's goal was to further peaceful compliance of the court decision, *whatever* the decision. SANE took no position on the merits of desegregation or busing. It opened an office in the heart of downtown Wilmington conveniently located near the federal courts, DuPont Company headquarters, and the city and county offices in the Public Building. SANE hired an executive director and a secretary. The financial arrangements of SANE were never made public. Rule received pledges for $150,000 from local corporations (including four banks, the three chemical corporations, the utility company, and the telephone company).

SANE's major strategy was to provide information encouraging peaceful implementation. In January 1977, it hired Spiro and Associates of Philadelphia, a public relations firm, to determine whether a public information campaign in the Wilmington area was required, and if so, to design the campaign. First, Spiro's account executive interviewed community leaders to assess the situation. Second, it approached the University of Delaware to conduct a poll to identify the types of people that might threaten community property and tranquillity. Barry Morstain and I represented the College of Urban Affairs and Public Policy in discussions with Spiro; negotiations broke down when the we had to insist that any data that the university gathered or analysis that it made should be released publically. Spiro wished to keep such information confidential and turned to an outside polling firm for the poll and analysis. Spiro evaluated SANE's material on desegregation in other communities and submited a list of public relations / informational activities for the sponsoring body to consider.

SANE subsequently printed and distributed copies of the various court decisions and other factual information and encouraged a judicious tone in the mass media coverage of desegregation news.[20]

On the recommendation of Spiro, SANE pressured governmental officials to open a Press Information Center. The intergovernmental task force did plan to do this but while they delayed SANE continued with its own informational activities and plans for its own press center. Task force leaders asked SANE to back off so that an official center could be opened. The two groups clashed over this issue. SANE leaders later said that they were in existence only to help if others did not do what needed to be done. A governmental Press Center was scheduled to begin operation in August 1977, but the stay led to a year's postponement.

Another part of the Spiro plan was a campaign to direct people's thinking in a positive direction. Spiro had tested a number of slogans and had recommended "Keep the peace, so kids can learn in peace." Objections were raised because the slogan seemed to imply that there was an alternative to keeping the peace.[21] Spiro and SANE changed the slogan to "Help keep the peace, so kids can learn in peace." That didn't answer the objections. In July 1977, the Board of Managers of the Alliance, a coalition of community groups supporting peaceful desegregation, met with representatives of Spiro and SANE. The Board was told that the slogan was intended for use only if violence occurred or was threatened. Finally, a television spot was produced by Spiro to be used in an emergency.

Spiro and SANE were involved in a number of other undertakings in support of peaceful implementation. SANE paid for the Alliance's newsletters, which were issued before the opening of school. SANE brought the mayor of Greenville and some other officials from other communities to tell Delaware leaders how they had coped with desegregation. Spiro suggests stuffing corporation pay envelopes with material urging employees to keep calm about the school situation, but no general campaign was organized to reach corporate personnel. Instead, SANE helped to set up some meetings on the issue in different companies.

All of these activities were in keeping with SANE's view of itself as an informational group. Community groups, however, persisted in seeing SANE as a source of funding. SANE had a financial pipeline to the corporate community and other sources were dry. By 1976 antibusing feelings made it impossible for local governmental funds to go to groups accused of favoring desegregation. Religious organizations, as always, had limited resources. Federal funds would not be available until desegregation began. Local fundations had virtually the same sources of support as SANE; requests to them seemed likely to be passed on to it. SANE could protest that it was not a rich uncle but rather a agency for planning informational campaigns; the fact remained that it had money and local desegregation groups needed it.

SANE did play the part of a granting agency, but it did so reluctantly and in ways that made no one happy. It never became the force of cooperation and coordination of effort that a central financial resource could have been. It left a trail of complaints about disappointed expectations, red tape, and power grabbing. Soon after SANE was formed, there was a planning meeting for representatives of almost a hundred community groups that were to form the Alliance. The SANE executive director brought along two home-baked pies. One of the organizers quipped, "Now we know what SANE will contribute." The joke was too near to the truth.

SANE and its chairman, Rodney Layton, perhaps merely reflected their business origins. Getting money from SANE was similar to a division getting authority for a special purpose from a parent corporation. It required elaborate justification and financial disclosure. SANE thought it was being prudent; its supplicants thought it was being patronizing. SANE was concerned with timing and did not wish to see funds wasted in scattershot and premature public relations exercises. Its critics thought that SANE was acting as if it had a monopoly on good judgment as well as on funds.

SANE had a particular dislike for funding school district-related operations, feeling that such matters were the responsibility of public officials. So they were—and if no public officials had been meeting these responsibilities, SANE would not have been needed in the first place. Once again, SANE appeared too legalistic and unsympathetic to those who sought its help.

The Alliance had many occasions to feel frustrated in its relations with SANE. On several occasions, Joseph Rule, the DuPont loanee whose GWDC report had led to the founding of SANE, offered help to the Alliance. He arranged for an office and a grant from the Crystal Foundation (the Crystal Foundation was headed by Irenee duPont, former chairman of GWDC). Some offers of resources were later retracted. SANE and Rule semed to be trying to control the Alliance by making secret offers, withdrawn at will.

Thus, although the Alliance and the other groups wrote proposals for SANE funds, to my knowledge no proposals were accepted until just before the expected September 1977 implementation date. One rejected proposal was the DCSD request for $79 to reproduce copies of UPDATE, a desegregation resource handbook developed by its staff.

The matter of control always seemed to poison relations between SANE and other groups. When the Alliance board previewed the "Keep the Peace" television spot, it reacted very favorably. The SANE executive director, Dorothy Marengo, and a representative from Spiro and Associates, Sandra Weiner, then asked if the Alliance would be willing to sponsor the spots if the situation warranted. The Alliance people wanted to know who would decide when an emergency existed that would necessitate use of the spots. According to the SANE executive director, SANE would. The Alliance Board insisted that the decision should be shared. They wanted the decisions to be made not by the board or chairman of SANE alone but by two people from SANE—Layton plus one other representative—and by the Alliance's cochairpersons. To the incredulity of many at that meeting, SANE resisted this idea, despite evident good sense of the alliance cochairpersons. It seemed purely a question of power. No agreement was reached at the meeting about who should decide on the need for the spot and who should sponsor it. (Months later the Interfaith Task Force and Effective Transaction Committee, probably unaware of the earlier controversy, agreed to sponsor the spot. Fortunately, the spot never had to be used.)

While SANE, defining its own role, was judging the worth of other groups and their plans, there was no way for others to judge SANE. SANE's closed-door method of operation aroused great resentment. The group seemed to know what everyone else was doing while community leaders knew very little about what SANE was doing. When SANE proposed to help the Alliance, it insisted that all preliminary discussions and decisions be made behind the scenes. There was one conspicuous SANE activity, but it was as irritating as the prevailing secrecy; SANE seemed to be spending money lavishly on lunches for leaders at the Hotel Dupont while other groups were hungry for subsistence funds. This seemed typical of SANE's insensitivity to the personal concerns of others. For instance, one afternoon at a conference center miles from my office, a center secretary pulled me out of a meeting to say there was a special message for me. Fearing a major family crisis, I rushed to a telephone. It turned out to be a courtesy call from a SANE representative to inform me before an official announcement was made that SANE was hiring Spiro and Associates. Perhaps I should have felt more honored: I was simply annoyed. The series of small and large incidents finally resulted in a split among community leaders.[22]

The business community's involvement in the process of school desegregation was limited to forming and supporting SANE. The symbolism was important; it signaled the corporate community's commitment to peaceful implementation of the law. But if the stated purpose of SANE was to keep the peace by providing information, a hidden purpose appeared to be to limit the pressures on the corporate community. The case of Delaware corporation and SANE closely resembled how Nader's Raiders had described previous business action on social issues.

Nader's group was wrong in one way. The business community had far less influence than it had hoped for and far less than the Nader critics assumed it had had. SANE and the business community had a style that made as many enemies as friends. Overall, business involvement had a marginally positive effect on the desegregation process, coming mostly from its funding of groups such as the Alliance and its encouraging of governmental officials to deal constructively with the issue. SANE encountered resentment because of its refusal to work openly. The business community, like most other groups in the state, chose not to risk direct opposition to the opponents of busing.

RELIGIOUS AND BUSINESS ROLES

Religious desegregation groups took public stances very similar to those of the business community. After DEEP's positive advocacy of desegregation made it the target of public hostility, other groups began to avoid any discussion of choices for effective desegregation. Both business and religious leaders stressed their neutrality and emphasized the first word rather than the second in the phrase, "peaceful implementation." There were few calls to action on the ground that desegregation was wise, just, or good. The emphasis was on the community's common interest in a smooth process and not on the moral reasons for the policies. Neither sector wanted to develop alternative plans to do something that the community did not want done at all.[23]

Although constrained in their public attitudes, the active groups in the religious and business communities did see the desegregation issue as a natural outgrowth of their previous work. To groups like the NCCJ and the DEA, desegregation was part of a larger commitment to intercultural harmony. To GWDC, desegregation was a threat to the stability of the community and economic position of the city. Individuals active in religious organizations were motivated by a personal commitment. Their positions put them on the front lines, where business leaders hired professionals to carry out the necessary tasks.

A characteristic pattern of involvement developed. Both business and religious leaders first consulted people on the national scene who were experienced in desegregation implementation. Both then worked through their ongoing umbrella organizations and developed new organizations that focused on the desegregation issue. Initially, the religious community worked through DEEP; after abandoning the probusing group, they formed the Interfaith Task Force. The business effort began with the existing GWDC and led to the formation of SANE.[24] Formation of new groups served to protect the old group from the storm of controversy and to concentrate desegregation resources and responsibilities.

Each sector first moved to prepare, and organize their own leaders and members. As the situation developed, leaders in each sector began to pressure school and governmental authorities to do "the correct thing." Much time and effort was spent on local and state authorities suggesting how and when they should begin implementation preparation. It soon became clear that the authorities were not as eager to prepare as were the community leaders. To fill this vacuum and encourage official action, each group began to develop its own programming. DEEP and NCCJ held conferences, SANE planned information and media centers, and NCCJ expanded its human relations training. Each brought in national authorities to consult with local leaders on desegregation implementation. Both the business and religious groups were hampered by limited legitimacy and limited resources in their efforts to convince the public that peaceful implementation should be everyone's goal. To counter these weaknesses, each sought to form coalitions with groups in other sectors.

The business and religious groups' styles differed. The business approach to a tranquil transition did not seek public participation. The public, if absolutely necessary, would be addressed through an advertising campaign. The corporate community was not able to work harmoniously with local community groups. It resembled Phelan and Pozen's elephant dancing among the chickens. Religious leaders, on the other hand, were able to involve many people through DEEP memberships and conferences, social action committees in congregations, and NCCJ human relations programs. In addition, they worked closely with police agencies and acted as the leaders in various community coalitions. Both groups, however, were elite groups with no close control or support from grassroots members. As in the desegregation controversies of the fifties, church officials tried to support ideals that were not fully accepted among their own members. Business groups could not risk alienating customers. Thus GWDC could take a role impossible to the Chamber of Commerce or a retailing association, and the NCCJ could take a position that would disrupt a congregation in a working-class area. Both GWDC and the NCCJ relied primarily on donations from the community elite.

The efforts of the religious community appear to have been the more successful. They worked closely with governmental, school, and community leaders in relative harmony and mutual respect. Business groups faced more conflict and suspicion. The different impacts resulted from the personalities involved. Business leaders showed business virtues; they were analytical, secretive, very confident, and calculating. They often failed to understand the politics and pressures constraining school personnel. Religious leaders were morally inspired, open, and people-oriented, willing and eager to demonstrate their personal commitment to desegregation. These traits were those expected of church people. Since desegregation is more a political rather than a rational or technical issue, the religious leaders' skills were more useful in the implementation process.

Although business sector financial resources were greater than those of religious groups, more business money went to pay salaries. The religious community was able to contribute the time of several key leaders and to obtain volunteers from its grassroots organizational network in churches and synagogues. The money was important, but the sense of commitment at the grassroots was even more significant. Person-to-person involvement at the local level was essential for successful communication. The business community was unable or unwilling to utilize its own networks within the various corporations. In any event, with or without financial or moral resources, neither sector had the legitimacy needed to reach and persuade the vast public.

SUPPORTIVE COALITIONS: CONSENSUS OR ACTION?

The groups from the business and religious sectors of the community showed that attempting to support desegregation guaranteed that operations would be from a very narrow base. There were more diverse groups also in the field. The DCSD had been formed early in the desegregation process. Later, as the DCSD strived to overcome its limitations, a group of community leaders instituted the regular Breakfast Group with school and government officials where the progress of implementation was discussed. Out of this breakfast came the Alliance, a coaliltion of community groups to support the public schools. Were these broad-based groups more successful than the business or religious groups in supporting peaceful and effective desegregation? Were they able to fulfill the roles that politicians abandoned in the highly charged situation? For answers, let us examine the DCSD, the Breakfast Group, and the Alliance in turn.

The Delaware Committee on the School Decision (DCSD)

On January 21, 1975, Governor Sherman W. Tribbitt established the DCSD by executive order. Set up as a statewide committee of fifty, the DCSD was asked to "develop methods to assist the Governor, County Executive, Mayor, State Board of Education, and the people of the State of Delaware to accept and implement, if that should prove necessary, the decision of the court." By this order, the governor expanded the Committee of Twelve that County Executive Melvin A. Slawik had established in (May 1974) "to seek ways to react constructively to the federal court decision whatever it may be."[25]

The fifty members of the DCSD were appointed by the governor, county executive, and mayor of Wilmington and served without pay. The DCSD included leaders from many different types of organizations concerned about the court order, including antibusing groups (PAC, Neighborhood Schools Association, Committee for the Improvement of Education), prodesegregation groups (Urban Coalition, ACLU, NAACP), groups favorable to peaceful desegregation (American Association of University Women, Delaware State Education Association, the League of Women Voters), parent organizations (State PTA, Wilmington Home and School Council), religious groups (Roman Catholic Diocese, Jewish Federation of Delaware, New Castle County Presbytery, National Conference of Christians and Jews), business groups (Greater Wilmington Development Council, Central Wilmington Businesses, Inc.), social agencies (YMCA, La Borinquena Recreation and Development Center), and governmental agencies (governor's office, State Human Relations Commission, Wilmington Community Affairs Office, New Castle County executive's office). Liaison with several New Castle County school districts, including the Wilmington School District, was also established.

The DCSD held regular monthly meetings; its thirteen-person Executive Committee met monthly, and oftener as needed. The DCSD included several program-oriented task forces dealing with students, teachers, and public information. The chairman, the Rev. Robert B. Moore, was the executive presbyter of the New Castle County Presbytery, the fifty-five Presbyterian churches in Delaware and the Eastern Shore of Maryland. Vice-chairman Stuart Young was a Wilmington attorney and cochair of the NCCJ. Members had children in a majority of the school districts in the county.

In November 1974, I joined the Committee as staff director; I was hired with general revenue-sharing funds from the county through a contract with the University of Delaware. It was my responsibility to help the Committee define its appropriate role and organize activities to accomplish its objectives.

Because of problems caused by the unpopularity of busing and the interdistrict nature of the Wilmington case, the DCSD was forced to perform a number of functions not possible for regular governmental institutions.

1. Public involvement. In spring 1976, the DCSD held public meetings and conferences to solicit from the public concerns and ideas

about implementing desegregation. These ideas were forwarded to the State Board of Education and other decision makers, including the court. The Committee petitioned the court for *amicus curiae* (friend of the court) status so it could argue for an impartial monitoring commission to be established to oversee desegregation. In its brief, the Committee stated its availability to help establish such a group. The court accepted the Committee as an *amicus* but rejected its request for a monitor.

2. Mobilization. The Committee spearheaded plans for implementation by working on the human relations and student orientation aspects of desegregation, developing an Information Center proposal, helping to involve the religious and business communities, serving as consultant to groups that wanted to take constructive action on desegregation, and, in general, trying to deal with desegregation problems a few months ahead of everyone else.

A major effort of the Committee was to bring together representatives of the school boards and other parties concerned with the suit to discuss implementation problems. As we have seen, implementation became virtually undiscussable in public. After several futile attempts, the Committee succeeded in fostering communication through the Breakfast Group described below.

3. Legitimization. The Committee took on the unpopular task of helping the general public understand that a desegregation order was a strong possibility. The Committee tried to answer specific questions raised by the public about the case and school desegregation through means such as newspaper articles, pamphlets, a home-coffee program, and television interviews.[26] A proposal for an Information Center, later adopted by the state government, was used to encourage cooperation and discussion among key organizations and agencies before the court order was handed down. Afterward the committee met with public officials to pursuade them to take a positive approach.

4. Critiquing desegregation plans. Several members strongly urged the Committee to develop its own desegregation plan, but it never was able to do so. Any discussion was thwarted by the disparate stands taken by blacks ("Keep the Wilmington School District"), antibusing people ("no busing"), and several other holders of strong viewpoints (such as those favoring a county district over smaller districts). The Committee was limited to critiquing plans proposed by others.

The diverse membership of the DCSD was both a strength and a weakness. The diversity generated many ideas for committee activities and resulted in increased understanding across racial and ideological lines. There was, however, a constant conflict between members' commitment to their individual goals and the need to compromise to achieve the purposes of the overall group. The best the DCSD could do was to maintain a precarious neutrality on the issues of implementation.

Public opinion studies have indicated that people with more extreme views tend to be more politically active. Few people are passionately committed to neutrality. In the case of the DCSD, the two groups most active politically—the NAACP and the antibusing Positive Action Committee (PAC)—were the least active in their DCSD work. Their public demands that individuals and groups stand up and be counted were not compatible with quiet work for moderate solutions. As the community became polarized, the DCSD was attacked from both sides. One side charged that since the DCSD was not antibusing, it was really probusing; the other side wanted the group to prove its virtue by taking a more positive stand on the side of black community interests.

The DCSD strugged hard to remain neutral, but it soon had to do so with a greatly diminished antibusing presence. Over a year before implementation began, all antibusing leaders resigned from the Committee, several to become leaders of the PAC. One resigned publicly, blasting the DCSD as probusing; a second resigned quietly, saying that she wanted to devote all her energies to antibusing activities. Except John Trager (the staunch antibusing PTA activist who resigned before the 1976 election to run for a school board seat—he lost) no vocal antibusing individual was active on the committee in its last year. Some persons who questioned the wisdom of busing remained, but they were not antibusing leaders. Because of this lack of antibusing voices, the president of PAC could claim that DCSD was probusing, "greasing the wheels" for a "massive busing order."

If the DCSD had to struggle with its collective neutrality, its members had to cope with their own ambivalent feelings about desegregation and protest. This internal struggle was greatest for those members who had been active in civil rights and desegregation causes. They themselves doubted the wisdom of busing and they had supported the use of protest against the Vietnam War. They could not condemn protest against busing, which the Committee was trying to minimize, as inherently harmful. They were uncomfortable at seeming to place blind faith in a future court order. Over time, this discomfort was relieved as the DCSD asserted that its support for whatever the court ordered was not based on blind faith but rather on the belief that obeying the law was the best way to protect the safety of the children, the quality of the public schools, and the community as a whole.

Another dilemma facing the DCSD was whether to function as a debate or action group. The DCSD was composed of informed, active, and competent spokespersons for the groups and agencies they represented. In many ways, the DCSD served both as an excellent forum and as a representative body on the busing and desegregation issue. In other ways, the DCSD faced the classical difficulty of having too many leaders and not enough followers. The first commitment of many of the members was to the groups they represented, not to the DCSD. The Committee easily achieved a debate, but with such a diversity among members, it had a difficulty in focusing for action. Some members were leaders of antiestablishment protest groups not experienced in designing or implementing programs. Others could not or would not commit themselves to serve on time-consuming committees or in quasi-administrative posts. Some refused to serve out front as spokespersons for the DCSD because doing so would jeopardize their leadership in their own organizations.

This conflict of interests manifested itself in various ways. Some members played to the press during meetings by making statements not relevant to Committee business. Other members effectively represented the position of the group they represented but did not interact constructively with other Committee members. A few members tried to engage in time-wasting debate rather than to move on to specific actions.

As a result the Committee was dependent on its staff to accomplish its goals. The Executive Committee was formed to reduce unproductive debate and to spearhead action. Its approach was that, although the Committee was not the authority responsible for implementing a desegregation order, it would undertake action if the appropriate authorities did not play their proper roles. The Committee worked to establish mechanisms or structures through which others could learn and act. For example, the small discussion group program referred to as the home-coffee program (funded through the Delaware Humanities Forum) was a demonstration to groups such as churches and civic associations that such programs were feasible and productive.

A third DCSD dilemma was posed by the gap between its responsibility and its means to carry it out. The DCSD was given rather broad responsibility by the governor and county executive. Its level of leadership and access to up-to-date information enabled it unofficially to monitor the process of implementing school desegregation.

The Committee was, however, an advisory body that was constrained by its lack of permanent and strong ties to any governmental body. Robert Salisbury argued in the sixties that for urban school districts to be dependent on the political system could be beneficial to them because it would open the door for them to seek and receive support.[27] The DCSD's relative independence from government was thus a mixed blessing. In its last year it had access to no funds for out-of-pocket expenses. Previously, federal revenue-sharing and Comprehensive Employment Training Act (CETA) funds had been funneled through the county administration. If the Committee had been more directly tied to the county or state government, however, it would have had a less free hand. That is one reason that the DCSD suggested that the court appoint it as a monitor—it wished to derive authority from the court. The court refused the request.

The governmental ties that the DCSD did possess were not necessarily fortuitous. First, the originator of the Committee, County Executive Melvin A. Slawik, was convicted of lying to a federal grand jury about zoning and kickback investigations. He was removed from office by the governor on May 20, 1976, about two years after he had appointed the Committee of Twelve. Second, three governmental executives who were tied to the Committee were all Democrats. The Committee had to deal with rumors that it was a Democratic Party front. Third, the DCSD was affected by the overall atmosphere of antigovernment feeling. Finally, since the governmental executives appointed the Committee's members, the Committee was not so broad or open in its membership as it would have preferred. For example, Governor Tribbitt appointed several people from outside the desegregation area who were totally inactive and he did not appoint David Weber, DEEP chairman, who had sought membership and had been recommended by the Committee for over a year.

If the DCSD faced serious internal dilemmas, it met equally difficult ones in the outside world. The court decision was one long-standing source of uncertainty. Among the issues that remained undecided were the total cost of desegregation and which pupils would be transferred. This uncertainty not only made planning difficult but led individuals who believed that they were unlikely to be affected by a court order to remain uncommitted to the DCSD. Lacking the specific details of remedy, neither the DCSD nor the public could confront the reality and immediacy of desegregation.

The DCSD filled the vacuum that existed as long as the responsibility for implementing a desegregation order remained unspecified. Its most successful efforts were creation of the Information Center, the Breakfast Group, and the Alliance to coordinate efforts among various agencies and groups concerned with desegregation.

The state of public opinion often presented the DCSD with difficult choices between symbolism and substance. The spring 1977 poll (see Chapter 2) indicated that blacks were evenly divided about busing.

The white suburban areas were solidly opposed to busing and most insistent that their political representatives also be. These suburban areas were where a frank discussion of the issue was most needed, but an avowedly neutral committee had limited credibility there. Gaining popularity would have required giving up neutrality. Thus the Committee was regularly attacked from both sides.

Two incidents illustrated this dilemma, in which the DCSD had opportunities to take a symbolic antibusing stand without substantive significance. In the first, the most vocal antibusing member of the Committee called on the Committee to demand the resignation of presiding judge, John J. Gibbons, on the grounds of bias. This member declared that Gibbons' call for a "hard" plan was an antisuburban act; others thought that in saying "hard" Gibbons had meant definite or specific. Gibbons had called for an interdistrict plan a year earlier in the original *Evans v. Buchanan* decision. The Committee declined to attack the judge. In the second incident, the county executive asked the Committee to use its *amicus* status to ask the judge to delay implementation. Again the DCSD declined, believing that its *amicus* status was limited to arguments concerning a monitoring commission. Thus the Committee placed its objectivity and neutrality before concessions to public passion, but it left its hindering probusing image unaltered.

On July 25, 1977, in the Delaware Legislature, Senator Tom Sharp introduced a joint resolution which stated—

> WHEREAS, that Committee has received large sums of money to fund it in the last several years; and
> WHEREAS, the Committee's output has not been such as to warrant such a large expenditure of money; and
> WHEREAS, The General Assembly has enacted laws and the appropriate agencies are working toward a goal of voluntary busing; and
> WHEREAS, the "Delaware Committee on the School Decision" has-outlived its usefulness[28]

—the governor should abolish the DCSD immediately.

Two members of the Legislative Committee on Desegregation talked Sharp into allowing the resolution to be sent to the Legislative Committee for consideration of its legal and other implications. DCSD leaders were tipped off that the Legislative Committee would vote on the resolution at a noon meeting on the following day. With the help of a sympathetic legislator, they arranged to talk with the Legislative Committee at the meeting. It was the first time that I, as the DCSD's staff director, had met with the Legislative Committee on Desegregation. Several committee members were abusive, apparently using the

DCSD and me as an outlet for their hostility toward the judges and the federal orders for busing. With the aid of the governor's counsel, the Legislative Committee's lawyer, and a second sympathetic legislator, however, the legislators decided in a closed vote to keep the resolution bottled up.

There were several major factors in their decision. There was a question whether the resolution would have any effect—for example, the DCSD had been established by an executive order of the governor but in fact received no state funds. It was pointed out that passing the resolution might damage the state's legal contention that state action did not impede desegregation. In October 1977, the governor did abolish the DCSD to make way for the blue-ribbon Effective Transition Committee with authority over desegregation implementation (but the ETC was not appointed until August 1978). Forewarned of the governor's plans and agreeing with this action, the DCSD asked the governor to replace itself. (This was a rare instance of a committee voting for its own abolition.)

Despite the problems of consensus building—personal commitment to other positions by many members, attacks by those holding strong views, difficulty in reaching agreement on action—the DCSD was able to arouse and coordinate governmental and community efforts in support of peaceful implementation. Public meetings to inform the public about desegregation; early resolution of the police jurisdictional issue; establishment of the Information Center, which required cooperation among various groups and agencies; convening of the Breakfast Group; and creation of the coffee program, which helped many organizations (especially churches) to begin dealing with desegregation—all were significant contributions of DCSD. An important secondary effect was creating a cooperative, supportive, and friendly atmosphere among community leaders. In many ways the best measure of the success of the DCSD was the achievement of the two groups it helped to establish to overcome its own limitations—the Breakfast Group and the Citizens' Alliance for Public Education.

Breakfast Group

In January 1976, the Community Relations Service of the U.S. Department of Justice helped to arrange a two-day visit to Louisville, Jefferson County, Kentucky, which was made by three members of the DCSD: the staff director, the state PTA president, and the chairperson of the State Human Relations Commission. (No Wilmington parent or school representative was able to join the delegation although they were invited.) The metropolitan situation in Jefferson County was particularly appropriate to our study, for the county and city school districts had merged just before implementing their metropolitan desegregation plan. One Kentucky activity that impressed the Delaware delegation was a daily meeting of agency representatives involved with desegregation. The Delaware representatives decided that the complexity of the New Castle County case would necessitate a similar group.

The idea of a monthly or biweekly meeting of key staff and community leaders was presented to the DCSD, which endorsed the idea.

Earlier, a number of school districts, state agencies, such as the attorney general's office and the Department of Public Instruction, and community group leaders met under the auspices of the state police and DCSD to discuss joint planning for a countywide information center. The major reasons why the DCSD wanted this meeting was to encourage more practical coopertion across city, suburban, community, school district, and governmental lines. It was the state police representative, Norman Cochran, who placed enormous importance on establishing an information center. He said that if others failed to act, the state police would establish their own center, but a cooperative approach would be much more productive. (Ultimately the state agencies and the governor took control and responsibility for the center.)

The DCSD had made two attempts to bring a few key community leaders together with superintendents from Wilmington and several suburban schools quietly to discuss implementation rather than legal, which is to say inflamatory, issues. The Wilmington School District officials voiced support of discussions, but they failed to attend either meeting. The suburban representatives who did attend helped to lay a foundation for further cooperation across traditional lines of authority.

In winter 1976, David Weber lamented that people in leadership positions were no longer meeting spontaneously at various court hearings. He felt that an informal meeting place was needed to replace the old courtroom rendezvous.

Finally, on March 12, 1976, inspired by the DCSD, there was a meeting of about fifteen agency, school district, and community leaders over breakfast. These first participants included the chairman of the suburban superintendents, the Wilmington superintendent, and representatives of teacher unions, several state agencies, several community groups, and the Community Relations Service of the U.S. Department of Justice. The Rev. Robert B. Moore, chairman of the

DCSD, chaired the meeting. (I was later a chairperson, and then the NCCJ executive director, Helen Foss, served as chairperson.) Eventually the group acquired its name—the "Breakfast Group"—and met everyone other week to discuss issues and problems in planning for school desegregation implementation—matters such as student preparation and crisis intervention.

Regular participants in the Breakfast Group included people from

government:
  Governor's Office
  Community Relations Service, U.S. Department of Justice
  Delaware State Police
  State Human Relations Commission
  New Castle County Police
  Attorney General's Office
  City of Wilmington Mayor's Office (sometime including the mayor)
  Wilmington City Council
  New Castle County Executive's Office

education:
  New Castle County Suburban Superintendents' Task Force on
      Desegregation
  Delaware State Education Association
  Delaware Federation of Teachers
  State Department of Public Instruction
  Interim Board of Education and New Castle County Planning Board
      of Education
  Wilmington School District
  Mt. Pleasant Citizen's Committee on *Evans v. Buchanan*

parent:
  Wilmington Home and School Council
  Delaware Congress of Parents and Teachers
  Wilmington Title I Advisory Board

community groups:
  Greater Wilmington League of Women Voters
  North Brandywine Council of Congregations
  SANE of Delaware, Inc.
  AFL-CIO Community Services
  Delaware Equal Education Process Committee
  Methodist Action Program
  National Conference of Christians and Jews

The Breakfast Group occasionally invited representatives of the State Board of Education, the State Legislature, and local school boards.

The Breakfast Group served a variety of functions:

1. Discussions about desegregation took place before, during and after breakfast among key individuals involved in implementation. Messages were exchanged without the formality of a letter, a memo, or even the telephone.

2. Information was exchanged at meetings—announcements of future meetings, reports of future agency or organization plans, analyses of the content and implications of court opinions, and descriptions of activities in other communities.

3. Introductions were important. When a new individual entered the desegregation process, the breakfast offered a convenient way to introduce him or her to many key people. Similarly, when studies were being made by a group such as SANE or the Rand Corporation, the researcher was introduced at the breakfast and often held interviews after the meeting. Names were related to faces and often trust was established across geographical and functional lines.

4. The meetings served as an idea exchange. Evaluations of the current situation, ideas for future activities, specification of problem areas, and other ideas, plans, and reflections were offered at each breakfast. For example, when representatives of the mass media described their elaborate plans to cover the first week of school, they were advised first to discover what the schools were usually like during opening week (how many buses were usually late, how many children tended to be absent) so that they would not interpret ordinary confusion as desegregation-related.

5. The Breakfast Group served as an advisory body both to its regular participants and its guests. Governor duPont, County Executive Jornlin, and legislators met with the group and received suggestions. After his election, Mayor McLaughlin regularly took part. Although much of the effect of these meetings was subtle, there were examples of obvious impact. For example, the group criticized the training for Information Center employees and the DPI quickly set a revised training program in motion. Later, the Breakfast Group advised the Information Center director to keep the Center open on the evening of the teachers' strike vote.

6. New ideas were sometimes generated at the breakfast. The most significant of them was that the Alliance should be established.

7. The meetings served as consensus achievers and conflict resolvers. The breakfast helped participants to discuss and agree on major needs like an alliance and school crisis intervention teams.

8. The breakfast was a frustration reducer. It provided a place for participants to let off steam, criticize each other, complain, and even grill key officials—all outside the glare of press coverage. It was one place where individuals were not treated as if they were crazy for believing desegregation would occur.

9. The breakfasts were a testing ground. The capabilities of various people were measured by their success in filling their role in the group. Some showed great ability to handle responsibility.

10. The meetings helped to maintain saliency. Having a regular breakfast ensured that the desegregation issue would remain prominent in the minds of government and community leaders. In the press of daily affairs, the breakfast was a constant remainder of the community's long-range dilemma.

The importance of the Breakfast Group was confirmed when it met on September 14, 1978—the fourth peaceful day of school busing—by the attendance of County Executive Mary Jornlin and several other school and governmental officials. Their presence assured breakfast participants that the meetings had played a significant role in the smooth transition to a desegregated county school system. The Breakfast Group did have a number of problems, however. First, the lack of formal rules and authority meant that decisions often were made (or at least appeared to be made) arbitrarily. For example, who should be invited? What should the agenda be? The chairperson usually had to make such decisions with no strong guidelines or input from the other breakfast participants.

A second drawback was lack of participation of the Wilmington School District superintendent and representative. The superintendent came only twice and the representative hardly said a word. Early in the process, the representative suburban school superintendent was an active participant but never reported back to the other superintendents. This not only limited the impact of the Breakfast Group but also caused resentment among the other superintendents, who were excluded to keep the meeting small and to avoid domination by school interests.

A third aspect of the Breakfast Group that might have caused difficulty was the lack of formal minutes. The meetings and discussions were confidential, which encouraged frank discussions but may well have resulted in the loss of some good ideas. It seemed paramount that people feel totally at ease within the group, however, so any lost ideas were considered less important than the ease and frankness that prevailed.

Secrecy was the price that had to be paid for the consensus achieved at the breakfast, but because of this secrecy, the breakfast could take no public stance or action. Those in the group who felt the need to take an open stand urged the formation of a coalition that could "go public." The result was the Citizens' Alliance for Public Education.

Citizens' Alliance for Public Education

On March 24, 1976, at Longwood Gardens, the luxurious former estate of Pierre S. du Pont, the NCCJ held a conference for business, labor, professional, and religious leaders on preparing for desegregation. School officials pointedly were not invited. The invitation was signed by top religious, labor, and business leaders in the county. Distinguished national business leaders who were familiar with the role that business could play in desegregation addressed the conference: Bruce M. Rockwell, chairman of the board of Colorado National Bank, Denver; Robert Lampere, vice-president of John Hancock Mutual Life Insurance, Boston, and chairman of the Trilateral Commission on Quality Education; and Kathy Straus, executive director of PRO-Detroit. Straus' description of the Detroit coalition reinforced my decision, as DCSD staff director, to work for the formation of a large coalition. (Straus was also a consultant to SANE and later supplied me with ideas and materials.) The decision to seek a coalition was further reinforced when some NCCJ activities a few weeks later showed a lack of information about the work of the DCSD, the Breakfast Group, and others. The need for a public group to coordinate action was reemphasized.

The lack of coordination among the local school district desegregation task forces, along with their great variation in levels of information, experience, and activities, led the Breakfast Group to suggest a special breakfast meeting for representatives of all such local organizations. The president of the state PTA, Betty Lewis, called and chaired the meeting, which was primarily devoted to a description of the history and activities of each group present. The personal contacts made there proved to be very valuable, then and later.

On May 19, 1976, the Community Relations Sevice and the National Center for Quality Integrated Education (related to the National Educational Association) held a day-long national conference in

Washington, D.C. on coalition formation in school desegregation situations. A large delegation from the Wilmington metropolitan area attended. By the end of that afternoon, a number of Delawareans had been impressed by the information made available to them. One thought-provoking statement was, "There is never a good time to begin a coalition. You are always too early for some and too late for others." It was a very fortuitous happenstance that the federal court ruling came that very afternoon, the one that stayed implementation for one year and established an interim board of education to plan for desegregation. Now there would be plenty of time to build coalitions.[29]

One participant in the Breakfast Group, a black elected official, persistently argued that desegregation was primarily a political process. He declared that a group was needed to serve as a counterforce to those working to disrupt school desegregation. Specifically, a group was needed with leaders to speak for peaceful implementation, to coordinate activities and statements of all existing groups, to coordinate and focus outside resoures, to generate grassroots support, and so forth. The Breakfast Group decided to ask a representative of each of the religious, educational, business, labor, and community groups, and parent organizations to meet to plan a large meeting to develop a coalition. The planning group met several times, drew up a list of invitees, created an organization structure, decided on coleaders of the meeting (the state PTA and Wilmington Home and School presidents), and established an agenda. Members of the Breakfast Group personally invited the various leaders to the meetings.

The first meeting was held on June 22, 1976. Almost everyone invited attended. Ninety-two groups were represented from the school, religious, business, and social agency sectors. Participants reviewed the preliminary organizational plans for the coalition. Small groups were led by people such as a school board president and a city councilman. There was little discussion of whether a coalition was required. That was already accepted. Individuals were named to develop the structure and functions of the coalition further. An ad hoc steering committee was asked to report back to the full group in one month.

During the formation of the Citizens' Alliance for Public Education (the Alliance, for short), serious organizational issues had to be faced. The desire to make the new organization a true coalition, bringing together blacks and whites and various sectors of the community, posed several problems. Inefficiency seemed inherent in a coalition of this sort, considering the vast variety of opinions that would be represented. While members of the planning committee agreed that a black cochair from Wilmington and a white cochair from the suburbs would symbolize the joining of interests, all favored the efficiency of a single executive head. Eventually the cochairman system was chosen. Similarly, while a representative steering committee was preferred, it was expected that the resulting large committee would be a clumsy decision-making mechanism. Ultimately the coalition serving method prevailed over the business-like approach. A board of managers composed of the following individuals was named:

President, Delaware State PTA (cochair)
President, Wilmington Home and School Council (cochair)
President Elect, Delaware School Boards Association
Member, Wilmington City Council
Pastor, Bethel AME Church
Vice-President, Wilmington Home and School Council
Leader, Committee to Improve Education
Former Chairman, Mt. Pleasant School Board
President, Greater Wilmington League of Women Voters
Cochairman, Mt. Pleasant Task Force on *Evans* v. *Buchanan*
Leader, North Brandywine Council of Congregations
Director, Green Circle Program
Aide to County Executive for Hispanic Affairs
Past President, Suburban Newark Civic League
Director, Community Legal Aid
Community Services Director, AFL-CIO
Title I Parent Coordinator, Wilmington
President, Newark League of Women Voters
Executive Director, Children's Bureau
Executive Director, Methodist Action Program

Joseph Rule, Jon Chace, and I were named as resource persons. It seemed advisable to utilize us as resources rather than to jeopardize the legitimacy of the Alliance by including us directly as members.

The goals of the Alliance were clear from the start: support for the public schools, informed citizen involvement, and peaceful and effective school desegregation if ordered by the courts. The Alliance board met with legislative leaders to give support for public schools even if that were to mean busing as included in a desegregation order. With the financial help of SANE, the Alliance published newsletters to inform people throughout the county (circulation was 3,000) of its activities and the desegregation situation. The strongest Alliance effort was to increase citizen involvement in the desegregation process.

One of the first chances for the Alliance to work toward its goal of citizen involvement came in October 1976, as the Interim Board began considering alternative desegregation plans. The Alliance quickly marshalled its forces through an ad hoc committee and a special board meeting. A "communications proposal" was presented to the Interim Board within a week arguing that

> Interim Board consideration of decisions about the planning process and the specific plans should involve two key criteria: technical adequacy *and* public acceptance. It should also be noted that both are relative concepts—any plan will have its strengths and weaknesses and public acceptance will not necessarily be complete.[30]

The Alliance urged the Interim Board to arrange regional public hearings, to appoint community people to existing task forces, to appoint countywide citizen, student, and school district advisory groups, and to establish community relations, safety, human relations, and extracurricular activity task forces. Although the Interim Board did not acknowledge the influence of the Alliance, it did hold one public hearing and it did establish advisory groups of parents and students to the sixteen task forces. None of the other Alliance recommendations were adopted.

Dilemmas faced by the Alliance were similar to those faced earlier by the DCSD. Diverse membership and leadership limited and slowed the pace of activities. The Alliance could not undertake programs of great scope because few individuals gave it their first loyalty, few were willing to give it a large block of their time, and funds were unavailable for an executive director. Although school officials had helped to launch the Alliance, they would neither recognize formally nor give it an official role in the desegregation process. The general public remained suspicious of any group not devoted to the antibusing cause, which limited the Alliance's ability to recruit those who were against busing. Antibusing leaders refused to join the Alliance, calling it the CAPE behind which probusers lurked.

The success of the Alliance was more due to the individuals who led it than to the organizations it brought together. The two most impressive leaders were its cochairs, Betty Lewis and Ruth Graham.

Betty Lewis had expertly guided the state PTA through the Scylla of the obstructionist antibusing forces and the Charybdis of those morally commited to desegregation of any post. Attacked from both sides, she used reason, intelligence, sweetness, and political maneuvering to steer the PTA to merely symbolic stands against busing while simultaneously guiding her group in substantive action to prepare for desegregation. Just as Dave Weber was behind virtually every religious activity aimed at peaceful implementation, Betty Lewis was a constant source of advice and ideas for those active in educational organizations.[31]

If one had to go to the Delaware Division Emergency Room, one would hope to be treated by a nurse like Ruth Graham. The same direct, no-nonsense, intelligent approach that led to her success as a teacher of nurses served her well in dealing with school issues. She was recognized for her leadership qualities in the city as was Betty Lewis in the suburbs. In August 1977, Governor du Pont named her to the Wilmington School Board.

As capable as were its two leaders, the Alliance was limited in its ability to achieve its goals. Unlike the DCSD, the Alliance had no executive director to bring its diversity into agreement on action and, when agreement was reached, to be responsible for executing the proposed action. Both cochairs devoted their time to their role as spokespersons, leaving the role of implementor vacant. The Alliance did receive funds for an office and a secretary from the local Crystal Foundation and as noted above, funds for a newsletter from SANE before busing began. In July 1978, the Newark City Council donated $5,000 to the Alliance for community education programs, and the Wilmington City Council soon made a similar contribution. These government commitments were a symbolic as well as a practical help, but they did not permit hiring a full-time executive for the Alliance.

SUMMARY

While it is difficult to pinpoint the exact influence of supportive community groups on the desegregation process, it is clear that the groups in New Castle County did have a number of effects.[32] Community groups were able to pressure school officials into involving the public, although not to the desired extent. Supportive groups were able to push governmental executives to prepare for desegregation, although not as quickly as they wanted. Community groups did force school and governmental officials to establish new structures to implement the order, although doing so was anything but easy.[33]

Community coalitions performed a number of significant political and administrative functions that government and school officials were unable or unwilling to perform during various phases of desegregation process in Delaware.[34] While the diversity of views within the coalitions made it no easier for them than for public officials to agree on a desegregation and reorganization plan, they were able to work in harmony for peaceful, effective school desegregation. They all had to struggle to reach more than a few thousand people. Yet, in the absence of other voices speaking for their position, the existence of these groups was significant for they gave legitimacy to the court order.

For a short period at the beginning of the DCSD, antibusing leaders worked within the DCSD for peaceful implementation. As the next chapter indicates, by 1976 busing opponents were putting all their efforts into a large organization using conventional political means to fight busing. Community groups did manage to play the mediation role occasionally.

The DCSD pushed for agreements between the county police and state police on their respective desegregation responsibilities and urged all parties to establish an information center. The clergy joined teams of school officials and police in training for crisis intervention. In 1978, Alliance leaders were asked to help find a solution to teacher negotiation problems.

The coalitions were most successful in mobilizing various sectors of the community to prepare for desegregation and in coordinating their efforts. The Breakfast Group was acknowledged by many to have been a significant factor in the desegregation process, for it established a structure in which key leaders could reach agreement on implementation issues.[35] Given the interdistrict nature of the *Evans* v. *Buchanan* remedy and the comprehensive impact of desegregation on the metropolitan community in general, the opportunities for communication provided by this group were sorely needed.

The DCSD and the Alliance pushed hard for public involvement. Their activities encouraged school authorities to open up the desegregation process somewhat to members of the public. The Breakfast Group also provided a means for community leaders to participate. While the resistance of school officials to widespread public involvement was never fully overcome, hundreds of community leaders did participate in programs stemming from these coalition groups.

Finally, pushing governmental officials to prepare for the possibility of protests, school incidents, and violence, the community groups helped to establish the mechanisms to ensure the safety of the school children.

In virtually every dimension of implementation, coalitions proved to be the dominating force. Although building and maintaining consensus were major limitations on their ability to act, coalitions were able to help achieve administrative and political goals. While these supportive coalitions were forming, maturing, and struggling to fill the void left by the inaction of school and governmental officials, however, an antibusing community group was organized to counter implementation of the desegregation order.

7 / Organized Opponents of Busing

With the white suburban public almost unanimously against busing, it was inevitable that organized antibusing efforts would figure strongly in the desegregation process. Begun in February 1975, the Positive Action Committee (PAC) became the single antibusing interest group, replacing the Neighborhood Schools Association (the group that helped John Trager of Wilmington, though a bachelor, win the State PTA vice-presidency in 1968) as the largest and most vocal antibusing organization in Delaware. PAC's efforts to stop busing, and its slogan, "It's time to wake up, folks," generated a great amount of local publicity. While community groups supporting school desegregation abandoned, rejected, or never even considered ideological appeals, PAC was highly ideological from the start. It claimed over 10,000 members (the dues were $2.50 per member), spent over $15,000 in printing materials to distribute throughout the county, held well-attended public meetings, and was an active lobbying force in the State Legislature. But despite its large membership, committed leadership, and public support, it was not as influential as its leaders had hoped. PAC remained a threat to politicians throughout and was highly influential with the State Legislature, but it failed in its major goals—to stop busing, to force a major confrontation between state and federal officials, and to punish those who did not subscribe to its goals.

THE LEADERSHIP AND IDEOLOGY OF PAC

The fortunes of PAC were tied to those of its president, James Venema. Venema was a salesman in the cosmetics side of the Glenn Turner organization, Dare To Be Great, which was under federal indictment for fraud when PAC was formed early in 1975.[1] The Turner business was built on a pyramid system, which served as a model for PAC activities. After leaving the Turner organization, Venema started a small sign manufacturing business.

Until February 1978, Venema was registered as an Independent but his politics were conservative Republican. Before the 1976 election Venema said that, if he had any political hero, it was Ronald Reagan. In August 1977, Venema outlined his conservative philosophy in a newspaper column entitled "Robin Hoodism and Its Perils":

> In my opinion, a predominantly white anti-busing group, like the Positive Action Committee (PAC), could not survive if its motivations were racist in nature and if it were devoid of any underlying basic philosophy. From its inception in early 1975, PAC has referred to forced busing as but the "tip of the iceberg," though we never attempt to fully define the iceberg because that would have led us into a myriad of other issues, and we had neither the time nor the money to educate the public on a number of issues. As we've discovered, due to its overwhelming complexity, it's nearly an impossible task to educate people on just a single issue. While this may strike some as harsh, and perhaps even condescending, it is nevertheless true.
>
> I prefer to label PAC as a "conservative" organization, the "iceberg" as rampant "liberalism," and forced busing as the most absurd example, and disastrous manifestation, of liberalism run amuck. Liberalism feeds upon itself and it has reached cancerous proportions in this country. Its ultimate endpoint, if not indeed its goal, is socialism or, for those who prefer (and there are many), that other unmentionableism.[2]

In some ways Venema had the style of a politician. He was young (thirty-five years old in 1975), well dressed, suave, attractive, and out for whatever publicity was available. Venema and several other leaders of PAC, however, were distinctly unpolitical in their frequent use of sarcasm, attacks on people and organizations, and extreme rhetoric. PAC's circulars displayed a school bus labeled "The Kidnap Express"; PAC's leaders associated their opponents with brainwashing, Nazi propaganda, and control over children; and Venema ruled out any sort of compromise or accommodation with implementation.[3]

Several PAC leaders had small business ties. For example, William D'Onofrio, once PAC's second in command and named president in April 1978, was a self-employed tax accountant active in civic associations. D'Onofrio described himself as a conservative and, true to conservative form, was very critical of liberals. "I found that most people involved in civic work . . . were liberals or middle of the roaders. That's why we have so many problems."[4] D'Onofrio's conservatism extended to the schools: "The finger points ominously at the advocates of 'progressive education' as the principal cause of this state of affairs [that] young people cannot read [or] write."[5] Other leaders of PAC also had middle-class backgrounds and conservative philosophies. A newspaper writer concluded, "PAC has tapped a wellspring of frustration with big government and public decision-makers perceived as being out of touch and unresponsive."[6] According to Venema, "Forced busing put it all in one neat little package."[7]

PAC's Tactics

PAC's declared that forced busing was the last provocation in the erosion of our freedoms. As one leader put it, "In slightly over 200 years we have regressed to the sort of tyranny and injustice the British government imposed on the people of that time. . . . [The judiciary is extracting] yet another freedom from out already dwindling supply."[8] Forced busing, according to the Positive Action Committee, took away parents' rights, harmed the education of children, caused people to flee the public schools, and was very costly. PAC leaders believed that the reprehensible loss of freedom had to be stopped, even if it meant confrontation between local and federal officials or between voters and their representatives.

PAC leaders disavowed both disruptive tactics and cooperation in connection with implementation. Venema said in July 1975 that PAC would not "cooperate in implementation of a forced busing plan" but still opposed "vandalism, racism, and violence."[9] Anticipating a "massive busing order," Venema told his followers, "Keep your cool. Stay calm. Don't start running, hooting, and hollering and tipping over buses. . . . I'm sure the opposition is just waiting for us to lose our cool."[10] Venema thought that stoning buses would not be effective. PAC leaders, however, refused to accept the possibility of neutrality or peaceful implementation. They claimed that groups like the DCSD, SANE, and the Alliance were probusers in disguise. For example, Venema indignantly rejected a "begging" attempt by Jon Chace of the Community Relations Service to involve PAC in the Information Center. When PAC judged that school and public officials had gone too far in complying with court orders, it accused them of being coopted. "Let the court pull the trigger," said Venema.[11]

PAC saw the State Legislature as the instrument for a confrontation with the federal government over busing. Venema declared, "We're going to get this issue to the voting booth. The General Assembly is the last line of defense between federal power running crazy and the citizens. We want them to stand up and fight for the people.[12] Venema was not concerned with whether his proposals were constitutional; he believed that it would be good for the courts to throw out 250 pieces of antibusing legislation. The challenge to federal power was the issue. PAC believed that State Board members should "resign" and that the court-directed Interim Board should have told the court to "go hell."[13] To quote Venema, "The people out there don't want busing. If we get a large enough membership, we can put in or take out any politicians we want."[14]

PAC held public membership drive meetings with the following speakers:

Sue Mills, member, Prince Georges County School Board
Lino Graglia, attorney, Austin and other desegregation cases, and author of *Disaster by Decree*
Nick Thimmesch, national columnist
Jean Ruffa, chairman, Jefferson County (Kentucky) School Board

One speaker was advertised as Edward P. Langerton, author of the *Busing Coverup*. It was said that he used a pseudonym in order not to jeopardize his two million dollars in federal grants at a well-known large midwestern university. The *News Journal* revealed that Langerton was Ralph Scott, a professor at the University of Northern Iowa and a former candidate for governor of Iowa on the American Party ticket.[15] The newspaper also revealed that Scott had received no federal funding for at least ten years; in fact, the entire university did not receive as much federal support as Langerton/Scott claimed for himself. It was later revealed that Scott and PAC leaders had received travel expenses from the Pioneer Fund, a group whose policies have been called racist.[16]

PAC concentrated on membership drives, mailings, mass meetings, letters to the editor of the *News Journal*, and pressuring public officials. Its strong, aggressive, threatening approach backfired on occasion. Early in 1976, I heard Governor Tribbitt tell a small group of DCSD leaders about a relatively serene meeting with a PAC delegation. At the end of the meeting, he said a well-dressed female PAC supporter leaned over his desk and said, "Governor, we know that you are against busing, but Governor, you'd better watch your ass on this one." Such abuse did not sit well with governmental officials and clashed with the PAC claim that their leaders and followers were respectable citizens and concerned parents, not racists. Soon afterward Governor Tribbitt wrote a letter attacking Venema's leadership (see Chapter 5).

School officials tried to protect themselves when dealing with PAC. In one school district, officials watched PAC meetings from an observation booth above the auditorium. When PAC officials spoke at one meeting of the Superintendents' Council, the session was recorded. (At this meeting PAC leaders reportedly threatened to destroy the public school system if busing took place.)

The PAC solution to the court-order problem was a voluntary transfer or freedom of choice plan. At one point they discussed supporting the abolition of the Wilmington schools (that would have entailed one-way busing, for black children only). As a last resort PAC would have considered abolishing the state's public schools. They reasoned that since busing would ruin the public schools anyway, Delaware might as well stand and fight busing to the end in order to stop it nationally.

PAC leaders accomplished their short-range goals. They became the visible and recognized spokesmen for the antibusing public. If an antibusing view was required, Venema was called. PAC received widespread radio, television, and press coverage. It could distribute up to 50,000 brochures door-to-door throughout the county whenever it liked. Several members of the General Assembly, including the chairperson of the Special Legislative Committee on Desegregation, were PAC members. PAC leaders regularly exhorted their followers to action and the PAC literature was full of recommendations: sign up your neighbors as new members, write your senators about a constitutional amendment to ban busing, and so on.

PAC and the Nation

As the desegregation case dragged on, PAC increasingly turned its attention to the national scene. Leaders of PAC were instrumental in forming the National Association for Neighborhood Schools (NANS) in August 1976. Jim Venema served as NANS chairman. Early on, PAC leaders were in contact with antibusing activists in Boston, Louisville, and other cities. As the Delaware case progressed, PAC officials sought more actively to form a national coalition against busing.[17] From the start Jim Venema described the PAC cause as part of a war that would be won or lost on the battlefield of Delaware.

Much PAC correspondence went to the White House, Congress, federal judges, and other national addresses. In a four-page single-spaced letter dated December 1, 1975, Venema warned "pro-busers" in the U.S. Senate to look out for "raped Middle America" whose outraged citizens intend to "foul you."[18] PAC officials constantly kept watch over Senators Roth and Biden, generally praising the former and chiding the latter. In summer 1977, the Newark *Weekly Post* wrote that Venema was considering a race against Senator Biden on the Republican ticket. As we saw in a previous chapter, Biden had by then become a staunch opponent of busing. In August 1977, Venema contributed the "Thinking Out Loud" column in the *News Journal*, applying his conservative philosophy to many political issues. In February 1978, Venema declared his intention to run against Biden.

Thus, at the top, PAC was a highly ideological organization. To leaders, their antibusing campaign was a matter of conservative principle. Their language resounded with strong symbols. They proselytized at the local and national level. They refused to compromise and demanded that public officials place their principles above compliance with the federal court.[19] But what of the followers of PAC?

PAC ACTIVISTS AND FOLLOWERS

The spring 1977 poll of New Castle County parents (see Chapter 2) suggests that the broad ideology of PAC's key leaders was not shared by those generally active in the organization (those who paid dues and attended meetings) and those who followed PAC affairs less closely (those who read PAC newsletters). PAC activists and followers did not come only from a narrow segment of society. In background and attitudes, PAC activists and followers were strikingly like their non-PAC suburban counterparts.[20] PAC members were distinguished mainly by their attitudes toward desegregation and busing and by the actions they would take to oppose them.

When we compare PAC activists to people with no PAC affiliation, we find no percentage difference between the background characteristics of the two groups greater than 7 percent (see Appendix 2). Similarly, political party affiliation and willingness to see the government guarantee jobs (an indicator of liberalism) are not related. PAC activists are more cynical about government, in general, although they are also more satisfied with neighborhood services. The percentage differences are in the 10–15 percent range. PAC activists are only slightly more positive than others about the quality of the local schools, and they are about as trusting of local school authorities.

The first major differences between PAC activists and those without PAC contact appear in the reactions to busing and its effects and the actions they had already taken with regard to busing (Table 7-1). PAC activists were much more likely to strongly oppose busing (79 percent versus 57 percent), disagree with the statement that the order should be obeyed (49 percent versus 63 percent), believe that busing will have negative consequences (the average percentage difference is over 16 percent), report already taking action on this subject (an average of over 50 percent versus less than 10 percent), and report they will attempt to avoid the consequences of the order (an average of about 33 percent per avoidance item versus 12 percent). Note that PAC follow-ers in general fall between the two extremes of PAC activists and those who have no contact with PAC.

Table 7-1
PAC Affiliation by Desegregation Activity (Suburban Parents)

Busing-related Activity	PAC Activists (67)	PAC Followers (89)	No PAC (144)
Have written letter	54%	21%	13%
Have joined group	72%	29%	9%
Have voted for candidate	60%	37%	15%
Have gone to meeting	82%	38%	19%
Have participated in a rally	15%	2%	1%
Would not go along with a plan where child's school is desegregated but child not bused	58%	37%	27%
Would move	18%	4%	2%
Would send child to private or parochial school	31%	21%	11%
Would keep child out of school	24%	9%	7%

Source: Spring 1977 poll.

As Table 7-2 indicates, PAC activists are not confined to blue-collar school districts. Of the eighty-one PAC activists in the spring 1977 poll, thirty-five or 43 percent lived in blue-collar districts. This is close to the percentage of respondents living in blue-collar districts (37 percent). In all types of suburban school districts, PAC activists comprised at least 12 percent of the sample, and at least 37 percent of those in each suburban category were PAC followers or activists. Thus, PAC ties were prevalent and PAC leaders were strong through-out the suburbs. Their influence could not be easily ignored in any one type of suburban school district. It must be stressed that over half of the people questioned in the suburbs reported receiving at least some information from PAC.

IMPACT OF PAC

PAC had developed into a vocal, active, single-issue interest group during 1975. With ten thousand members and several committed leaders, PAC seemed poised to play a major role in the political process in Delaware. What effect, then, did PAC have on government officials, political parties, and school policies?

Table 7-2
PAC Affiliation by Type of School District (Total Sample)

	PAC Activity		
Type of School District	Activists	Followers	No PAC
Upper class (95)	12%	32%	57%
Middle class (209)	16%	30%	54%
Blue collar (175)	20%	17%	63%
Black (401)	0%	1%	99%

Source: Spring 1977 poll.

PAC and Policies

PAC had a major influence on the Delaware State Legislature's approach to desegregation. Much of the legislature's action was symbolic rather than substantive, however.[21] The best example of a symbolic gesture was the November 1977 resolution calling on President Carter to remove Judge Schwartz from office. Such a request was not the proper procedure for removing a federal judge, and was unlikely to have any practical effect in any event. The legislature, as was noted in Chapter 5, did refuse to take some more extreme symbolic actions; it once held off from subpoenaing a federal judge.

It must be noted that legislators were not more sympathetic to busing before PAC came in the scene than after its rise to power. PAC pressure, however did push the legislature to become more vocal in its opposition and to take collective action, however symbolic, to satisfy the antibusing forces.

PAC did not succeed in involving the legislature in a no-holds-barred conflict with the federal judiciary over busing. The legislature as a whole showed no sign of being willing to be in contempt of court on the issue of financing or any other issue, although individual legislators expressed more extreme views. Nor did the legislature react against public education. When the governor asked for major budget reductions in public education in 1977, including some that would have greatly increased the pupil-teacher ratio in secondary schools, the legislature greatly limited the cuts.

The legislature did take several PAC-approved substantive actions. In particular, it enacted a voluntary transfer plan and examined magnet school plans. The voluntary transfer plan did have an impact on education and finance in Delaware, but nothing came of the flirtations with magnet schools. One major side effect of the PAC pressure was an increased amount of state money going to lawyers, as legislative leaders more and more sought legal advice. This fostered a legally conservative approach to the issue. It also seems to have educated both the legislature and the public on the relative power of state and federal authorities. The 1977 and 1978 polls showed only 36 and 39 percent of suburban parents believing that action by the legislature could stop busing. If a poll had been taken in 1975, that percentage would certainly have been far higher.

PAC lobbying did help to block passage of the crucial four-district plan in December 1977 (see Chapter 5). PAC leaders presented the vote as a referendum on busing. Since groups supporting implementation generally did not lobby for or against the four-district plan, the contest was between the governor and school officials and the PAC. The defeat of the bill was seen as a victory for PAC.

As the busing conflict intensified, the city suffered in noneducational areas. One legislative leader said privately that some of his colleagues were asking of every new bill: how does this affect Wilmington? Their intentions were not protective. Several pieces of legislation important to the city were affected negatively by this mood. Authorizing legislation was need for the city to build a planned jai alai fronton near a soon-to-be-built highway and a new office building. The facility promised increased tax revenue. The legislature whittled away at Wilmington's percentage of the handle and then failed to enact the needed legislation. Although there was political disagreement on which firm would build and operate the facility, anticity feelings loomed large in the turndown.

A second legislative issue was even more important to the city. Wilmington depended on a 1.25 percent wge tax for about 25 percent of its annual revenue. In 1977 a suburban legislator filed suit to have the wage tax declared unconstitutional because it had been enacted as legislation (by a simple majority) rather than by the charter process (which required a two-thirds vote). Again, there were political considerations—suburban feeling against the wage tax had been strong and movement of some hospital facilities to the suburbs had been blocked by the city—but the city-suburban split over busing certainly gave impetus to the new suit.

Finally, in October 1977, Governor du Pont nominated the Rev. F. David Weber, the chairman of DEEP (the pro-desegregation group), to chair the antipornography commission recently established by the legislature. The Senate overwhelmingly rejected the nomination.

Thus, PAC seems to have had some impact in areas outside of education, primarily by intensifying anticity feeling.[22] In the legislature it stopped the four-district plan and supported voluntary desegregation plans. It was successful mainly in generating symbolic gestures against busing. If PAC obtained little change in educational policies, then, how did it affect the fortunes of political candidates?

PAC and the 1976 Elections

Although desegregation litigation had been reopened in 1971, public attention in New Castle County had been slight until 1975. By 1976 PAC was riding a wave of vocal and active public opposition. By 1976 PAC claimed over ten thousand members and was able to attract up to a thousand people to its antibusing meetings. PAC concentrated its attention on the State Legislature, demanding that legislators take a stand against busing and enact specific antibusing legislation.

By October 15, 1976, PAC had announced all its endorsements for the State Legislature and other state and local races. With few voices calling for reason and busing scheduled to begin in the following fall, PAC appeared invincible. The major political question was: How much would PAC affect the 1976 elections?

All twenty-nine seats in the Delaware lower house were at stake in New Castle County in 1976. PAC endorsed twenty-one candidates. Ignoring the six races in the City of Wilmington, PAC endorsed sixteen Republican and five Democratic candidates in the remaining twenty-three races. Of the twenty-one endorsees, fourteen were incumbents; all five of the endorsed Democrats were incumbents.

PAC based its endorsements, in part, on what it considered antibusing votes in the State Legislature (e.g., for example, a vote against the $50,000 funding of the Legislative Committee on Desegregation was a bad vote). Of the fourteen House members highest on the PAC voting index, eleven were Republicans; of the fifteen lowest, twelve were Democrats. Even excluding the six representatives from the city, seven of the ten lowest on the index were Democrats. The PAC endorsements were thus favorable to Republicans. Although PAC leaders claimed that their board was composed of seven Democrats, seven Republicans, and five Independents, it seemed to several nonendorsed Democrats that Republican party affiliation figured favorably in endorsement decisions.

At first glance, the PAC endorsements may appear to have heavily influenced the 1976 Delaware House races. Sixteen of the twenty-one PAC-endorsed candidates were elected. Even allowing for the four of the twenty-one who were unopposed, 70 percent of the PAC endorsees battling for contested seats (twelve of seventeen) were elected. All five democrats endorsed by PAC won, as did eleven of the sixteen Republicans.

Nevertheless, it is difficult to say whether the PAC endorsements or other variables caused this result. There are alternative explanations for the success of PAC endorsees. PAC endorsed incumbents; incumbents often win. Similarly, PAC endorsed four candidates who had no major party opposition; perhaps other PAC-endorsed candidates had only token opposition. Finally, PAC may have endorsed the most popular candidates, ones who would win independent of PAC support.

The most obvious question to ask is whether the candidates endorsed by PAC in 1976 fared better than their counterparts in the 1974 election, when busing was not an issue and PAC did not exist. Table 7-3 compares the 1976 and 1974 results.

In the fourteen races contested in both 1974 and 1976 where PAC endorsed a candidate, the PAC endorsees improved upon the 1974 showing of their party's candidate in ten races. The average increase for a PAC endorsed candidate was a modest 2.7 percent over the candidate's party showing in 1974. This difference did not necessarily result from PAC's support. The other factors named above (such as incumbency) may have accounted for it. Multiple regression is a statistical method that can be used to distinguish the effect of PAC from other influences on the results.

Multiple regression analysis identifies different factors that may affect a situation, assigns them particular values, and tests their effects singly and together on the outcome. Without going into all the calculations, the PAC endorsement seems to explain less than 1 percent of the variance in the 1976 election. Other factors such as the vote in the preceding election, party strength as measured by registration, incumbancy, and district location explain most of the result.

To illustrate the extent to which the 1976 results reflect past election and party strength as opposed to PAC influence, Table 7-4 presents the percentage of the vote predicted through multiple regression analysis for Democratic candidates. Only four variables—the 1974 Democratic vote, 1976 Democratic registration, incumbency, and district location—explain over 80 percent of the variation in the 1976 vote. The predictions vary from the actual results by over 5 percent in only seven of the twenty contested races. Two of these seven races did not even involve PAC endorsements, so the four non-PAC variables are relatively good predictors in the three-quarters of the races that involved PAC.

Table 7-3
Democratic Candidate Percentage of the Major Party Vote,
Delaware House, 1974 and 1976

District	1974	1976	Increase for PAC Candidate (1974–1976)
1	59.4%	60.0%	No PAC endorsement
2	100.0%	100.0%	No PAC endorsement
3	71.3%	72.0%	No PAC endorsement
4	67.4%	58.7%	No PAC endorsement
5	66.8%	74.5%	No PAC endorsement
6	48.4%	42.8%	No PAC endorsement
7	0%	0%	0%
8	45.2%	58.1%	No PAC endorsement
9	38.2%	32.8%	+5%
10	32.5%	0%	No contest (+33%)
11	0%	31.0%	No contest (−31%)
12	0%	35.0%	No contest (−35%)
13	30.8%	23.1%	+8%
14	53.7%	66.0%	+12%
15	71.3%	69.1%	+2%
16	64.1%	65.5%	−2%
17	100.0%	64.0%	No contest (+36%)
18	100.0%	72.0%	No contest (−28%)
19	32.4%	0%	No contest (+32%)
20	65.2%	58.7%	−6%
21	87.0%	100.0%	No contest (+13%)
22	42.5%	35.9%	+7%
23	43.4%	40.4%	+3%
24	52.1%	49.8%	+2%
25	49.7%	45.4%	+5%
26	49.0%	51.9%	No PAC endorsement
27	67.5%	59.9%	+8%
28	52.0%	61.9%	+10%
29	49.8%	66.4%	−16%
			2.7% average

The PAC-endorsed candidates fared an average of only 1.6 percent better than predicted. Eight fared better than the prediction; five fared worse. Only one candidate, William Oberle, running against incumbent Dick Le Gates in the Twenty-fourth District, went from a projected loss (42.4 percent) to an actual victory (50.2 percent). In all other races the candidate projected to win indeed won. This table

Table 7-4
Predicted versus Actual Vote, Contested Delaware
House Races (1976 Democratic Vote)

District	Candidate	Actual	Predicted	Democrats, Actual less Predicted	Predicted vs. Actual Increase for PAC Candidate
1	George	60.0%	58.7%	+ 1.3%	No PAC endorsement
3	Johnson	72.0%	69.5%	+ 2.5%	No PAC endorsement
4	Rispoli	58.7%	67.6%	− 8.9%	No PAC endorsement
5	Jonkiert	74.5%	71.4%	+ 3.1%	No PAC endorsement
6	Thomas	42.8%	40.7%	+ 2.1%	No PAC endorsement
8	Loughney	58.1%	48.2%	+ 9.9%	No PAC endorsement
9	Burke*	32.8%	37.1%	− 4.3%	+ 4.3%
13	Reed*	23.1%	27.1%	− 4.0%	+ 4.0%
14	Maxwell†	66.0%	55.4%	10.6%	+10.6%
15	Byrd*	69.1%	73.1%	− 4.0%	+ 4.0%
16	Kelley†	65.5%	64.2%	+ 1.3%	− 1.3%
20	Ferguson†	58.7%	66.9%	− 8.2%	− 8.2%
22	Jahren*	35.9%	46.5%	−10.6%	+10.6%
23	Williams*	40.4%	41.6%	− 1.2%	+ 1.2%
24	Le Gates*	49.8%	57.7%	− 7.9%	+ 7.9%
25	Brown*	45.4%	43.3%	+ 2.1%	− 2.1%
26	Anderson	51.9%	51.0%	+ .9%	No PAC endorsement
27	Worthen*	59.9%	57.3%	+ 2.6%	− 2.6%
28	Cain†	61.9%	59.5%	+ 2.4%	+ 2.4%
29	Brady*	66.4%	56.0%	+10.4%	−10.4%
					+ 1.6% average

*Opponents endorsed by PAC.
†Endorsed by PAC.

makes evident that the PAC endorsement may have helped some candidates and hurt others, that overall the effect was less than 2 percentage points, and that PAC made the difference between victory and defeat in one race. Table 7-4 when compared to Table 7-3, suggests that PAC endorsements increased the average endorsee's vote by less than the apparent increase in the vote from 1974-1976.

The variables mentioned so far are not the only ones that may explain the slightly better showing of the PAC endorsees. What of the quality of the candidates themselves? Were they more active, more attractive, or more widely supported by other interest groups than were their opponents? If so, was their better showing a result of such factors rather than the PAC endorsement? Several measures of the quality of the candidates and their campaign were entered into the regression equation. Although none were ideal, each measured an aspect of candidate quality.

Campaign expenditures are one measure of how active a candidate is. Endorsements show something of the extent of support and what part of the electorate is appealed to; candidates endorsed by the *News Journal* received some added publicity and may be considered "better" candidates on at least a middle-class reform scale. Finally, age differences between candidates may be a measure of their attractiveness to the voters.

Allowing for these factors in the 1976 campaign, the most striking finding is that the difference in campaign expenditures between the Democratic and Republican candidates explains none of the vote. As for the ages of the candidates, older ones seemed less able to garner votes, but this explains little of the variance. For Democratic candidates, age explains about one additional percent of the vote.

When we look at the effect of endorsements, those of the *News Journal* explain more of the variance than those of PAC. The PAC variable continues to explain about 1 percent of the variance, the *News Journal* about 2 percent. Neither variable is statistically significant.

Thus, allowing for candidate quality fails to explain away the slight advantage conferred by PAC endorsement and also fails to explain more than a very small added percentage of the variance.

In brief, PAC endorsements had little impact on the 1976 Delaware House elections. Candidates endorsed by PAC tended to win, but primarily because PAC tended to endorse incumbents and candidates in noncompetitive races. Party rather than PAC accounts for the vast majority of the 1976 votes cast.

This conclusion is consistent with the finding the candidate expenditures were not related to the vote. Neither PAC nor publicity in the 1976 campaign changed voters' long-standing political allegiances or loyalty to incumbents.

PAC endorsed candidates in all six of New Castle County's Senate races in 1976. Two of the four Republicans endorsed by PAC won; one of the two Democrats endorsed by PAC won. PAC endorsed just one of five incumbents; he was victorious. There was only one victor among the four nonincumbents running against an incumbent endorsed by PAC. Thus, on the face of it, PAC endorsements were not related to victory (unlike in the lower house races) and this may be explained by PAC's failure to endorse incumbents.

Did PAC-endorsed candidates perhaps fare better than their counterparts in 1972? That is, did the PAC endorsements increase the votes, but not enough for victory? Table 7-5 indicates that this is

Table 7-5
Candidate Percentage by Major Party Vote,
Delaware Senate, 1972 and 1976

	1972		1976	
District	Democratic	Republican	Democratic	Republican
8	42.5%	57.5%	42.5%	57.5%*
10	35.5%	64.5%	35.5%*	64.5%
11	40.2%	59.8%	65.3%*	34.7%
12	62.0%	38.0%	54.9%	45.1%*
13	100.0%	No candidate	58.1%	41.9%*
15	41.6%	58.4%	48.8%	51.2%*

1976 average PAC percentage of vote	49.4%
1976 average PAC percentage of vote (without District 13)	50.9%
1972 average of 1976 PAC party candidate (without District 13)	45.9%

*Endorsed by PAC.

improbable. In two of the five Senate races contested in 1972 (Districts 8 and 10), the PAC endorsee received exactly the same percentage of the vote as their party's candidate in 1972. In two districts the PAC endorsees fared better (Districts 11 and 12) and in one the PAC endorsee did worse (District 15). The PAC endorsees did an average of 5.0 percentage points better than their 1972 counterparts—all because one candidate increased his party's vote by 25.1 percent. However, this candidate (Senator Cicione) had switched parties between 1972 and 1976. A PAC nonendorsee also switched parties (former Senator Isaacs) and lost 7.2 percent. These party switchers confuse our analysis (as well as political observers and participants), but it seems probable that the effect of a PAC endorsement is probably no greater in the Delaware Senate than in the Delaware House.

PAC also endorsed candidates for the U.S. Senate (Roth, Rep., over Maloney, Dem.) and county executive (McGinnes, over Jornlin, Rep.). To influence the outcome of these elections, PAC endorsements would have had to encourage voters to cross over traditional party lines. The 1976 Republican Party registration was almost perfectly related to the Roth and Jornlin vote. Furthermore, since PAC supported Roth and endorsed Jornlin's opponent, a PAC endorsement effect should have resulted in a lower party vote relation for Jornlin than Roth. The opposite was true. Finally, Ford, du Pont, and Evans received almost the same percentage of the vote as was registered to their parties.

Analyzing this another way, 98 percent of the variance in Roth's vote across New Castle County is explained by 1976 registration percentages, the 1972 Nixon percentage, 1972 and 1974 legislative vote percentages, and the location of the district in the city or suburbs. At most, PAC could explain only a trivial amount of the vote.

In brief, there is no evidence that PAC endorsements affected any of the key statewide and county races.

There are a number of likely explanations for the failure of a PAC endorsement to have a major effect. First, party identification traditionally plays a major role in state legislative races. Voters who deviate from their political loyalties are the exception. Among those who saw busing as beyond the control of state legislators, this would be even more true. It would mean that the burden of proof is on who believes that one *should* expect a change in voter loyalty.

Second, organizations most affect elections by mobilizing voters, not by changing their views. In a partisan, presidential-year election, interest is so high that even political party organizations cannot greatly increase turnout. And PAC was in no way as organized or active as a political party or union. PAC endorsed candidates but did not actively work for them. To my knowledge, the most PAC did was to hand out fliers. Political organizations keep lists of sympathetic voters and try to be sure that all of them go to the polls. PAC did not undertake such a campaign. Perhaps its leaders believed that endorsements would be enough.

Third, the candidates did not differ very much in their views toward busing. PAC-endorsed candidates may have stressed the issue more or have been less inclined to consider busing inevitable, but their opponents also opposed busing strongly. In the Twenty-seventh District, for example, Sandra Worthen, one of the most liberal candidates, a good-government type, made strong antibusing claims.[23] After the election, PAC endorsements were criticized on just these grounds. It was charged that the PAC rankings of legislators were based on insignificant differences in voting records. Indeed, PAC's main area of success may have been its great effect on the legislature where it pushed every candidate to take a strong antibusing position. Its subsequent endorsements could point only to minute differences among legislators, which voters, assured of the antibusing positions of all candidates, could ignore.

Fourth, PAC seems in retrospect somewhat of a newspaper tiger: its ability to get press coverage caused the public to exaggerate its ability to mobilize its members or friends. All interest groups try to exaggerate the support behind them; by election time, one legislator told me, PAC's ability to draw a thousand people to a meeting had long since passed. A few can look like many to a sensitive group like the state legislators, but the ability of a few to mobilize others across a diverse county over a long time may be quite limited.

In the months after the 1976 election a letters-to-the-editor battle raged in the Wilmington *News Journal*. Critics chided the Positive Action Committee for making inappropriate endorsements in the 1976 elections and PAC officials defended their choices. My analysis suggests that the conflict of letter writers was much ado about nothing, for PAC had at most a minor impact on the 1976 elections.[24]

PAC and the 1978 Elections

While driving my car to a school desegregation meeting a few days before the start of busing, I heard a news reporter begin a sentence: "PAC announced today that four—" Immediately I imagined four mass demonstrations and my heart began double-pumping. The announcer went on however: "—four candidates running for State Legislature were being endorsed by PAC." I thought to myself that the battle for a peaceful transition was over, for not only was PAC still relying on conventional political action but also it was narrowing its electoral scope. Part of the reason for the low profile was Jim Venema's attempt to become a U.S. Senator.

In February 1978, Venema announced his candidacy for the U.S. Senate seat of Joseph Biden, Jr., a Democrat. Venema stated his intention to change his party registration from Independent to Republican. Republican Party leaders, dismayed by the entrance of this Johnny-Come-Lately to their party and perhaps disturbed at Venema's possibly racist support, decided to enlist a tried and true vote getter to oppose Venema in the primary. When County Executive Mary Jornlin refused to run, James Baxter, a successful chicken farmer and businessman long active in Sussex County GOP activities, announced his candidacy.

The Venema-Baxter primary campaign was notable for its civility and lack of ideological conflict. Both candidates took conservative stances and strongly opposed busing. Both tried to reach out to new voters. Venema began by ignoring the busing issue, since people knew his position on that, and showing his conservatism and expertise on other issues. Baxter focused on cutting into Venema's antibusing constituency in New Castle County. Both candidates were criticized for having limited viewpoints. Baxter was accused of running for the U.S. Senate without rising above his small-town background; he could not shed the image of chicken farmer. Venema was chided for being a one-issue candidate, exploiting the busing issue for personal and political gain.

Table 7-6
Pac Endorsements and the 1978 State Legislative Elections, Percentage of Vote

| District | 1978 | | 1976 | Difference |
	PAC Candidate	% of Vote	% of Vote	
House				
8	Loughney (D)	53%	58%	− 5%
15	McBride (D)	80%	69%	+11%
20	Ferguson (D)	100%	59%	
24	Oberle (R)	79%	50.2%	+29%
Senate				
9	Sharp (D)	58%	60%*	− 2%

*The last race in this senatorial district was in 1972.

Despite Venema's relatively well-known name, strong antibusing credentials, ties to populous New Castle County, and more cosmopolitan style, Baxter won. Venema received 61.8 percent of the 15,466 votes cast in New Castle County, but Baxter won 87.7 percent of the 7,063 downstate votes. Venema had not been able to broaden his electoral base. Baxter's upstate votes gave him 53.7 percent of the total primary vote (22,529).

In the general election, Senator Biden crushed Jim Baxter. Biden received 58.5 percent of the 160,409 votes cast, Baxter 41.4 percent. In suburban New Castle County, Baxter tried to paint Joe Biden as a chameleon on busing but did not succeed. Biden received 57 percent of the vote in the Wilmington suburbs, just a bit under his statewide percentage.

Although Venema's loyalty to the Republican Party was still being questioned after the general election, Venema won a regional GOP post in December 1978. In winning the party leadership position, Venema said, "I put the cart before the horse in running for the Senate."[25] Presumably, Venema will make another political horse race in the future.

PAC endorsed four candidates for state representative and one for state senator in 1978. One of the five candidates ran unopposed. Two of the four remaining candidates improved their party's vote from the last race, two fared worse. Bill Oberle, running as an incumbent, received 79 percent of the vote, a vast improvement over his 1976 showing. The remaining three candidates averaged 1.3 percent more of the vote than in the previous race. Oberle was the one example of PAC's electoral influence. There was also a possibility that PAC had had a small effect on the votes for the General Assembly.

SUMMARY

PAC succeeded in putting the antibusing issue high on the legislature's agenda and in the public's consciousness. PAC determined the policies and influenced the statements of the State Legislature. It may well have colored Senator Biden's action and words on busing. It established a climate in which it was difficult for officials to work for peaceful implementation of the court orders.

PAC failed, however, to force a confrontation with the courts, to recruit fifty thousand members, to stop the political executives and school officials from working for effective implementation, or to defeat politicians it rated unfavorably. Most importantly, it failed to stop busing. Of course, its failures are explained in part by the magnitude of the goals. PAC leaders thought big throughout the desegregation conflict. But they made several miscalculations.

PAC's strident and ideological tone narrowed its constituency. The New Castle County public was neither so conservative nor so receptive to rhetorical overkill as PAC's leaders suffered from an image of extremism.

Like other community groups, PAC ran into the power of long-standing political forces like political parties and the local school establishment. An attack on the public school system was an attack on the livelihood of school officials and they were not likely to yield to it. PAC's abrasiveness also turned off political figures like Governor Tribbitt who were used to receiving respect rather than threats.

Finally, as the desegregation process dragged on and PAC failed to stop busing, its support lessened. By 1978 it could claim only seven thousand members, about half of its 1976 estimate. In essence, the major limitation on PAC was that the public, the school officials, and the governmental executives did not share its conservative philosophy. There was no mass market for its policy of ideological confrontation.

In the end, there was a great irony in the work of PAC. Its methods had helped to guarantee a smooth desegregation process. It had adopted conventional political means to further conventional political objectives. It tried to affect elections, the legislature, the U.S. Senate, and the voting public.

PAC did not turn to protest, disruption, overt racism, and other more inflammatory tactics. By channeling the tremendous feelings of public frustration into relatively conventional political activity, it effectively preempted the ground from more extreme individuals and groups and thus contributed to a relatively tranquil desegregation process.[26]

8 / Early Consequences of Desegregation

Desegregation Begins Quietly, Peacefully

School Opening Draws High Marks

Police 'Happily Bored' With Deseg Implementation

Teachers, Students Delighted

First Day is Breeze; 4th R is for Routine

Busing: 3 Days' Practice Makes (Almost) Perfect[1]

New Castle County was under the microscope of national and local media attention, and happily no educational illness could be found. In September 1978 the New Castle County schools opened peacefully, and New Castle County received praise from Philadelphia to Los Angeles.[2]

Peaceful implementation of court-ordered desegregation was no mean feat. In Louisville-Jefferson County a few months before, the National Guard had had to accompany school children to school. The conflict in Boston had raged for years. Although 90 percent of suburban parents were reported as opposing busing, New Castle County was not the scene of disorder, protests, or violence as busing began in September 1978.

Not everything went perfectly the first week of school. There were minor snags ranging from the pathetic to the funny. One second-grade boy from Wilmington got on his bus too early; he had a ninety-minute ride to Newark and back before the bus's second run took him to his assigned school.[3] A Newark father, anxious about the long bus ride for his fourth-grade daughter, personally put her on the bus. He was not reassured when the bus driver asked for directions to Wilmington. There were not enough buses for special education students.[4] On Thursday a fight in the old Conrad High School, converted to a middle school by the desegregation plan, led to a boycott of classes.[5] But by the second week most of the snafus were either corrected or being addressed. Over 60,000 school children, 20,500 now bused for desegregation, were being educated in 99 schools in a new county school district.

The goal of the court order was, of course, more than just peace or tranquility. The court had ordered local and state officials to desegregate the schools, but the results were far from predetermined. Orfield has noted that "even where desegregation is feasible, implementation may be impossible," for it is not clear that "a judiciary with limited administrative capacity and power [can] transform urban public schools."[6] Simply put, school desegregation may lead to a rapid loss of white students, resulting in a Pyrrhic victory for desegregation. As James S. Coleman put it, collective action may be thwarted by individual noncompliance.[7]

We must also consider whether the other effects of desegregation were equitable for the previous victims of segregation. The complex interaction between the court and state and local leaders resulted in a plan with economic, educational, sociological, and political impact. Without drawing premature conclusions, we can begin to analyze some of the implications of the metropolitan desegregation plan.

In sum, this chapter looks at Delaware's early response to the court's challenge by addressing two questions: Were the schools desegregated? To what degree did the plan treat blacks equitably?

WHITE FLIGHT

The spectre of white flight haunted New Castle County for half a decade. As the federal court was making its decisions on *Evans v. Buchanan* and the future of the schools in New Castle County, the decline in white enrollments after desegregation was grabbing headlines in the national media.

James S. Coleman gave currency to the concept of "white flight" from desegregated schools. I have just quoted Coleman's dictum that individual decisions have offset collective decisions; that is, busing orders have led to a rapid exodus of whites from the affected public schools. But after the initial publicity given Colemen's arguments, other researchers offered more limited conclusions about white flight.

Coleman and Pettigrew and Green disagree on the merits of busing but agree on the relative lack of white flight in metropolitan areas.[8] In a metropolitan plan, there are a limited number of places to which people can flee to escape desegregation; the cost of leaving the affected public school system is likely to be high. The financial (and psychological and social) costs of moving from a central city like Boston or Detroit is far less than the cost of such a move outside the metropolitan area. In Florida, where school districts encompassed entire counties and all districts were desegregated, white flight was minimal, for moving outside of the desegregation area meant moving outside of the state.[9] However, there is one possible escape from metropolitan desegregation. In the Nashville–Davidson County Schools, almost 10,000 students left the public schools to attend private and parochial schools.[10] Such options available to those considering leaving the public schools within a metropolitan area must also be considered.

The situation in the Wilmington metropolitan area presented a mixed picture for white flight. The desegregation area defined by the court encompassed all parts of the state not previously desegregated; thus parents could not move within the state to avoid desegregation. However, New Castle County was close to Pennsylvania, Maryland, and New Jersey: in fact, the official SMSA metropolitan area included a Maryland and a New Jersey county. On the positive side, the percentage of black students in the desegregation area was only about 20 percent, less than what many have considered a racial tipping point. However, some plans offered by the Wilmington Board would make some schools close to majority black.

While some communities had a short time to react to a federal school desegregation order, New Castle County residents had years to consider the implications of busing. In July 1974, the court declared that the Wilmington schools were segregated and ordered the secondary schools to be desegregated in September 1976. Stays were granted so that September 1977 and September 1978 also figured as implementation deadlines. Thus there was time for parents to begin new private or parochial schools, to move to an unaffected area, or to place their children in established private or parochial schools. If there was time for anticipatory white flight, there was also time for parents to accept the court order. Thus in the Wilmington metropolitan situation, the existence and magnitude of white flight can be studied over a period of time.

The analysis of enrollments below is divided into two parts. First, a methodology for analyzing enrollment declines is established by examining enrollment changes from 1971 to 1977, the years before busing began. The enrollment decline from September 1977 to 1978 is then analyzed. The analyses suggests that, while enrollment declines are easy to measure, explanations for the declines are problematic. The analysis does indicate that white flight has occurred in New Castle County but, compared with other communities, on a limited scale.

Decline in Enrollment before September 1978

In the 1970s enrollments have declined in the public schools in New Castle County (see Table 8-1). White enrollment has declined while black enrollment has held steady. Over 73,000 white students were enrolled in New Castle County public schools in September 1971. In September 1977, white enrollment had declined to 58,200, a decrease of 20 percent. During this time, black enrollment rose slightly (about 2 percent) from 16,376 to 16,716, and other racial groups (Spanish-speaking and Orientals) increased from 0.6 to 2.3 percent of the total enrollment. As a result of these changes, white presence in the public schools of the county declined from 81.2 to 75.4 percent; black presence rose from 18.2 to 22.3 percent.

Table 8-1
New Castle County Public School Enrollments, 1971–1977*

Year	White		Black		Other		Total
	No.	%	No.	%	No.	%	
1971	73,011	81.2	16,376	18.2	569	.6	89,956
1972	71,811	80.5	16,539	18.5	896	1.0	89,246
1973	69,989	79.8	16,500	18.8	1,207	1.4	87,696
1974	67,961	79.1	16,557	19.3	1,383	1.6	85,901
1975	65,104	78.4	16,373	19.7	1,602	1.9	83,079
1976	60,335	76.8	16,608	21.4	1,627	2.0	78,570
1977	56,480	75.4	16,716	22.3	1,720	2.3	74,916

*Enrollment figures include vocational schools, the Appoquinimink School District, special schools, and special classes. The DPI reports enrollments based on September 30 counts each year.

Clearly the decline in white enrollments predated the first of the desegregation decisions. It was July 1974 that the three-judge panel ruled that the Wilmington schools segregated and one judge called for a metropolitan plan. But a few weeks later the Detroit or Milliken decision apparently limited the federal courts' discretion in imposing metropolitan desegregation plans. It is therefore unlikely that the September 1974 white enrollment loss is due to the threat of desegregation.

From September 1974 to September 1977, white enrollments declined by 11,481 or 16.9 percent. The reasons for this decline are not self-evident. To understand it, we begin by examining where the students went.

Declining Birthrates New Castle County families had slowed their rate of baby production by the early 1960s. That, and a sharp drop in county births beginning in 1972, would have led to some decline in public school enrollments independent of desegregation. Births in the county decreased from 7,313 in 1960 to 6,567 in 1966, a drop of 10 percent.

The 1974 New Castle County public school enrollment figures partially reflect the number of children born to residents of New Castle County from 1957 to 1969. For example, most children born in 1969 would be in kindergarten in 1974. Obviously the relation between births and public school enrollments is not perfect, for deaths, migration, attendance at nonpublic schools, and dropouts normally affect actual public school enrollments. However, the number of births in the county during the corresponding years does give us some indication of the pool of possible future public school enrollees.

In New Castle County, 75,966 children were born to white New Castle County residents between 1957 and 1969. This was the pool of children on which the 1974 enrollments partially drew. The 1977 pool—the total of white births in the county from 1960 to 1975—was 71,658 or 4,308 less. This represents 4,179 children surviving to school age using the 0.97 survival rate. However, in 1974 only 85.4 percent of the county's pupils were in public schools, so the pool difference should be reduced to 3,569. Thus, 31.1 percent of the 1974–1977 white student decline of 11,481 could be attributed to the birthrate decline in the county. Since parents could not avoid having children because of a court decision that would come later, this part of the loss cannot be attributed to white flight.

Movement to Nonpublic Schools While public school enrollments have declined in the 1970s in Delaware, private and parochial school enrollments have increased. Table 8-2 indicates that, in September 1971, slightly over 16,000 Delaware resident students were in Delaware's nonpublic schools but by 1977 about 19,000 of Delaware's students were in parochial or private schools in the state—an increase of almost 20 percent. In New Castle County the nonpublic school enrollment was 16,731 in 1977, up 2,035 or 13.8 percent from 1974.

This increase is less than the actual loss of public school pupils to nonpublic schools. The nonpublic school increase occurred while the total school-aged population was declining, and thus the nonpublic schools also should have had an enrollment decline. To determine the loss of public school students to the nonpublic schools attributable to events unique to the period of 1974 to 1977, it is necessary to determine how many students would have shifted independently of these events.

Table 8-2
Nonpublic School Enrollments of Delaware Residents,
1971–1977

Year	New Castle County	Kent County	Sussex County
1971	15,067	1,008	147
1972	14,944	1,077	156
1973	15,020	1,171	187
1974	14,696	1,268	242
1975	15,070	1,500	343
1976	16,427	1,672	475
1977	16,731	1,756	477
Increase (1971–1977)	11.0%	74.2%	224.5%

There are several ways to project the historical pattern of nonpublic enrollments to 1977. The most obvious method is to project the ratio of nonpublic to the total nonpublic and public enrollments of New Castle County residents from 1971 to 1974, to 1977 (Table 8-3). When this is done, the projected number of nonpublic school students is 13,930 students. (This is simply the projected ratio of 0.152 times the total 1977 school enrollment of 91,647.) The actual nonpublic school enrollment in 1977 was 16,731, or 2,801 more students than the projected number. Thus, it is reasonable to see the 1974—1977 movement to nonpublic schools in New Castle County as 2,801 or 766 more than the absolute increase of 2,035 from 1974 to 1977.

This loss to the public schools of 2,801 students is not necessarily due to white flight. National estimates of nonpublic school enrollments show a stabilization in the absolute number of nonpublic enrollments and an increase in the percentage of elementary and secondary students in nonpublic schools.[11] Widespread dissatisfaction with the public schools, the back to basics and fundamentalist school movements, and the options available to increasing numbers of two-wage families may explain the reversal of previous declines in nonpublic school enrollments.

One way to separate white flight from these national trends is to assume that these national trends operated in both northern and southern Delaware from 1974 to 1977. In Delaware's southern counties, the increase in the nonpublic to total enrollment ratio doubled

Table 8-3
Ratio of Nonpublic to Nonpublic and Public Enrollment,
1971–1977

Year	New Castle County	Kent and Sussex Counties
1971	.143	.025
1972	.143	.027
1973	.146	.029
1974	.146	.033
1975	.154 (projected = .149)	.040
1976	.173 (projected = .149)	.047
1977	.183 (projected = .152)	.049

from 1974 to 1977 compared with 1971 to 1974 (from 0.025 to 0.033 against 0.033 to 0.049). If this increase in the ratio occurred in New Castle County, then 14,480 New Castle County residents would have been in nonpublic schools in 1977. This suggests that 2,251 students (16,471–14,480) in New Castle County would have left the public schools for the same reasons as in southern Delaware. If this assumption were valid, then only 550 (2,801–2,251) students would have been lost for reasons peculiar to New Castle County, presumably the threat of busing.

The difficulty with this estimation is that the assumption is questionable. For example, southern Delaware had few nonpublic students in the early 1970s and it could be argued that these counties were catching up in nonpublic enrollments. Since the southern schools were desegregated in the late 1960s, it could be argued that the movement there was not independent of the white flight phenomena. It could also be argued that it is invalid to compare southern and rural Delaware to urban New Castle County. With this reasoning, all the movement to nonpublic schools could be considered the result of busing.

Thus, it appears that 2,801 students, 24.4 percent of the whole loss, shifted to nonpublic schools from 1974 to 1977. The extent to which this shift was due to the threat of busing is not clear.

Dropouts In recent years the Delaware Department of Public Instruction has collected statistics on dropouts, those students "who leave school or discontinue . . . schooling for any reason, except death, before graduation or completion of a program of studies and without transferring to another school." In the suburban districts of New

Castle County, 926 dropouts were identified in 1974–1975 and 1,096 in 1976–1977. If this increase of 170 dropouts is extrapolated for one more year, an estimated 255 or 2.2 percent of the white loss can be attributed to an increased dropout rate. Desegregation may have been a reason for some students to dropout, but a 1978 analysis of reasons for dropping out in Delaware ranked it near the bottom of a list of reasons.[12]

Migration   In every community in a given year some residents migrate elsewhere and others replace them. But desegregation may bring a change in the net flow of families or the number of families with school-age children who replace those who departed. Migration, of course, occurs for many reasons besides desegregation. Economic conditions, tax rates, and personal goals may change over time and affect an area's relative attractiveness.

One way to determine the impact of migration on pupil loss from 1974 to 1977 is to examine cohort losses during this period.[13] That is, the total number of resident students in grade one in the public and nonpublic schools of the county can be compared with the number in the schools in grade four, three years later.

Table 8-4 presents the relevant cohort data. In 1974, 35,445 students were in the county's public elementary schools. In 1977, this cohort was in fourth through ninth grades. It is estimated that an additional 1,550 county white students were in the nonpublic schools of the county in 1977 across these grades. The total cohort lost 1,880 more students than it gained from migration. If the same percentages held across all thirteen years of school, then a net of 4,073 students would have left the county for other pastures. This number is 35.5 percent of the white loss from 1974 to 1977.

A second way to determine the number of pupils lost to migration is to assume that this factor accounted for the loss of white pupils not accounted for by birthrate declines (3,569), movement to nonpublic schools (2,801), or dropouts (225). This suggests that 4,856 students would have been lost from 1974 to 1977 because of migration.

The two approaches suggest that between 4,073 and 4,856 students were lost to migration from New Castle County. But how many were lost because of desegregation? That is, to what extent would people have moved away independently of busing.

David Armor has used census statistics from 1950, 1960, and 1970 by age cohort to project later enrollments.[14] He then has compared these census-based projected enrollments with actual enrollments just before and after the carrying out of busing plans in communities

Table 8-4
1974 New Castle County Grades 1–6 Cohort Enrollments,
1974 and 1977

1974 Grade	Public	Nonpublic*	1977 Grade	Public	Nonpublic*
1	5,683	839	4	4,516	1,118
2	5,406	832	5	4,627	1,064
3	5,543	847	6	5,062	1,126
4	6,073	878	7	5,599	1,136
5	6,260	907	8	5,841	1,129
6	6,480	944	9	6,370	1,124
Subtotal	35,445	5,247		32,015	6,797
Total	40,692			38,812	

Loss: 1,880 students

*Estimated from suburban New Castle County residents in nonpublic schools.

throughout the nation. Although his method would be valid in communities where migration patterns after the 1970 census would have or did remain constant, his estimating procedure cannot be used in Delaware. The 1950 and 1960 censuses indicate a net inmigration of whites into the county which then continues, but at a slower pace, from 1960 to 1970.[15] If we had no post-1970 figures and therefore were to assume that inmigration would have continued after 1970, we would view the subsequent outmigration as white flight. This would probably greatly overestimate this phenomenon. Fortunately, Census Bureau population estimates are available for the years 1971 through 1975.[16]

Table 8-5 reports the ratio of the estimated number of children in the school-age pool to the pool of the number of births to New Castle County mothers in the corresponding years. This ratio is a measure of the degree of net inmigration over time affecting the school-age pool in any year. The ratio has declined at a startlingly steady pace from 1970 to 1974. This suggests that net outmigration was a characteristic of New Castle County's school-age population before busing became an issue.

We can use these statistics to estimate the net outmigration of students that would have occurred if the 1971 to 1974 trend had continued for three more years. Table 8-6 reports the school-age population change after correcting for New Castle County birthrate changes. From 1971 to 1972 the net inmigration partially offset the

Table 8-5
Relationship of School-Age Population to Birth Pool
for New Castle County Whites, 1970–1977

Pool Year	School-Age Population (Census)	Projected Birth Pool	Census Population to Birth Pool Ratio
1970	88,745	77,649	1.14
1971	88,208	78,343	1.13
1972	86,571	77,568	1.12
1973	85,509	76,755	1.11
1974	83,690	75,966	1.10
1975	81,862	74,906	1.09
1976		73,597	
1977		71,658	

Table 8-6
School-Age Census Bureau and Birth Pool Estimates
for New Castle County, 1971–1977

Years	Actual Loss			Projected Net Loss		
	Census Loss	Birth Pool Loss	Net	Continuation of 1971– 1974 Trend	Continuation of 1972– 1975 Trend	Continuation of 1973– 1975 Trend
1971–1972	537	775	− 238			
1972–1973	1,062	813	+ 249			
1973–1974	1,819	789	+ 1,030			
1974–1975	1,828	1,060	+ 768	1,600	768	925
1975–1976				2,250	682	925
1976–1977				2,900	682	925
1974–1977				6,750	2,132	2,774

decline in earlier births. From 1972 to 1973 net outmigration was greater than the birth pool loss, and by 1973 to 1974 net outmigration was accounting for more school-age population loss than birth declines.

These figures suggest an increasing loss of school-age population that predated the busing controversy. If the trend had continued, the 1976 to 1977 loss would have been almost 3,000 children. The total

1974–1977 loss would have been 6,750 children. Thus, *all* the net outmigration could be considered to result from factors predating the busing controversy.

If we assume that the actual 1972–1975 outmigration average would continue through 1977, a school-age population loss of 2,132 children would have occurred from 1974 to 1977. Similarly, assuming the 1973–1975 trend, 2,774 children would have been projected to outmigrate from 1974 to 1977.

Thus, the most obvious projection method suggests that no net outmigration during 1974–1977 resulted from busing. Less reasonable assumptions suggest that about half of the outmigration could have been due to busing, but this seems quite unlikely. (For example, the neighboring states of Pennsylvania and New Jersey experienced net outmigration during the 1970–1977 period. Pennsylvania's rate was even higher than New Castle County's. This reinforces the conclusion that a substantial portion of the outmigration in Delaware from 1974 to 1978 was caused not by busing but by factors affecting the entire region.)[17]

White flight occurred in New Castle County from 1974 to 1977, but the amount is uncertain. The loss of 11,481 white pupils during this period is by no means all attributable to reactions to potential busing. Almost four thousand enrollees were lost because of the declining birthrate in New Castle County. How one describes the remaining decline of about 7,900 students depends on one's assumptions.

Those who remain steadfastly opposed to busing could make the following argument. The high net outmigration figure and nonpublic school shift could be attributed to white flight. Adding the increase in dropouts, this would account for 7,900 of the lost 11,481 white students or 68.9 percent of the white loss. Thus, over 7,800 white students fled the schools before busing began.

Proponents of metropolitan desegregation could dismiss each of the possible reasons for white flight. The increased net outmigration could be attributed to trends that predated desegregation. Nonpublic school increases could be attributed to a statewide and national trend toward private/parochial education. The increasing dropout rate could be attributed to factors like increasing family problems.

In my opinion, it is most reasonable to attribute the nonpublic school enrollment increases to white flight, but I would not attribute much of the net outmigration loss to anticipation of desegregation. Anticipatory white flight probably accounted for a loss of at least 3,000 pupils, but it is unlikely to have led to more than a net loss of

5,000 students. However, anticipatory flight, occurring before the busing plan is specified and enacted, usually is less than later flight. A remaining question is: How much flight occured after busing began?

Decline in Enrollment in September 1978

In September 1978, New Castle County schools opened with over 6,000 fewer pupils than the 74,916 on the rolls in September 1977 (Table 8-7). The decline included 5,757 white students, a 10.2 percent loss. There was a slight decrease in black students; the increase in "other" students continued. (Note that these enrollments include the Appoquinimink and Vocational School Districts as well as the county district.)

White Decline The pool of white children born from 1961 to 1973 in New Castle County totaled 69,585 or 2,073 fewer than the previous pool. Correcting this figure for survival rates and for those students (estimated at 18.3 percent) who went to nonpublic schools, the decline in the pool of students from 1977 to 1978 was 1,643. That is, of the reduced number of white students in the public schools in the September 1977 school year, 1,643 could be attributed to the decrease in births in the county.

Table 8-7
New Castle County Public School Enrollments,
1977–1978

Year	White		Black		Other		Total
	No.	*%*	*No.*	*%*	*No.*	*%*	
1977	56,480	75.4	16,716	22.3	1,720	2.3	74,916
1978	50,723	73.9	16,290	23.7	1,666	2.4	68,679

In September 1978, 18,127 residents of New Castle County were registered in nonpublic schools in the state. This was an increase of 1,396 over the 1977 figures, although only four new schools with a total enrollment of 350 students were begun. If the 1971–1974 pattern had continued through 1978, the ratio of nonpublic to total enrollments would have been 0.152. Given the 1978 public and nonpublic enrollment of 86,806, an enrollment of 13,195 might have been expected in nonpublic schools in 1978. The actual enrollment was

18,127, or 4,932 above this projection. Subtracting the 1974–1977 enrollment loss of 2,801 attributable to a movement to nonpublic schools, the 1977–1978 switch would be 2,131. (Based on southern Delaware nonpublic enrollments, the loss would be 2,161.)

If we assume a dropout rate of an additional 100 students (actual statistics are not yet available), that, along with birthrate declines and nonpublic school movement, would account for 3,904 of the 5,757 fewer students in 1978 than in 1977. This would leave a 1,853-student decline attributable to outmigration. (See Table 8-8.)

There is no way to determine exactly what percentage of outmigration is really white flight. Given the considerations discussed above, I would estimate that the people in flight number closer to 2,000 than 4,000.

Table 8-8
Summary of White Enrollment Loss, 1974–1978*

Loss Category	1974–1977		1977–1978		Total	
	No.	%	No.	%	No.	%
Outmigration	4,856	42.3	1,853	32.2	6,709	38.9
Birthrate	3,569	31.1	1,643	28.5	5,212	30.2
Nonpublic Schools	2,801	24.4	2,161	37.5	4,962	28.8
Dropouts	255	2.2	100	1.7	355	2.1
Total	11,481	100.0	5,757	100.0	17,238	100.0

*White enrollment for the public schools in the county for 1974 was 67,961; for 1977, it was 56,480. The white enrollment for schools in the future county school district was 64,679 and 52,764 respectively.

The percentage loss of white students from the public schools of New Castle County was about 6 to 8 percent in the first year of desegregation. The 1977–1978 enrollment declines beyond that expected because of a smaller birthrate pool could be labeled white flight. This was a loss of 4,105 students, or 7.8 percent of the enrollment in the schools that were to make up the new district in 1978. If we assume that none of the 1977–1978 dropout increase and half of the outmigration resulted from longterm factors unrelated to busing then the percentage of flight would be 5.8 percent.

A decline of 6–8 percent is a relatively low rate of flight. David Armor's analysis of flight in communities across the nation suggests that New Castle County was more successful than most in limiting white flight in the first year. In northern school districts with court-ordered school desegregation, Armor found a first-year 13.1 percent loss, where the decline due to the usual causes had been projected at 3.6 percent. Thus, the net loss, presumably was due to busing, was 9.5 percent. In southern school districts, the net loss was slightly higher (15.0-3.0, or 12.0).[18] In New Castle County, however, the total loss was under 11 percent and the net loss was only 6–8 percent.[19]

While studies have found less flight in metropolitan areas, few cases of metropolitan desegregation exist. Armor focuses on Louis-ville–Jefferson County, for the other metropolitan cases involve cities either within a single, rural, county school district or in Florida, where all districts were desegregated about the same time. New Castle County compares favorably with Louisville–Jefferson County. There the first-year net loss was 8.3 percent, higher than even the largest estimate of first-year loss in New Castle County.[20]

Los Angeles provides another comparison. Like New Castle County, Los Angeles began its busing plan in September 1978. There the white enrollment declined 15 percent, although some of this decline merely continued the previous white decline.[21]

It might be suspected that little white flight took place in New Castle County in the first year of busing because so much anticipatory flight had occurred in the years before busing began. However, this does not appear to be the case. White enrollment in the schools that were included in the desegregation area decreased by 17.8 percent from 1974 to 1977. If we use the same procedure as before, the amount of anticipatory white flight would range from 4.3 to 8.5 percent. To the extent that comparisons are possible, this is approximately the same as in Louisville–Jefferson County and the northern school districts analyzed by Armor.

School Desegregation   In September 1978, by almost any measure, racial segregation had been eliminated in New Castle County schools. Eighty-five of the ninety-three nonspecial schools had within 10 percent of the average percentage (24) of white students enrolled in the desegregated grades (that is, excluding kindergarten). Only eight schools did not have between 15 and 35 percent black students (Table 8-9).

One problem was apparent, however. Of the three schools with more than 35 percent black students, two were in Wilmington. Of the twelve elementary schools with 30–34.9 percent black students, half were in Wilmington and linked with the old Newark District.[22] (The

Table 8-9
Racial Composition by School Type

Percentage of Black Students	Elementary Schools	Junior High Schools	High Schools
0– 4.9	0	0	0
5.0–9.9	1	0	0
10.0–14.9	2	1	1
15.0–19.9	5	1	3
20.0–24.9	16	10	7
25.0–29.9	23	6	1
30.0–34.9	12	1	0
35.0–39.9	3	0	0
Total	62	19	12

one almost totally white school was located on the outskirts of the county and had been excluded from the assignment plan.)

In short, the schools of New Castle County were desegregated without a concentrated loss of whites. Limited white flight did occur, however, although the plan was a metropolitan one.

There remains a further criterion to apply in assessing the success or failure of the implementation: How equitable was the plan's impact?

IMPACT: THE BURDEN OF BUSING

Under the desegregation plan, De La Warr and Wilmington students were assigned to suburban schools for nine years. Suburban students were assigned to Wilmington or De La Warr schools for three consecutive years. (Kindergarten students were not reassigned across the previous school district lines.) That is, some students would be bused into the suburbs from predominately black areas, and other students would take the reverse route.

As I said in Chapter 4, it is difficult to decide whether or not this plan is equitable. It could be argued that the plan is not equitable because, on the whole, blacks are bused for three times as many years as are whites. In fact, one of the original plaintiffs in the reopening of the *Evans* v. *Buchanan* suit, Lillian Richardson, exclaimed "They can't do that!" when she heard the details of the plan.[23] Further, the schools that were downgraded from secondary to elementary schools were black schools. The exceptions were Wilmington High School, which was maintained, and Conrad High School, which was converted to a junior high.

In other ways, the plan does appear to be fair. If it is desired that all schools reflect the racial composition of students in the county district, then the 9–3 plan accomplishes that. The percentage of black students in the desegregation area in September 1977 (21.7) multiplied by twelve years of school equals 2.6 years. Since three years is closest to this average and corresponds most closely to traditional educational grade groupings (6–8, 10–12), a 9–3 plan is reasonable. Further, while blacks are bused for more years than whites, more whites than blacks are bused. Finally, while more schools in Wilmington and De La Warr were downgraded, more suburban schools were closed.

In summary, a strong argument can be made that the busing plan was fair for both black and white students, although, achieving racial balance inevitably put a greater burden on the minority black students.

School Facilities

On December 12, 1977, the New Castle County Planning Board of Education received a report from their Committee on Excess School Capacity.[24] This report placed schools buildings in three categories: (1) old and needing upgrading; (2) over fifteen years old but in good condition; and (3) new or modernized and in excellent condition. As Table 8-10 shows, the suburban elementary and high schools were given superior ratings. The schools in Wilmington had a better averge at the middle-school level. The overall school facility average favored the suburbs. All the differences were quite small, however.

Table 8-10
Average School Facility Ratings

Area	Elementary	Middle/Junior High	High School	Average
Wilmington	1.92	2.75	2.50	2.17
Suburbs	2.23	2.48	2.86	2.39

Before desegregation, Wilmington schools were not much worse than suburban ones, but facility ratings nevertheless increased for city children as a result of desegregation. A suburban high school, Conrad, and a city high school, P. S. Du Pont, became junior high schools under the 9–3 plan. Both held middle ratings and their conversion raised the averge rating for the city and suburban high schools. Since virtually all the city's high school students were assigned to suburban high schools that were rated more highly than the city high schools, on the average they went to a better facility. Several older city junior high schools were converted to elementary school use. Busing city students into superior suburban facilities again improved the city students' environment. At the elementary level suburban schools with a 2 rating were closed while city schools with poorer ratings were kept open. The suburban elementary school rating was increased, and this favored the Wilmington students, most of whom were bused to the suburbs for grades 1-3.

Taxes

Relatively progressive changes in school taxes resulted from desegregation. Table 8-11 presents the mean assessed value of residential property in each of the old districts, the tax rates and mean taxes paid in each, and the tax increase based on these means. In De La Warr and Wilmington, the uniform tax rate of 1.875 dollars meant a school tax saving.[25] The average saving in De La Warr was only 2 dollars; the Wilmington decrease was 80 dollars. The white blue-collar districts had mean tax increases of 70 to 84 dollars. Two of the middle-class districts had a smaller increase. In the affluent districts, the tax increases ranged from 100 to 200 dollars.

The residents in the white blue-collar districts had a disproportionately high change in their tax rates. The percentage of increase was high in these districts, ranging from 45.8 to 80 percent. These discrepancies, however, did not amount to much in actual money. The mean annual tax increase in Conrad, the district where the percentage increase was highest, was only 84 dollars.

Thus, imposing the uniform tax rate had progressive effects in all but three blue-collar districts. It led to a tax decrease for those in the majority black districts and progressively high tax increases for those in districts with higher average assessments. The plan was relatively fair in that it was based on the ability of those taxed to pay. The new tax rate also moved in the right direction in compensating for the effects of past racial discrimination.

Teachers' Strike

The first major disruption caused by the implementation of desegregation was a bitter thirty-one day teachers' strike.[26] Although New Castle County teachers had participated in the in-service week and open house before the schools opened and had worked in the successful first week of desegregation, they did not have a contract.

The failure to reach a contract agreement before school opening had led the New Castle County Educational Association (NCCEA) to ask

Table 8-11
Changes in Taxes Resulting from Desegregation

School District	Mean Assessed Valuation of Residential Property	1977–1978 Tax Rate*	1977–1978 Taxes	1978–1979 Tax Rate*	1978–1979 Taxes	Tax Increase	Percent Increase
Alexis I. duPont	$31,416	$1.239	$389	$1.875	$589	$200	51.4%
Alfred I. duPont	$22,606	$1.337	$302	$1.875	$424	$122	40.4%
Mt. Pleasant	$16,798	$1.280	$215	$1.875	$315	$100	46.5%
Stanton	$14,402	$1.553	$224	$1.875	$270	$ 46	20.5%
Marshallton-McKean	$14,433	$1.380	$199	$1.875	$271	$ 72	36.1%
Newark	$12,390	$1.730	$214	$1.875	$232	$ 18	8.4%
Claymont	$11,895	$1.290	$153	$1.875	$223	$ 70	45.8%
New Castle–Gunning Bedford	$10,803	$1.210	$131	$1.875	$203	$ 72	55.0%
Conrad	$10,068	$1.040	$105	$1.875	$189	$ 84	80.0%
De La Warr	$ 6,970	$1.914	$133	$1.875	$131	$(2)	– 1.5%
Wilmington	$ 7,486	$2.940	$220	$1.875	$140	$(80)	–36.4%
Mean	$13,151				$247		

*Includes operating, debt service, tuition, and bond taxes.

the help of a federal mediator. Mike Epler, president of the NCCEA and a Breakfast Group regular for two years, also asked several community leaders to observe the negotiations. Ultimately Betty Lewis, Ruth Graham, Helen Foss, and I formed a majority of a six-person parent observer group. Neither our presence nor the mediator's efforts seemed to improve the negotiating atmosphere.

On Sunday evening, October 15, negotiations between the NCCEA and the School Board stalled on the issue of salary. Teachers were upset because former city teachers were earning several thousand dollars more than suburban ones for doing the same job. The NCCEA insisted that salaries be leveled up immediately to the Wilmington standard. The Board insisted that it did not have the 22 million dollars that leveling up would require annually. As the teachers withdrew to a converted discount store for a strike vote, the Board offered to equalize salaries at the end of a three-year contract. The NCCEA said it would accept a one-year delay. Neither side would budge further and the teachers voted to strike.

On the following day, almost 80 percent of the teachers were out, in defiance of the state law forbidding teachers' strikes. Almost all secondary schools were closed; only a few elementary schools were operating and those with skeleton staffs. Schools did not function normally again until after Thanksgiving.

While money was the major issue at the bargaining table, there were underlying problems exacerbating negotiations. Judge Schwartz had ordered the desegregation of teachers as well as students. The involuntary transfer of black teachers from the city and white teachers from the suburbs upset many. Some teachers felt burdened by having to deal with a new mixture of pupils in their classrooms. Some were simply opposed to busing. Some teachers also were chafing at past poor treatment by public officials.

Reorganization had created another set of problems. Eleven different sets of working conditions and management styles had been merged in one large system. Teachers sought a leveling-up of working conditions or, at least, equity of treatment across the schools. Administrators sought flexibility for the difficult period ahead. The general problem was manifested in conflicts over particular issues. For example, there was a major negotiating battle over the length of the working day.

The teachers themselves were not united. Most former Wilmington teachers, realizing they had little to gain from the strike, crossed the picket lines. The NCCEA also faced a future challenge from the American Federation of Teachers (AFT) affiliate it had defeated in the spring bargaining election. It was under pressure to obtain a good contract that would defuse the threat from the AFT.

During the October 21–22 weekend, the Board offered and the teachers rejected an offer to level up salaries after two and one-half years. At this point, public sympathy for the teachers shifted to a general desire to see the strike ended. Governor du Pont intervened.

The governor assigned his secretary of labor, Donald Whiteley, to represent him at the negotiations. He turned down a request from NCCEA President Mike Epler and Superintendent Biggs to call the State Legislature into session to provide funds for leveling-up. Rather, he ordered his top financial aids to examine the school district's books to determine if money for additional increases was available.

The School Board rejected suggestions that teachers' salaries be leveled down. This would have achieved salary equity by lowering the salaries of former Wilmington teachers, a majority of whom were black. The parent observers first called for an independent financial audit, and when the teachers rejected this, they then widely publicized their view that money was the issue and the Board (and the school children) could not afford the teachers' demands.

The pressures came to a head in November. The governor's financial aides announced that the School Board offer would entail almost a 20 million dollar deficit over three years. The governor sent a letter to all the teachers asking them to face the financial reality. He called a special meeting of over a hundred parent leaders on November 11 to repeat these arguments. I addressed the meeting as a representative of the parent observers. I urged parents to unite behind our "parents plan," which called, in part, for the teachers to accept the Board's latest financial offer. The plan also asked the governor to help recoup state funds saved by not paying striking teachers and to appoint a committee to examine the state's collective bargaining law for teachers. As a result of this meeting, within a week almost all parent groups in the county (including PAC and the Alliance) had come to a common position even more critical of the teachers' demands.

On Thursday, November 16, the governor gave the screw a final twist. He informed the NCCEA and Board that unless a settlement was reached by Monday, he would not support the use in the settlement of state monies saved during the strike. On Friday the Board offered a complex financial package that froze the highest salary step until all other comparable county teachers had caught up. This leveling would occur at one and one-half years, but leveling-up would occur as the

Board had offered almost a month before. By Sunday an agreement was reached, both sides agreeing to keep the schools closed for a cooling-off period until after the Thanksgiving holiday.

Almost certainly, reorganization, not desegregation, was the immediate cause of the strike. Attaining equitable treatment of teachers in the county was the issue throughout the desegregation process. The question was when equity would be achieved.

If more funds were to be made available for teacher salaries, either the governor and state legislature had to act through legislation or the public had to act through a referendum. If no more funds were to be made available, the same parties had to make this clear. The strike occurred because of the failure of all these actors to reach a political compromise that would resolve this most difficult aspect of the court order.

On the positive side, the strike also illustrated the forces working for the success of desegregation in New Castle County. The teachers opened school instead of striking. They did not want to be blamed for preventing a peaceful, effective transition. The teachers' association involved community leaders in its efforts to avoid a strike (and obtain a good contract). After some misgivings, the Board agreed to having observers. During the strike, both sides tried to minimize tension, especially racial conflict.

The strike was ended with the help of relationships developed during desegregation planning. As in the planning process, public officials did not quickly rise to the occasion. The State Legislature was no help; it failed publicly to either restrict the funds available for salaries or to increase them. Even the governor, who did play a significant role, entered the situation after community leaders. But community leaders, who had worked together for years, organized the parents into a coalition that ultimately served notice on the teachers that their interests were in conflict with parental interests.

In all, however, failure to resolve the problems of reorganization before the opening of school clearly led to a breakdown in the desegregation process.

Second-Generation Problems

By January 1979, the New Castle County School District faced a number of second-generation desegregation-related problems. White parents were charging that there was a double standard of discipline; they felt that black students were being allowed to violate the student conduct code without fear of punishment. Minority parents, on the other hand, claimed that minority students were being suspended in disproportionate numbers. The superintendent admitted that many schools were tense because of racial conflict. Parents of high-achieving youngsters complained that teachers were watering down the curriculum. Other parents were disturbed at the time schools were spending in disciplining rather than in teaching. Reports of intraclass resegregation had to be investigated.

Superintendent Biggs summarized the problems succinctly at the Breakfast Group in February 1979. He observed that the New Castle schools were experiencing the problems that other communities had faced after the start of desegregation; they were just facing them a little sooner.

SUMMARY

In ending school desegregation, the start of busing in New Castle County was a success. The schools opened peacefully, almost all reflecting the racial composition in the district. The plan was relatively equitable and the financial effects, as measured by increases in taxes, were favorable to those who had been in the majority black districts.

The implementation could not be called a complete success, however, because of concerns about the future. Would white flight continue? Would the percentage of suburban white parents willing to send their children to schools in the city continue to drop? Would second-generation problems like class segregation and differential suspension rates be handled quickly and effectively? Would the animosity generated by the teachers' strike and the financial impact of reorganization long fester?[27]

Nevertheless, even limited success seems to be so rare these days that, when found, it deserves careful analysis. That will be the subject of the next chapter.

9 / Toward a Political Analysis

Many people caught up in the Delaware desegregation process blamed politics for every difficulty that arose. In part, I have written this book to counter the view that politics should and could be removed from the implementation arena. I want to make it very clear that achieving effective desegregation, far from being hindered by politics, is actually a political business through and through.

THE LIMITS OF APOLITICAL ANALYSIS

To understand the difficulties that resulted when apolitical analysis is applied to school desegregation, it is instructive to examine Richard Nelson's critique of the approach that dominates most considerations of urban problems.[1] Nelson begins with the familiar question, "If we can land a man on the moon, why can't we solve the problems of the ghetto?" He finds that three major intellectual traditions have attempted to analyze urban problems rationally in order to provide solutions: systems analysis, organizational analysis, and scientific analysis.

When we apply each of Nelson's categories to the literature on implementing school desegregation, we discover that rational analysis either masks, underemphasizes, or fails to help us understand a number of important difficulties. Let us look at each of the three in turn.

Systems Analysis

Under systems analysis, one states objectives or evaluation criteria and then measures alternatives along these criteria. The trouble with developing a school desegregation plan, however, is that inevitably there is a conflict among goals and means. Should, for example, black and white students be treated equally in the number of years that they are to be bused? Should the percentage of black and white students be kept equal across schools for maximum neighborhood stability? Should busing times be minimized overall to keep down costs? Each objective may be desirable, but realizing one is incompatible with achieving the others. Unfortunately, the more complex and stressful the situation, the less helpful is systems analysis in finding a solution.[2]

It is possible for majorities to dominate the decision-making process in pursuit of narrow operational goals. For example, it is tempting to use the systems analysis approach in arriving at pupil assignments in desegregation plans. Researchers at the Division of School Planning, North Carolina State University, have developed a linear programming model that can allocate students to schools on the basis of decision rules such as "minimize the percentage differences of minority students across schools" and constraints such as "bus no child for more than 30 minutes."[3] To date, however, computerized pupil assignment models have not been successful. John A. Finger, Jr., an expert at developing desegregation plans, has concluded that computer programs are not sensitive to considerations of equity:

> Assigning students to desegregated schools by computer has been attempted, but all the computer programs that I know of create residential instability and for this reason will not work effectively. A preliminary plan was prepared but rejected for Denver. I attempted unsuccessfully to use a computer program for Stamford, Connecticut, developed by the Desegregation Center at the University of Miami.
>
> A computer program which assigns students to schools and provides transportation routes would seem to be very desirable because it could simultaneously minimize number of students to be bused, travel time, and number of buses required. Unfortunately, minimizing these parameters results in some extremely undesirable outcomes. If students are selected on the basis of race and proximity to school, students residing in integrated neighborhoods would sometimes be assigned to black schools if they are white and white schools if they are black. Sending black and white students in an integrated neighborhood to different schools is not a desirable outcome of a desegregation plan. This problem could be avoided by an alternative procedure which assigns all the students in a city block or some other geographic aggregate to a school. However, both procedures create residential instability for several reasons. Some children of the same race will be bused all 12 years and others not bused at all. The residents of some areas of the city will be bused and other areas will not be bused.[4]

Other analysts have described similiar problems with computer models in Corpus Christi and elsewhere.[5]

As this discussion illustrates, the systems analysis approach tends to assume that goals or objectives are agreed upon and that the major task is to find the best alternatives for achieving them through rationally analyzing information. But conflict usually dominates desegregation planning—conflicts over the interests of blacks and whites as reflected in disagreements over the number of years that children of either race must be bused; conflicts over the meaning of goals like equity (should *intraracial* or *interracial* equity be a goal?); and conflicts over the desirability of busing and closing black or white schools. Such conflicts are at the heart of every discussion of desegregation plans. As Nelson says, rational analysis approaches "play down or ignore that many problems may be largely political, involving real conflicts of interest that cannot be dissolved by sweet rationalism."[6]

Organizational Analysis

Implicit in recommendations derived from organizational analysis is the assumption that improving the educational organization will lead to more effective school desegregation. The improvements may take many forms—upgrading personnel through in-service training, adding new organizational structures like a human relations office, altering teaching methods, or, as implied by Nelson, analyzing alternative organizational structures to maximize organizational outputs.[7] For example, we saw in Chapter 4 that the reorganization of school districts in an interdistrict desegregation case requires a determination of the most appropriate size of a school district (measured by pupil enrollment). But not only does no agreement exist on what should be the goal (efficiency? responsiveness?), there is no consensus on the relation between alternative school district sizes and these goals. Like systems analysis, organizational analysis masks conflicts among goals and means.

Even if school board members were agreed on organizational changes needed to comply with a federal court order to desegregate, one could not assume that making the changes would be a simple administrative task. Members of organizations resist changes that seem to threaten their values, routines, and interests. Conflict is not limited to decision-making bodies like school boards; organizational change also stirs up conflict of interests (over salaries and authority) and ideologies (over disciplinary codes and treatment of blacks in extracurricular activities) within the administrative hierarchy. Furthermore, school administrators, especially superintendents, are subject to many political pressures from their "constituents." The public is especially attentive to administrative action where desegregation is involved.[8]

Organizational analysis not only underemphasizes conflict over goals and means at the decision-making level, it also neglects the political problems of implementing organizational change.

Scientific and Technological Analysis

Some researchers believe that social science can establish general laws and thus general principles of action. On this assumption, a number of works have listed principles for achieving effective school desegregation.

In its report on school desegregation in Boston, the United States Civil Rights Commission lists ten objectives that "can be used by other communities to plan and implement successful desegregation."[9] It added four more conclusions to a report the following year.[10] The most comprehensive study in this area—by Al Smith, Anthony Downs, and M. Leanne Lachman—located "one set of basic principles [which are] most universally applicable to the achievement of effective desegregation." This set includes meeting desegregation requirements established by the courts, avoiding major disruptions in the schools and community, and achieving quality "unified" education for all students.[11] The Smith, Downs, and Lachman handbook is based on an analysis of over a thousand separate studies, correspondence, and additional materials.

Forehand and Ragosta studied nearly two hundred schools to determine what "positive action . . . can be taken to maximize the educational benefits of integrated schooling," focusing on policies within schools, not "community politics." They identify a number of "generalizable principles" that can serve as "guides to evaluating and formulating actions."[12] Orfield's focus is also on the adaptation of schools rather than entire school districts.[13] Orfield is careful to point out that those "educational requirements for successful desegregation" that he identifies (such as changes in teaching methods anc curriculum) are based on "little systematic, carefully controlled research on educational processes within desegregated schools."[14] Another published example is the report of the national conference sponsored by the U.S. Office of Education and the Council of Chief School Officers; it presents a long list of "ideas that work" and "successful, positive steps" that can be taken to help improve education after desegregation.[15]

All these various principles, objectives, conclusions, and conditions regarding effective desegregation raise two important questions. Is there a consensus on what to do to achieve effective school desegregation? And, if such a consensus exists, why don't local officials act on it.

Perhaps the agreements in these presentations—on the need for public involvement in planning and implementation, positive positions by community leaders, mobilization and coordination of all sectors of the community to support implementation—are too general. Further, each study seems to add significantly to the shopping list. The total list may be too long to be of much use. To some extent Smith, Downs, and Lachman recognize this when they suggest that working toward a good desegregated school system is essentially moving toward a good school system. In the USOE / Council of Chief School Officers' report, *Take a Giant Step*, it is suggested that decisionmakers fully revise the curriculum, retrain and desegregate the staff, involve all elements of the community in planning, develop contingency plans for all negative possibilities, and so on. An all-inclusive prescription like this list offers decisionmakers a checklist but no priorities. Unacknowledged is the political problem of choosing among items on the checklist and allocating resources among priorities. Similarly, these recipes do not indicate how much of a recommendation is enough. How much teacher retraining should be offered and what kind of training is desirable? How much emphasis on communications is necessary? Presumably "enough" will be apparent after the fact: if things go well, decisionmakers did enough. Again the political problem of allocating priorities is obscured by seemingly neutral principles.

If all these uncertainties and generalities do in fact add up to a course of action, we are still faced with the question of why decisionmakers do not do the "right things." However satisfying it is to blame prejudice and incompetence, a political explanation appears more realistic. Actions that are required in order to achieve effective school desegregation run counter to the ways that school systems typically operate in the United States. It may be illuminating here briefly to compare Roscoe Martin's conclusions about suburban schools with the principles of effective desegregation. Martin says that schools and educational decisionmakers are relatively isolated and insulated from the public; that the superintendent and professional educators dominate the decisions; and that, in general, schools operate like bureaucracies:

> Four bureaucratic progeny of the public school mythology may be singled out for brief mention. First is the reverence for form, at whatever expense to substance. This reveals itself in deep respect for procedural rules, affection for familiar things, and suspicion of innova-

tion. Second is the brisk defensiveness which flows spontaneously from sensitivity to criticism. This state of mind arrays the schoolmen, as the defenders of the public school faith, against the critics, even the sympathetic critics, who are regarded almost uniformly as attackers. This leads inevitably to the we-they dichotomy: we who defend the public school vs. those who seek to destroy it. Third is the bland assumption of professional rightness, manifest in the invocation of tradition and in *a priori* reasoning—the assertion of firmly held beliefs as facts. Fourth is the homogenized character of the practitioners—their common origins, their uniform (and well nigh universal) belief system, their uncommon loyalty and dedication to the pursuit of common goals.[16]

These school operational principles, enunicated by Martin and substantiated by many others, are in conflict with the desegregation principles noted previously. For example, the need to involve the public clashes with the isolated and closed nature of American public education.

It may seem that inertia, conservatism, or resistance to change accounts for the reluctance of decisionmakers to act in accord with the principles of effective desegregation. I suggest, however, that the opposition actually results because the principles call for a redistribution of power away from those who hold it to those who seek it. As I have just noted, a key principle is opening the school decisionmaking process to the community. But local educational administrators have sought isolation to protect themselves from the conflicting demands of the public.

When communities become battlegrounds over sex education, patriotism, permissiveness, and religion in schools, school administrators develop the habit of keeping their heads down. To be caught in the open, in a position of leadership, can be professionally fatal. More than one Delaware superintendent has reminded me of the consequences that may befall superintendents who lead a desegregation effort. For example, Roland Jones, superintendent of the Charlotte-Mecklenburg School District, was fired on the air during a televised school board meeting. He had taken a positive approach to busing in a "confidential" meeting with ex-President Ford, as suggested by *Take a Giant Step*. Word leaked out and that was that.

Apolitical and Political Assumptions

Using Nelson's framework from *The Moon and the Ghetto*, let us take a closer look at the problems of rational, apolitical analyses of school desegregation.

First, as we have seen, the rational model assumes that goals and objectives are agreed upon. All that remains is to administer the consensus successfully. The rational model is apolitical; it sees unity instead of conflict. Conflict, however, is inherent in desegregation problems. They are therefore better understood from a political perspective, which assumes conflict, than from a technical or administrative viewpoint, which does not.

Not technical but political tasks are essential to achieving desegregation—working to reach agreement on goals and means in a desegregation plan; persuading school officials to yield power in the implementation process; minimizing interjurisdictional and policy differences between officials who must work cooperatively to prepare for implementation; and getting a resistant public to support compliance with a disagreeable court order.

In Delaware, changing circumstances and value conflicts long prevented the development of clear objectives. The federal judges in the case specified no objective more definite than the general order to desegregate. The Interim Board, the organ of decision making for over a year, early abandoned its attempt to specify objectives and rationally evaluate means to reach them. Where there is basic conflict over the desirability of a goal, an apolitical analysis of how to reach it is not much help in understanding the problems.[17]

Second, the rational model assumes that solutions exist. But, where one side or the other in a conflict must give up some of its perogatives, neither technological nor administrative methods can offer an outcome that will satisfy all parties. When the questions are ones that concern power—which teachers should be transferred to achieve more of a racial balance in the staff? what schools shall be closed? how much authority will be given to appointed citizen groups? the issue is not what is the best solution but whose interests the solution will favor.

Third, the rational model places great faith in the effectiveness of information in dealing with problems. Research, analysis of alternatives, and data are treated as the keys to selecting superior solutions. Early in the Wilmington desegregation experience, school desegregation experts made presentations to parent audiences, who failed to be impressed. One of the consultants remarked belatedly that desegregation is a process, not a content issue: *how* something is done or said is more important than *what* is done or said. During one crisis in Boston, for example, emotions ran so high that blacks and whites met in different rooms. William Leary, the former school superintendent, served as messenger between the caucus of white parents in one room and the caucus of black parents in the other. The desegregation process often finds leaders of the probusing and antibusing groups, politicians and school officials, and state and local and federal officials not talking to one another. When tensions are high, creating an atmosphere in which people will be willing to meet and exchange information becomes more important than the agenda.

Similarly, who presents information may be more significant than the content. The credibility of the source often determines whether the message will be accepted. On emotional issues, people tend to be concerned first of all with which side the speaker favors, not whether the information being presented is useful or valid.

In Rittell and Webber's terminology, desegregation poses "wicked," not "tame," problems.[18] Agreement is lacking even on the nature of the problem. Some see a problem called "segregation" in segregated schools, but many suburban parents and educators see no problem at all—at least no problem that they should have to deal with. Some see school district size as the critical factor where others hold job-retention as the most important consideration. Some argue that equity requires all white children to attend "black" schools for two years, and others argue that equity requires greater busing of whites and less of blacks. All of the problems are interrelated and multifaceted. There are no solutions but only compromises, and such compromises come from political processes and analysis rather than from technical expertise and recommendations.

POLITICS OF IMPLEMENTATION

Even political scientists have been slow to move beyond the study of decision making to the study of the content, the implementation, and the consequences of those decisions.[19] Until the late 1960s political scientists followed the maxim, "It's not whether you win or lose but how you play the game." As Kenneth M. Dolbeare has written:

> At least since the end of the decade of the thirties, empirically oriented political scientists have concentrated almost exclusively upon aspects of the political processes through which policies are made. Voting behavior, political parties, interest-group activities, decision making in institutions, etc., have all been prominent fields of concentration for those who specialize in American politics. Analysis starts with a claim made for government action of a particular kind and ends when a statute is passed, a decision rendered, or a regulation issued in that subject area. Relatively little attention has been paid to the content of the policies produced through these processes or to the effects which they may have on the people and problems which are their objects.

Even the policy-oriented approaches finally developed in political science had limited utility according to Dolbeare:

> Patently, these approaches neither have taken nor will take us very far into the substance of public policy; they ask why policies have their present form, and they look for answers exclusively within certain narrow subareas of the visible political process. At no time do they ask what difference it made to people or problems that such policies were enacted. Only in the area of judicial-impact studies do political scientists ask such questions, and then only with regard to whether or not compliance with a Supreme Court decision was forthcoming. In short, what government does is studied chiefly in terms of how it came to be that way, not in terms of whether it was effective or ineffective, better or worse than some other way of solving a problem, or good or bad in the absolute or overall sense.[20]

What was true of political science in general has been relatively true of the research in school desegregation. The study of the politics of Northern school desegregation has concentrated on the decision whether or not to desegregate.[21] Further, since both positive and negative decisions seemed to lead to little actual student desegregation, such research, to quote the authors of one of the most elaborate studies, seems "to be documenting an enormous effort that failed."[22] In recognition of this, political scientists began to concentrate on policy content, implementation, and impact.

Recently a number of political scientists have focused on school district compliance and noncompliance (that is, resistance), primarily in the rural South.[23] The key concern has been to identify factors that lead to compliance. In the related literture on the politics of federal enforcement efforts, the most significant finding has been that federal coercion is very closely related to compliance.[24] However, studying how people complied and how they implemented the law may be more useful in understanding the dynamics of school desegregation. It would seem to be helpful to study processes that have worked rather than efforts that have failed.

I have argued that any attempt to facilitate school desegregation must assume the existence of conflict and attempt to manage it. No approach that treats the community as a unified whole can be effective. The problem must be seen as political.[25] Two political frameworks may help us to understand the school desegregation process: the ideological model, which assumes a bipolar or polarized distribution of attitudes, values, resources, and interests in the community, and the pluralistic model, which assumes a polycentric distribution. In the preceeding chapters, elements of these models shaped my description of the attitudes and actions of the general public, courts, educational officials, governmental officials, and community leaders in Delaware. At this point, I wish to return to the responses of the various players over the decade of the 1970s, placing them within these broad, political frameworks. Doing so may help to clarify the broad implications of this analysis of the Wilmington metropolitan school desegregation case.

It is tempting, having rejected an apolitical approach, to select one of the two political models as a guide to discussion. The Delaware desegregation process could be seen as either an ideological or a pluralistic conflict. Alternatively, models could be applied en ser-iatim as Allison has so effectively done.[26] That is, the desegregation process could be examined first as an ideological confrontation and then, for further insights, as a pluralistic conflict.

Nevertheless, I believe that a simultaneous consideration of both the ideological and pluralist models is necessary to understand the Delaware case and the implications beyond. The real world of deseg-regation implementation is too complex to be reflected by a simple use of models.

Delaware Dynamics

In short, this book has described the attempt of pluralist institutions to resolve an essentially ideological conflict.[27]

Paul Peterson has described an ideological conflict as one in which: (1) participants in the policy-making process include groups commit-ted to broadgauge objectives who become involved in a range of policy questions; (2) such groups find similar allies and similar enemies across a range of policy questions; (3) there are enduring and signi-ficant linkages between inclusive social groups and important politi-cal factions and (4) groups prefer the defeat of the opposition to "reasonable" compromise.[28] In the ideological model, actors are moti-vated by broad and diffuse goals based upon deep cleavages in socie-ty. Race is probably the best example of such a cleavage. For an ideological conflict, words like freedom and equality are more signi-ficant than tax rates and school facilities. In fact, in ideological con-flict, symbols play at least as large a role as do tangible outcomes. Participants in the conflict are committed to their view of the world and tend to form permanent and dichotomous alliances. Since con-flict is over principles and symbols, compromise is difficult, if not impossible. Decisionmakers are motivated more by their principles and their view of what is right than by group pressure.

In the pluralist model, on the other hand, groups focus on narrow issues of self interest, alliances shift according to the issue, and differences are compromised in order to reach resolution. Decision-makers play the role of broker in arranging compromises among the contending groups. Today's losers may become tomorrow's winners. Conflict is not intense or deeply rooted; rather an equilibrium of sorts is reached across a wide range of issues.[29]

In Delaware, the desegregation process was rooted in ideological conflict. The pluralist forces were partially successful in imposing upon this ideological structure a pluralist framework.

The desegregation conflict in Delaware in the 1970s was rooted in past racial antagonisms. Delaware's educational system had been separate and unequal by law, and the state was the scene of a major confrontation over the implementation of the Brown decision. By 1970, New Castle, the northern county of Delaware, was racially segregated on a geographical basis. The Wilmington public schools served a majority black school population while the suburban school districts served almost all white children. Racial differences were reinforced by class differences in the city-suburban split. Further-more, the emphasis on localism in both government and education in Delaware reinforced the separation of blacks and whites. The reopen-ing of the Evans v. Buchanan suit in 1971 was an outgrowth of these ideological and racial antagonisms.

Black power was nonexistent outside the city. Within the city, blacks ran the school district and led the parent organization. The racial division was also coterminous with divisions of wealth and income. The city limits enclosed the bulk of the poor, black residents of the county; the suburban areas held almost all the affluent whites.

The distribution of public opinion further illustrates the ideological nature of what came to be called the busing issue. Virtually every suburban white parent opposed busing. The only supporters of busing were black city parents (although they were themselves divided). Furthermore, white opposition to busing was not simply a matter of self interest (see Chapter 2) but rather reflected white attitudes about blacks and the relations of blacks to government. That is, to both whites and blacks busing was more than a battle over specific desegre-gation plans. The rise and success of the antibusing organization, PAC, was due to the general white opposition to busing and was led by strong conservative ideologues.

The federal court orders required that the public institutions of Delaware—all levels of government, all public schools—face up to the racial issue, which had been a nonissue for years.[30] The courts did not impose a remedy. They acted more like stern but nonauthoritarian parents, requiring cooperation and responsibility among quarrelsome siblings. The District Court was motivated by a judicial theory of restraint that discouraged judicial interference with local decision making. The court wanted the parties in the suit to negotiate a settlement (through the Interim and New Boards, the State Legislature, and direct discussions) and shoulder the responsibility for implementing the final plan.

These institutions, which should have played integral roles in the bargaining process, were unable to agree on a desegregation plan. The State Legislature, hounded by PAC, continually took an ideological approach: it passed symbolic resolutions, indulged in rhetorical over-kill, and failed to enact an acceptable desegregation plan. The school boards also failed to live up to the court order. None of their plans were acceptable to the city and to the suburban school boards and to the court. Their plans reflected white, suburban domination. Political executives who tried to force a compromise had no luck. The parties to the suit were too ideological to consider compromising on a plan. To blacks, for example, magnet schools symbolized white treachery; and to whites any plan calling for even minimal involuntary busing amounted to a sellout.

Political executives, beginning with the county executive in 1974, did establish pluralistic mechanisms in order to reduce conflict and to prepare for desegregation. The Committee of Twelve, later the Delaware Committee on the School Decision, the Information Center, the four-district plan, several initiatives for a negotiated settlement, and the governor's Effective Transition Committee—all were created in the hope that bringing people together would minimize the sense of crisis. But in an ideological conflict, contact may not further agreement, and ideologues may refuse to play the game. It happened that way in Delaware. DCSD lost its antibusers, no negotiated settlement was developed by the court-directed boards, and the State Legislature did not enact the four-district plan until it was too late for the court to accept it.

A negotiated settlement and adequate preparation were hindered not only by the ideological nature of the conflict but also by the pluralistic responses. Hargrove's "essential insight" was borne out, that implementation is a political process in which individuals and groups vie for control of programs or to defend themselves against them.[31] To put it another way, the court placed the desegregation of the schools at the top of the public agenda in Delaware. Once the issue had been forced on everyone, many individuals and groups did treat the issue as a pluralist issue, asking: What can we gain through this process and what must we protect?

No reorganization plans were agreed upon and preparation was delayed partly for pluralistic reasons. School superintendents were interested in maintaining, if not improving, their positions; school board members wanted to protect their districts; and politicians sought to expand their constituencies. Preparation was delayed because educators were reluctant to involve the public in school affairs, because politicians told people what they wanted to hear, and because both sought protection from the antibusing white public.

As we have already noted, this brings us around full circle. The courts looked to the institutions that had both created and failed to undo an illegal pattern and required those same institutions to remedy the situation. Understandably, these institutions did not develop a totally acceptable plan. However, no Delaware official obstructed the implementation of the plan, some helped to develop a plan, and a number helped to prepare for the plan's implementation. Thus, despite the problems described above, Delaware did desegregate peacefully and effectively in September 1978. While not an absolute success, desegregation in New Castle County certainly was a relative success compared to the traumas that occurred in Boston and Louisville–Jefferson County. Why?

ACHIEVING EFFECTIVE DESEGREGATION

Most of the population in the New Castle County desegregation area was strongly against busing. At the same time, the public, especially blacks and middle-class whites, supported the public schools, wanted tranquility in the community, intended to obey the law, and held to the principle of desegregation. It was the middle-class school districts and the middle-class representatives dominating the State Board of Education who were the major spokespeople on the issue. The areas of the highest potential resistance—the blue-collar districts—were unable to dominate either the State Board or court-directed boards. Only in the State Legislature were obstructionist forces very strong. The relatively low percentage of blacks in the county was not overly threatening to whites. Thus, unlike Boston, or some Southern states of the 1950s, there was never any question that school officials or governmental executives would obey the law, nor was there ever much support for extremist actions in Delaware.

Officials and Their Constituency

The nature of the constituency in Delaware allowed public and school officials some latitude in approaching busing. Some public officials took the initiative in establishing pluralist mechanisms to smooth desegregation. That is, they tried to transform the ideological conflict into a situation in which all advocates could sit down together and reach some agreement.

Among these mechanisms, the one that showed most risk and foresight was County Executive Slawik's establishment of what was to become the Delaware Committee on the School Decision in 1974. In 1977, Mayor McLaughlin's efforts to deal constructively with the issue and Governor du Pont's management approach were also significant factors in smoothing the process.

The efforts of public officials to deal with school desegregation pluralistically were aided immeasurably by Jon Chace of the Community Relations Service. As a broker, Chace helped to bring and keep together the various governmental representatives.

If New Castle County had been able to depend only on community preference for tranquility and the pluralist initiatives of three governmental executives, however, it is unlikely that effective desegregation could have been achieved. Two other forces were necessary—community organizations and the courts.

Community Substitution

As noted in Chapter 5, Rossell has listed the political and administrative functions that mayors should fulfill in the desegregation process. In Delaware, in the absence of governmental action, it was community groups, especially coalitions, that fulfilled many of these functions. For example, the DCSD and the Citizens' Alliance for Public Education rather than governmental and school officials took responsibility for informing and preparing the public for school desegregation; the Breakfast Group helped coordinate efforts to implement the law; the National Council of Christians and Jews conducted human relations programs in the schools; and SANE prepared a public relations campaign to cool things off if problems got hot. All of these groups lobbied school and governmental officials, encouraging them to obey the law and prepare for desegregation. The actions of the groups were thus in the spirit of pluralism—encouraging citizen involvement, bringing diverse people together, pressuring officials, and trying to force a planned resolution (although not any particular plan).

It was not only the actions of community support groups that averted the much-feared violence and disruption; ironically, the relatively conventional political tactics of the nonsupport group PAC also contributed. PAC preempted every other antibusing effort and channeled its energy into the mainstream of the political system. The State Legislature, Congress, and school boards were the targets of PAC, and its leaders judged that protest and demonstrations would not help them to reach their goals. Their rhetoric was fiery and intransigent, but their tactics were conventional. When Jim Venema announced his candidacy for the U.S. Senate in spring 1978 at the same time that several PAC leaders began movements to start private schools, the conventionality of PAC was cemented. No protests were planned for the start of busing. The antibusing movement had accepted the immediate inevitability of the busing order.

Court Wisdom

The ingredients were available for a tranquil movement to desegregation by September 1977. Although feelings had cooled, however, school and governmental officials were still lacking a sense of unity and inevitability. At that time, one bad cook might have spoiled the broth. Fortunately U.S. District Judge Murray Schwartz turned out to be both a Solomon and a Julia Child.

Judge Schwartz's decision to stay implementation from September 1977 until September 1978 was the final factor that helped to maintain the calm. The added year was a blessing, for time itself reduced the uncertainties. The U.S. Supreme Court refused to hear the Delaware case in October 1977 and the nature of the desegregation plan became known. Both developments nourished the necessary feeling of inevitability.

A survey of city and suburban parents in early 1978 indicated that almost all suburban parents (90 percent) and three-quarters of city parents (74 percent) believed that busing was inevitable, and about one-half of the suburban parents felt that public officials should accept, if not work for, peaceful implementation of the court order. This was a substantial shift from the previous year; in spring 1977 only two-thirds of the suburban and half of the city parents had thought that busing would eventually come. With the shift came a willingness to deal more realistically with desegregation preparation.[32] The many to whom busing was a fate worse than death were able to come to terms with it because of Judge Schwartz's decision. During that extra year, school officials shaped a county school district, governmental officials set up a full operational information center and media center, and community groups and officials became deeply involved in cooperative preparations.

Judge Schwartz also contributed to peaceful desegregation and equity by ordering the 9–3 pupil assignment plan. This plan had been developed by the New Board's pupil assignment committee, after the judge had disengaged it from its mother board. Also, in his opinion on

January 9, 1978, Judge Schwartz ordered the New Board to undertake a number of preparatory and remedial actions. Judge Schwartz's various decisions minimized the antibusing (and antipreparation) pressures on governmental decisionmakers, defined a compromise plan that had been avoided by city and suburban officials, removed political pressures from the pupil assignment committee, and removed from the New Board the political onus of having to prepare and undertake appropriate remedial actions. In short, Judge Schwartz changed the political climate by fiat.

The success in Delaware represented artful politics in many quarters. Let us consider its implications for other situations.

Implications

At the beginning of this chapter, I discussed the problems that result from a rational/technical/administrative approach to implementing school desegregation. Those who take this path tend to focus on the technical leadership of school professionals. They hope that politicians, at best, will ignore the issue; they fear that the baser sort of politician will exploit it. They see the public as a passive group who should be informed of the court decision and the details of the plan, but only as necessary. People will comply with a desegregation order because it is the law. The development of the plan is the most critical part of the process. Like other implementation steps, development is treated as a highly technical and rational matter. Using this model to achieve effective desegregation, local leaders would have topflight educators devise the best plans possible, would try to keep politicians and the public at bay, and would stress the positive educational aspects of the plan when it became necessary to discuss it in public.

Such is the model. Procedures under a political model stand in marked contrast (Figure 9-1).

The Pluralist Approach   The pluralist approach emphasizes the process, not the content, of school desegregation. Paul Geisel, who joined blacks, brown, and whites in the development of a plan for Dallas, says, "If [there is a] lesson from Dallas, [it is] don't pay attention to what we did—the specifics aren't important and probably won't last ten years—but look at how we did it."[33]

Pluralists focus on the role of political executives in desegregation. Believing that the literature overemphasizes the leadership of school superintendents and principals, Rossell and Dunaway prescribe action by the mayor to further desegregation (see Chapter 5). The mayor

Figure 9-1
Comparison of the Implications of the
Apolitical, Ideological, and Pluralist Models on
School Desegregation Implementation

	Model		
	Apolitical	*Ideological*	*Pluralist*
Distribution of Values, Resources, Attitudes and Interests	Unitary	Polarized	Polycentric
Focus	Technique	Symbols	Process
Leadership Role	Professional	Legitimizer	Broker
Process Model	Instrumental	Expressive	Negotiated
Implementation Strategy	Compliance	Conversion	Compromise

is needed to involve the public and serve as a broker, striking political bargains among all groups involved in the desegregation process. The public in turn can mobilize to convince the mayor that it is in his or her political interest to take a constructive role in peaceful implementation.[34]

To achieve peaceful desegregation, the public must feel well represented by leaders; and those leaders must be involved in the bargaining process. For maximum public participation, community coalitions must be formed. Coalitions bring people together so that compromises be made and political figures may be encouraged to support effective desegregation. Coalitions in addition can serve as countervailing forces to antibusing groups.[35]

Public compliance results from public participation in the desegregation process. Through participation, members of the public reach partial fulfillment of self-interest through influencing the content of the decision. Under the pluralist model, the public is instrumental in completing the process. They speak their minds; some are satisfied when the decision favors them; others may have achieved some modification in the result or only have had their position recognized; all become a permanent part of the final decision. The pluralist model receives its power from public participation.

Under the pluralist model, effective desegregation implementation requires that many assorted individuals and groups cooperate to implement the law.

Norton Long once described the process of local government as an "ecology of games." In Long's view, local political processes were a mesh of various conflicts, each played by different rules, with different players, and for different stakes.[36]

To implement the court orders, Delaware's players should all have been playing the "school desegregation game." Instead they seem to have been playing different games with different goals. The legislature's football strategy was to play with style, the political executives' baseball goal was to avoid a loss, the court's checkers objective was to end the game by mutual agreement, and the school officials' desire was to keep their chess set. Often these four sets of decisionmakers also played solitaire, each with its own set of spectators. The legislators worked closely with PAC, political executives worked with supportive community groups, the court worked with lawyers, and school officials worked somewhat with local educational leaders. Very few interactions occurred.

A number of forces keep people from working together on desegregation. As Lewis Dexter noted about Congress years ago, people tend to talk to those with whom they agree.[37] On an issue like desegregation, where emotions run high, talking with those on the other side can be especially upsetting. Approaching the other side may seem like, and indeed may be, a wasted effort. On the other hand, different groups may perceive accurately that their political impact will be greater in one decisionmaking area than another. Thus PAC, whose major resource was numbers, had enormous influence in the State Legislature, where members count votes. Supportive community groups had fewer but more influential members, and they were successful in influencing administrators and advisors to governmental executives.

A further divisive force was the decisionmakers' natural suspicion of each other. Legislators saw themselves as watchdogs of the executive and school officials, courts ruled on the constitutionality of legislative action, and school officials feared politicians as threats to their financial status. Finally, the self-interests of the actors often dictated that they keep independent from each other. For example, in Delaware the superintendents wanted to maintain or increase the number of administrative positions after reorganization but they realized that the legislature would be very unsympathetic. The legislators, on the other hand, were concerned with avoiding blame for desegregation; they were anxious to demonstrate their independence of the courts.

The pluralist recommendation to community leaders, then, would be to treat the desegregation process much like an election campaign.

Like politicians, leaders must forge coalitions among diverse elements and across political roles. Support for peaceful desegregation, like votes, must be earned by meeting the interests of the public. Timing is critical, for support should not peak prematurely. Public relations campaigns should coincide with the start of busing. Otherwise, money and time may be wasted or, worse, good will that was created too early may dissipate.

Some recent case studies of desegregation show the usefulness of the pluralist bargaining approach. The Dallas Alliance, a business group, successfully established a committee of five blacks, five browns, and five whites to develop a desegregation plan acceptable to both the court and a significant proportion of the community.[38] In Milwaukee, school officials set up a community participation program led by black and white cochairmen that resulted in relatively successful school desegregation.[39] In Atlanta, a bargain was struck that gave blacks more educational positions in return for their relinquishing some of their desegregation demands. In all three cities, peace has not been seriously threatened.

The pluralist approach is not foolproof, however.[40] Because minority groups often have little power in local politics, they may be unable to protect their interests in negotiations. Revisionists are now suggesting that inequities have arisen from certain pluralist bargains. Some pluralist compromises have created disadvantages for blacks, disadvantages that have been ignored in analyses of these plans. In Milwaukee, for example, critics charge that almost all those who have volunteered to change schools have been black, and in Dallas and Atlanta they observe that many blacks continue to attend segregated schools.[41] In Delaware, the court established several pluralist mechanisms but had to reject all desegregation plans that were produced because they were all inequitable.

The greatest limitation on the usefulness of pluralist strategies in desegregation is the intransigence of the different ideologies that are in conflict. In order to succeed, pluralist strategies need to be supplemented, whenever possible, with approaches that take account of ideological obstacles.

The Ideological Approach   When ideology dominates the desegregation decision-making process (as in Delaware), those working for peaceful implementation have limited options. The ideological model has many fewer possibilities for change, whether by information (using the rational model) or political resources (using the pluralist model). To quote Nelson, "It is apparent that many of the more optimistic believers in the power of rational analysis overestimated their power." Such believers "possess an enormous amount of confidence that it is possible to find technically correct answers to important policy problems; they play down or ignore that many problems may be largely political, involving real conflicts or interest that cannot be dissolved by sweet rationalism."[42] What Nelson says applies to pluralism, as well; political methods may offer no complete solution because they too ignore the ideological basis of conflict.

While the rationalist focuses on technique and its results and the pluralist on process, those who follow the ideological model recognize that symbolism plays a large role in public debate. Therefore, workers for peaceful implementation take care in choosing their symbols. In Delaware, for example, community leaders learned quickly (in part from Louisville advisors) that appeals to follow the law may have swayed a few lawyers but had little effect on the general public. Arguments for ensuring the safety of children and maintaining good public schools seemed to be better received. Also effective was the reassuring presence of respected leaders in the community who gave measured support to calm, peaceful approaches and thus further legitimized the court order.

McConahay and Hawley concluded that self-interest was not, as pluralists would suppose, the major determinant of busing attitudes in Louisville–Jefferson County. They found that busing is a symbolic issue similar to prohibition and anticommunism (see Chapter 2) and that the power behind the symbol was a subtle racism: "Parties to the debate argue as if they were concerned with harm to children or the family or the community or the nation, but only shout past one another because the debate is really over whose values will dominate public life and whose group will receive the concommitant public respect."[43] Choice of labels furthers the symbolism; nobody is "pro-busing" or "anti-desegregation." "Busing" is the cry of those who oppose the change, "desegregation" the banner of those who favor it.

Because labels and language affect the audience so strongly, all leaders of groups within the process must constantly guard against unwittingly stepping on any toes. Symbols can trigger devastating reactions in emotional situations like those accompanying desegregation.

Under the ideological model, the most important task for the politician who wants to further effective school desegregation is to legitimate the court's action. Because people in an ideological conflict tend to believe "You are either for us or agin' us," appeals to their self-interest do not get through. The more politicians are caught up in the ideological model, the less they will consider compromise. They will either express their own ideological view, if it will please the public, or avoid the issue entirely to avoid offending anyone. The rhetoric of the Delaware State Legislature definitely conformed to the ideological model.

The ideological model explains why people who do not believe that busing can be stopped may still demonstrate against it (see Chapter 2). They act to express their feelings rather than to gain immediate rewards from government. Threatening opponents of busing with the costs of noncompliance may only strengthen their resolve to defy the court order. Community leaders, under this model, may encourage participation because it is therapeutic to the public, not because it will improve the plans. The antibusing public will feel better after venting its anger. Informational campaigns cannot change attitudes because attitudes are based on emotions and symbols, not on information. In order to convert the antibusing factions—to reach and teach the public—small-group programs on attitudes and values are necessary. In Delaware such a program was established to discuss desegregation in a setting that permitted changes in attitudes.

While the pluralist model suggests an approach like an election campaign, the ideological model recalls a less benign analogy. One observer of the Delaware situation noticed that the community in facing court-ordered desegregation produced the same series of reactions typical of an individual facing death. Researchers have found that fatally ill persons first disbelieve the diagnosis (denial); second, they lash out at the diagnostician or doctor (anger); third, they try to negotiate to avoid the inevitable (bargaining); fourth, they enter a period of deep depression (depression); and fifth, (if there is time) they acquiesce in the verdict and make preparations for death (acceptance).[44]

This analogy readily fits the actions of Delaware state legislators. They resorted to denial by initially ignoring the issue, anger at Philip Kurland and the courts when faced with the court opinions, bargaining when they attempted to propose magnet schools, depression when they passed resolutions condemning federal judges and the New Board, and, finally, acceptance when they enacted the four-district reorganization plan (see Chapter 5).[45] Because individuals go through these several phases before accepting an inevitable and feared happening, time may indeed be valuable in dealing with death and busing. Delaware, for example, was helped by the time it had to adjust between the initial court decision in July 1974 and the actual implementation in September 1978.[46]

An effective way to aid the process is to increase the pace at which the community confronts these acceptance phases. The early efforts of the DCSD to convey the inevitability of busing to the public in January 1975 helped to create public acceptance in September 1978. Although pluralists from their viewpoint may not wish to address the busing issue too early, those aware of the ideological model will push for immediate public discussion of the issue. The stronger the impact of ideology, the less chance there will be for a desegregation plan to be formed by political compromise among the forces in the community. Where ideology dominates, the desegregation plan will almost certainly have to be imposed by the courts. Where local politicians to develop a plan, the ideology of the white majority leadership would overwhelm the black interests. Where community attitudes are polarized and political power is unbalanced, the court must specify the plan in order to avoid an inequitable result.

In summary, a community seeking a peaceful transition and facing ideological conflict over busing cannot rely solely on pluralist techniques. A combination of methods will best serve the cause. Leaders must shift the focus of the conflict so that the issue is joined over less devastatingly emotional symbols. They must enlist whatever segments of the public are willing to join forces. They must then identify respected individuals in the community willing to legitimize the court order. The public must be involved, both to allow the inevitable to be faced as soon as possible and to vent emotions well before the children became the targets. Time must be used as an ally to help so that the community faces the issue and ultimately reaches the stage of willingness to prepare for school desegregation.

FEDERAL DESEGREGATION POLICY

The three models—rational, pluralist, and ideological—not only describe community reactions and suggest approaches for local leaders facing the necessity of desegregation; they also have profound implications for federal assistance in such situations.

All policymakers hold implicit or explicit models of the implementation process and base their policies upon them. Since the 1964 Civil Rights Act, the executive branch of the federal government has attempted, at least in principle, to help achieve school desegregation.[47] Unfortunately, almost all federal help has been based on the least satisfactory model—the rational.

Under the Civil Rights Act, Title IV, General Assistance Centers were established to help school districts plan and implement school desegregation (they act, for example, as consultants for in-service training).[48] Until recently, such centers have not been permitted to work directly with community groups. Emergency School Aid Act (ESAA) funds have been available only after desegregation plans were set, and then only to finance educational support programs not mandated by the court order (such as tutorial programs and in-service training). Since the rational model assumes that technical information and analysis are critical, it is not surprising that federal resources are primarily available to provide technical assistance for educational organizations and not long-term political help for community bodies. This view is reflected in other federal educational policies; Wayson has argued that the Elementary and Secondary Education Act assumes that local educational authorities are the decision-making units, each one a hierarchy directed by administrators who wield power through rational means.[49]

If a doctor has an unsatisfactory model of the human body, his or her treatments are unlikely to work. Since federal desegregation aid is based upon an overreliance on the rational model, it is less helpful than it could be. Federal aid based upon the political models would be the best medicine. (In fact, preventive medicine—federal help for voluntary metropolitan plans—would make many of these cures unnecessary.)

An exception to rationally based federal aid is the work of the Community Relations Service of the Department of Justice. The CRS efforts are based upon the pluralist model. In Delaware, CRS help was instrumental in achieving peaceful desegregation. CRS representatives were very sensitive to the political nuances of the situation. They helped local community leaders to solve many kinds of problems. CRS work included everything from helping to bring blacks and whites together to meet common goals to making peace among warring suburban superintendents.

If more federal aid were to be based on the pluralist model, the following points should be considered. Aid is most useful early in the process to prevent a multitude of independent groups from forming, to allow the development of staff and lay leadership before actual implementation, and to initiate programming early enough to offset the usual strength of antibusing groups. In Delaware, early federal aid would probably have forced the centralization of resources (people, money, ideas) in the DCSD, SANE, NCCJ, and the Alliance. Under current federal regulations only 10 percent of the ESAA money allocated to local communities is for community groups, and these funds are released only after a plan has been officially accepted by the court or federal authorities. It is a classic case of much too little, much too late.

In the pluralist model public acceptance results when benefits are offered to participating groups. Many whites, however, see only loss when the court intervenes in their schools. The pluralist model suggests that public acceptance would increase if more federal aid for education were available to an area under court order.[50] This would not "reward" those who had violated the Constitution. People whose children must be bused are far removed—by time and space and circumstances of every kind—from the officials who created the situation the court wishes to correct. In areas like metropolitan Wilmington, for example, a substantial part of the population did not live in the area in 1971, when the suit was reopened, much less in 1957, when *Evans v. Buchanan* began.

The pluralist approach recognizes that all issues and all communities are different. To be effective consultants and advisors, federal officials must understand the local situation, know the local participants, and develop a relationship built on trust. Results will be based on their interpersonal abilities rather than their technical expertise. The staff of the General Assistance Center headquartered at the University of Pittsburgh and spread thinly over a number of sites, was of little help in the Delaware case. The CRS, on the other hand, had people in their Philadelphia office who knew the Delaware people and the Delaware situation. CRS people might have been even more effective if they had opened an office in Delaware earlier, but they were in town frequently enough to develop relationships useful in their work.

Another great source of help to community leaders in Delaware was their personal contacts with their counterparts in communities in similar situations. During visits and conferences, the practical aspects of coalition building, involving the public, and challenging school officials were discussed. The federal government might well encourage and support appropriate conferences, handbooks, and continuing contacts among leaders so that the expertise of veteran desegregation leaders could be shared where needed.[51]

These comments on federal aid are most applicable in metropolitan cases. The Delaware case illustrates well how metropolitan interdistrict desegregation by its variegated nature requires additional pluralist-based aid.

No official meeting ground for city and suburban school officials in Delaware existed at the onset of desegregation planning. It took almost two years for even the suburban school superintendents to begin to meet regularly. When the court created the Interim Board to bring city and suburban school officials together to plan, there were no established norms for decision making and administrative structure. The Board was torn by conflicting loyalties (each member was loyal to a home school district), heterogeneity (styles, goals, and values among its members varied), and differences in operating methods. The Superintendents' Council and various task forces were clumsy first attempts to restructure the decision making system. It seems obvious that pluralist help in bringing people together and not rational technical assistance is the first necessity in an interdistrict situation.

Interdistrict desegregation further requires that the State Legislature be involved in school district reorganization and finance as well as other substantive areas. One specific problem in Delaware was the conflict between equity in teacher salaries and the cost of reorganization, which led to a six-week strike in fall 1978. Moreover, the interdistrict nature of a case may well demand the reorganization of non-educational branches of both government and community, if they are to deal with the innumerable issues that cross city/suburban lines. All these are pluralist problems. Therefore, successful interdistrict desegregation is even more dependent on federal pluralist-based aid than is single-district desegregation.

Finally, as I argued parenthetically a few pages ago, a positive pluralist way to deal constructively with the issue would be federal and state action to encourage voluntary metropolitan desegregation. A Wisconsin law provides state aid for city districts whose pupils transfer to suburbia and for the suburban districts who receive the transfers. This approach offers both parties to a potential desegregation suit incentives to resolve their differences without a costly court battle. Federal and state legislation encouraging or mandating "voluntary" desegregation (for example, specifying a number of suburban seats for minority children) could prevent a pluralist conflict from developing into a full-blown ideological confrontation.

When a community conflict begins to follow an ideological model, useful federal assistance becomes very difficult. Federal aid, in the minds of those against busing, is transformed into federal interference in an ideological conflict.

The ideological model makes all actions of the federal government symbolic and thus very significant. Former President Ford's sympathy with antibusing sentiment fueled the movement in Boston and probably in other cities. President and Mrs. Carter's decision to send their daughter Amy to the integrated neighborhood school was a positive signal to places like Delaware. Such symbolic leadership can do more than discourage antibusing sentiment. It can raise the morale of those working for peaceful implementation. In Delaware and Louisville–Jefferson County, where about 90 to 95 percent of the suburban white population was against busing, people working for peaceful implementation often felt very isolated. An "Alice in Wonderland" feeling often prevailed where those working for peace were constantly facing unrealistic interpretations of the legal situation and suspicion and outright hostility on all sides. Federal support and acknowledgment of the problems would be invaluable in such situations.

Since no amount of aid will change the position of people ideologically opposed to busing, available aid should go to those who support the goals of peace and effective desegregation. These do not necessarily include the local school district or groups favored by the district.[52] Thus, giving a school district the power to veto ESAA funds proposed for a local community group puts an inappropriate constraint on federal ability to help.

Because under the ideological model it is mandatory to confront the desegregation issue as soon as possible, especially in cases of great ideological conflict, there is an obvious need for federal aid well before, not soon after, implementation. I have maintained that in some communities, federal legislation encouraging voluntary metropolitan desegregation plans could lead to increased desegregation. At the least, it might encourage communities to face this issue earlier in the legal process and therefore accept it earlier.[53]

Public officials also need funds to support planning for implementation early in the litigation process. Desegregation impact plans, along with the aid of CRS, would help to ensure adequate preparation for all of the spillover effects of desegregation.

A further lesson of the ideological model is that officials who are ideologically opposed to desegregation may have to be coerced by federal authorities to implement the law. Rodgers and Bullock found that school districts under federal coercion in Georgia were more likely to desegregate than those under black political pressure.[54] In fact, political and school leaders may well prefer to be coerced so that they will not be personally blamed for their behavior. As Peltason concluded almost twenty years ago, the role of the judge is partly to take the heat. Public officials often prefer to say, "The judge is making us [do it]."[55]

It is clear from this discussion is that the ideological and the pluralist models suggest an emphasis on political approaches to local community problems, a type of federal assistance quite different from any stressed in current programs.

Of course, the reliance of the federal government on technical rather than ideological and pluralist assistance is not mere wrongheadedness but reflects, in part, the political realities of dealing with local school district supporters.[56] A shift of federal aid from technical to political would give rise to one more conflict in a long series of dilemmas associated with to school desegregation.

DESEGREGATION DILEMMAS

Desegregation through busing presents many troublesome dilemmas for our nation. Both legally and philosophically, desegregation cases must balance the rights of black and other minority children against the rights of majority children. Black desires for educational equality through desegregated schools are opposed by white desires to maintain the freedom to send their children to their current schools. It would be easier if these two values were not in conflict, but in many circumstances, the choice has to be made. Federal court decisions have held that minority rights take precedence and have legal standing in most cases.

The basic dilemma raised by this conflict of values in places like Delaware is that the very institutions that have violated the constitution are called upon by the courts to remedy their violation. These local institutions nevertheless maintain their ideological bias and their white control.

Even when school and public officials respond to a court order and begin to cooperate in preparing for, planning for, and implementing desegregation, the public is generally against these activities. This opposition faces officials with the dilemma of being responsive to their public to maintain their positions or being responsive to the court to retain their legality. Further, the public opposes busing but their support is necessary for its success. Political leaders who seek to implement the law may find themselves having to use pluralist means to fight an ideological battle. This mismatch of tools and problems is a serious dilemma. Pleas for bargaining and compromise are lost on those who are ideologically opposed to busing.

Community leaders also face dilemmas caused by school desegregation. The narrow groups through which they usually work do not influence constituencies broad enough to affect the desegregation process. But attempts to form broad coalitions are likely to founder on the controversiality of the issues involved. Desegregation arouses a breadth of emotion, not consensus.

Unlike storybook battles, dilemmas are not won or lost; unlike puzzles, they are not solved.[57] The relatively successful desegregation of the New Castle County schools has raised a whole new set of problems—the possibility of white flight, how schools in a large district can be responsive to citizen needs, the new power and militancy of the teachers. The resolution of these problems is uncertain, but one conclusion is sure: Educational dilemmas will remain as long as society is made up of groups with conflicting values.

In writing this book, I have tried to do something about what Gary Orfield calls "one of the strange facts about desegregation planning, ... the tendency of each city to face its problems without being aware of solutions developed and lessons learned elsewhere."[58] I hope that other communities will profit from this account of the Delaware experience in the politics of desegregation.

Appendix 1 / Desegregation Plans

Phase 1:
Free-for-All

Author of Plan	Title of Plan	Description of Plan	Submission or Formulation Date
State Board of Education	Six-District Plan	Multidistrict plan with Newark recombined with Appoquinimink	April 10, 1975
Stanton School District	Center School	Grades 3–5 and 7 spend one day per week at centers (e.g., cultural arts); excludes districts not contiguous to city	June 13, 1975
Positive Action Committee	PAC Proposal (Voluntary Plan)	Voluntary transfer or freedom of choice	June 13, 1975
Kaylor, Wolfe, Bynum (citizens)	Delaware Academy Model	County divided into three service areas, high school (grades 11–12 magnet plan)	June 13, 1975
Marshallton-McKean School District		Statement supporting multidistrict plan	June 13, 1975
Maryanne Ennis (Mt. Pleasant parent)	Module	County district with modules where all children attend suburban schools for grades 1–4, 7–8, and high schools are magnet schools	June 13, 1975

Author of Plan	Title of Plan	Description of Plan	Submission or Formulation Date
Claymont School District		Statement supporting voluntary transfer plan	June 13, 1975
League of Women Voters		List of criteria (e.g., financial equity)	June 13, 1975
Wilmington School District	Metro Plan	Maintain local school districts, cluster schools, and list of ancillary issues (e.g., affirmative action)	June 13, 1975
Wilmington School District	Wilmington Only Plan	Redistribute white children within city	June 13, 1975
Wendell Howell	Multiple Option Preference System	County school district with magnet schools	June 13, 1975
De La Warr School District	New Castle County School System	County school district with four regional school attendance areas	June 13, 1975
Conrad Area School District	Voluntary Transfer	Modification of voluntary transfer plan	June 13, 1975
Alfred I. duPont School District	Center Plan	Center plan including all suburban school districts	June 13, 1975
John Zebley (citizen)	Voluntary Plan	Voluntary plan with magnet approach at secondary level	June 13, 1975
Newark School District		Statement on why Newark should not be included and criteria for plan (e.g., districts of 10,000–25,000 pupils)	June 13, 1975
Alexis I. duPont School District	Optional Transfer Plan	Open enrollment plan with 10 percent limit on transfers	June 13, 1975
Greater Wilmington Development Council		Statement favoring a single county district with three areas, each with superintendent	June 13, 1975

Author of Plan	Title of Plan	Description of Plan	Submission or Formulation Date
Community Legal Aid		Statement supporting bilingual programs and variable racial ratios so bilingual and Spanish-speaking programs can be provided	June 13, 1975
Rep. John H. Arnold		One-way busing with volunteers from Wilmington selected first	June 13, 1975
Sen. George F. Schlor	Senate Bill No. 57	County school districts for all of Delaware	June 13, 1975
State Board of Education	Modified Zone Transfer Plan	Five transfer zones with magnet schools and voluntary transfer program in each; retains existing school districts	Sept. 16, 1975
State Board of Education	Five District Reorganization Plan	Multidistrict plan excluding Newark and Appoquinimink	Aug. 4, 1975
State Board of Education	Wilmington Only Plan	Minor modification of Wilmington's version	Aug. 4, 1975
Mt. Pleasant and Conrad School Districts		Include Newark in plan	Dec. 1975

Phase 2:
Interim Board

Author of Plan	Title of Plan	Description of Plan	Submission or Formulation Date
State Legislature	Voluntary Transfer Plan		June 25, 1976
Legislative Committee on Desegregation	Zelon Plan	Secondary magnet schools for gifted in Wilmington and De La Warr with unspecified back up plan	Jan. 26, 1977
Interim Board	Center Plan	Grade Centers (5, 9)	Feb. 1977
Interim Board	ISA Six-District Plan	Multi-district plan	March 31, 1977

Phase 3:
But For

Author of Plan	Title of Plan	Description of Plan	Submission or Formulation Date
State Board of Education	"But For" Plan	One-way busing of students in public housing in city and on one side of the city; school districts maintained	June 16, 1977
State Legislative Committee on Desegregation	"But For" Plan	Reverse voluntarism: all Wilmington students assigned to suburbs unless they opt out	June 24, 1977
State Board of Education	Modified "But For"	One-way busing plan based on legislative plan of reverse voluntarism with expanded boards of education	July 5, 1977
Wilmington School Board	Plan 2	Feeder assignments	July 1977

Phase 4:
New Board

Author of Plan	Title of Plan	Description of Plan	Submission or Formulation Date
Judge Murray Schwartz		Creation of 5-member board to design single district	Aug. 5, 1977
New Castle County Planning Board of Education		Single district with four attendance areas, two consecutive year grade centers	Sept. 30, 1977
Wendell Howell	Plan W	Feeder pupil assignment with variable years bused within single district	Sept. 30, 1977

Phase 5:
Final Order

Author of Plan	Title of Plan	Description of Plan	Submission or Formulation Date
Judge Murray Schwartz	Final Order	Single district 9–3 pupil assignment plan; remedial services; tax rate set	Jan. 9, 1978

Appendix 2 / Positive Action Committee (PAC) Characteristics

PAC by General Attitudes

	PAC Activists	PAC Followers	No PAC
Republican	25%	20%	18%
Republican lean	8%	15%	8%
Independent	24%	17%	18%
Democrat lean	8%	6%	4%
Agree: Over the past few years, the government has paid too much attention to blacks and other minorities	70%	61%	60%
Agree: The amount of prejudice against minority groups in this country is highly exaggerated	65%	55%	53%
Almost never trust the government in Washington to do what is right	34%	17%	21%
Agree: People like me don't have any say about what government does	51%	45%	40%
Agree: It's the duty of the government in Washington to provide jobs for all the unemployed who want to work	43%	38%	40%
Strongly agree: Black people should have the right to live in any neighborhood they choose	30%	28%	17%
Very satisfied with neighborhood quality of public services	61%	37%	43%

PAC by Background Characteristics

	PAC Activists	PAC Followers	No PAC
Income $10,000	9%	10%	13%
Income $10,000–20,000	53%	31%	50%
Income $20,000 +	38%	59%	37%
Protestant	55%	58%	51%
Catholic	40%	32%	31%
Male	36%	39%	42%
Female	64%	60%	57%
Professionals and Managers	23%	35%	26%
Craftsman, Operatives, Laborers	11%	7%	15%
Refused to reveal occupation	56%	40%	41%
College Degree	18%	36%	25%
Some College	31%	24%	22%
High School	51%	40%	53%

PAC by Educational Attitudes

	PAC Activists	PAC Followers	No PAC
Own school district's schools are good or excellent	85%	81%	75%
Almost never or some of the time can trust local school authorities to do what is right	42%	48%	46%
Agree: If enough people show they are against it, busing can be stopped	67%	61%	56%
Agree: The desegregation plan should be obeyed if it is ordered by the courts	49%	68%	63%
Disagree: same item	48%	29%	32%
Dissatisfied with reading, arithmetic, and other basic skills	16%	15%	19%
Strongly oppose two-way busing	79%	69%	57%
Day will come when children in neighborhood will be bused to achieve desegregation	60%	71%	67%
Will come next year	50%	45%	42%

PAC by Desegregation Outcomes

	PAC Activists	PAC Followers	No PAC
Agree: Better education for blacks	19%	22%	39%
Better education for whites	8%	8%	15%
More discipline problems	80%	81%	64%
White flight	91%	92%	75%
Reduce prejudice	10%	16%	34%
White test scores down	69%	53%	41%
Black test scores up	30%	20%	34%
Increase racial tension	87%	79%	73%
More parent problems	84%	75%	66%
Reduce extracurricular activities	88%	87%	71%
Safety risked	91%	78%	74%
Cost high	99%	99%	95%
Less say for parents	85%	75%	66%

Notes

Chapter 1

1. See the U.S. Commission on Civil Rights, *Desegregation of the Nation's Public Schools: A Status Report* (Washington, D.C.: U.S. Government Printing Office, Feb. 1979), for a discussion of pending metropolitan school desegregation cases.

2. Gary Orfield, *Must We Bus? Segregated Schools and National Policy* (Washington, D.C.: Brookings Institution, 1978), p. 196.

3. Steven V. Roberts, "Leaders of Wilmington, Delaware, Seek Smooth Start of Busing," *New York Times*, Feb. 2, 1978; William Trombley, "Strike Perils Busing Plan in Delaware," *Los Angeles Times*, Oct. 30, 1978, pt. 1, pp. 3, 16, 22–24; and Warren Brown, "Teachers' Politics Derail Wilmington Desegregation," *Washington Post*, Nov. 19, 1978, sec. A, p. 8. Among the national media, CBS Television News and the *New York Times* sporadically reported on Wilmington desegregation.

4. Charles V. Willie and Susan L. Greenblatt, "Comparative Community Analysis of the Conflict Resolution Process in School Desegregation," Harvard Graduate School of Education, proposal to the National Institute of Education, 1976; and Robert R. Mayer et al., *The Impact of School Desegregation in a Southern City* (Lexington: D. C. Health, 1974).

Daniel J. Monti and James Laue, "Implementing Desegregation Plans: The Social Scientist as Intervenor," *Education and Urban Society* 9 (May 1977): 369–384; and Gary Orfield, *Must We Bus?* pp. 124–125.

5. Daniel J. Monti, "Examining the Desegregation Process," *Integratededucation* 15 (Nov.–Dec. 1977): 41–46.

6. Christine H. Rossell, "The Mayor's Role in School Desegregation Implementation," *Urban Education* 12, no 3 (Oct. 1977): 247–270. This is a shortened version of her July 1976 processed paper.

7. There are several analyses of the usefulness of social science research for the federal court: *The Courts, Social Science, and School Desegregation,*

vol. 39 of *Law and Contemporary Problems* (Winter 1975), ed. Betty Levin and Willis D. Hawley; and Mary Von Euler. "Meeting the Courts' New Research Needs," *Education and Urban Society* 9 (May 1977): 277–302.

8. There is even a conflict over the best way to describe this policy alternative. Proponents of desegregation argue that "busing" isn't the issue, for many, if not most, suburban children are already bused to school. Opponents of "busing" argue that they oppose the involuntary transfer of children out of their present school attendance area and school district. Most opponents of busing claim that they favor desegregation when it is the result of individual choice but oppose forced desegregation, which they have labeled "busing."

In this book, I have tried to use the words that those involved would use, where appropriate. The reader should not misconstrue my use of the words desegregation or busing to indicate my predilections on this issue. For a negative statement on busing see Edward P. Langerton (pseudonym), *The Busing Coverup* (Cape Canaveral: Howard Allen Enterprises, 1975). For an analysis that presents evidence against busing see David J. Armor, "The Evidence on Busing," *The Public Interest* 28 (Summer 1972): 90–126. For a legal argument against busing see Lino A. Graglia, *Disaster by Decree* (Ithaca, N.Y.: Cornell University Press, 1976). For a more positive statement on busing see U.S. Commission on Civil Rights, *Fulfilling the Letter and Spirit of the Law: Desegregation of the Nation's Public Schools* (Washington, D.C.: U.S. Government Printing Office, Aug. 1976), and the refutation of Armor's work by Thomas F. Pettigrew, Elizabeth L. Useem, Clarence Normand, and Marshall S. Smith, "Busing: A Review of 'The Evidence,'" *The Public Interest* 30 (Winter 1973): 18–118. Armor replies in "The Double Double Standard: A Reply," *The Public Interest* 30 (Winter 1973): 119–131. For a sympathetic and relatively comprehensive analysis of busing see Gary Orfield, *Must We Bus?* For a balanced view of the social scientific evidence see Nancy H. St. John, *School Desegregation: Outcomes for Children* (New York: John Wiley and Sons, 1975). See also Patricia Bates Simun, "Exploding the Myths of School Desegregation," *Integrateducation* 15 (Nov.–Dec. 1977): 59–65.

9. Robert L. Crain, "Why Research Fails to Be Useful," in *School Desegregation: Shadow and Substance*, ed. Florence H. Levinsohn and Benjamin D. Wright (Chicago: University of Chicago Press, 1976), p. 43.

10. For a briefer analysis of the Wilmington metropolitan case see Jeffrey A. Raffel and Barry R. Morstain, "School Desegregation in the Wilmington Metropolitan Area: The Dynamics of Power and Ideology in the Educational Arena," College of Urban Affairs and Public Policy, University of Delaware, Aug. 1978. This work will appear as "Wilmington, Delaware: Merging City and Suburban School Systems," in Charles V. Willie and Susan L. Greenblatt, eds., *Community Politics and Educational Change: Ten School Systems under Court Order* (New York: Longman Publishers, 1980 tentative). See also Jeffrey A. Raffel: "Desegregation Dilemmas," *Integrateducation* 14 (Nov.–Dec. 1976): 38–41; "Political Dilemmas of Busing," *Urban Education* 11 (Jan. 1977): 375–395; and "The Politics of Metropolitan Desegregation: Ordeal by Court Order," *Phi Delta Kappan* 58 (Feb. 1977): 482–488.

David L. Kirp has raised an additional point about the utility of the desegregation literature. According to Kirp, "The desegregation case-study literature is modest in scope and, for the most part, predates the busing controversy." That is, the case studies written in the 1960s and early 1970s when desegregation plans were based on eliminating racial barriers to neighborhood school attendance may be of limited help to those faced with implementing desegregation plans involving the transfer of students outside of their neighborhoods in the 1970s and 1980s. See David L. Kirp, "Race, Politics, and the Courts: School Desegregation in San Francisco," Harvard Educational Review 46, no. 4 (Nov. 1976): 572–611.

Chapter 2

1. For a description of the suburbanization process, see Harry L. Miller and Roger Woock, Social Foundations of Urban Education (Hinsdale, Ill.: Dryden Press, 1973).

2. The demographic statistics reported here are from U.S. Bureau of the Census, Statistical Abstract of the United States: 1977 (98th ed.; Washington, D.C.: U.S. Government Printing Office, 1977). See also Robert A. Wilson and Charles P. Wilson, The Delawareans: Delaware Enters the 1970's (Newark, Del.: By the authors, 1972).

3. Daniel J. Elazar, "Are We a Nation of Cities?" The Public Interest 4 (Summer 1966): 42–58. Elazar concluded that the United States is not a nation of large cities but of moderate cities, small towns, and suburbs within metropolitan areas. Most Americans live in towns and cities with populations of less than 100,000. Most metropolitan areas (as defined by the Census Bureau as a Standard Metropolitan Statistical Area or SMSA) have fewer than 500,000 people.

4. Newark Planning Department, Newark, Delaware: Facts and Figures (pamphlet; Newark, Del.: The Department, Aug. 1978). For an excellent description of Delaware, its government and politics, see Paul Dolan and James R. Soles, Delaware Government (Newark, Del.: University of Delaware Press, 1976).

5. See Jay D. Scribner, ed., The Politics of Education (Seventy-sixth Yearbook of the National Society for the Study of Education, p. 2; Chicago: University of Chicago Press, 1977).

6. Frederick M. Wirt, "School Policy, Culture and State Decentralization," in Scribner, ed., Politics of Education, pp. 164–187.

7. Dolan and Soles, Delaware Government, p. 167. The authors see localism as a major influence throughout Delaware government.

8. Clyde Bishop, "An Analysis of the Delaware Educational Assessment Program," Ph.D. diss., College of Urban Affairs and Public Policy, University of Delaware, June 1976.

9. Some observers of Delaware education have criticized the local school districts as fiefdoms with the local superintendents as the lords of the manor. These critics point to the superintendents' salaries. Superintendents in three of the eleven districts had salaries greater than $50,000 in 1977–1978 and four more were paid over $40,000. These salaries are comparable to those of

superintendents of large school districts in other states with more than ten times as many students. Furthermore, sixteen county school officials earned more than the governor's $35,000 salary. See John Felton and Richard Sandza, "86 Who Are Paid More Than the Governor," *News Journal*, Sept. 25, 1977. pp. 1, 12–14.

10. See, for example, Miller and Woock, *Social Foundations*, pt. 1. In "A Discrete Multivariate Model of Neighborhood Choice" (Discussion Paper D77-5; Cambridge, Mass.: Department of City and Regional Planning, Harvard University, July 1977); David Segal has developed the following table, which shows the diversity across the suburbs as well as differences between the city and the suburban areas:

School District	1970 % College-going	1970 % of Pop. That Is White
Alexis I. duPont	71.0	96.7
Alfred I. duPont	81.3	99.0
Claymont	57.9	97.7
Conrad	37.5	97.6
De La Warr	36.4	66.9
Marshallton-McKean	54.6	94.3
Mount Pleasant	71.4	99.2
New Castle–Gunning Bedford	40.5	95.5
Newark	50.3	96.3
Stanton	50.3	98.3
Wilmington	32.6	55.9
Weighted average for 11 school districts	52.1	86.8

11. The 1973 scores were reported in the *News Journal* as follows:

School District	1973 DEAP Average (Grade 8)
Alfred I. duPont	57.9
Alexis I. duPont	57.1
Mount Pleasant	55.6
Stanton	53.1
Claymont	52.3
Newark	51.6
Marshallton-McKean	51.1
New Castle–Gunning Bedford	50.2
Conrad	49.8
Appoquinimink	48.2
De La Warr	43.0
Wilmington	40.4
State mean	50.0

The source for the scores was the Delaware Educational Assessment Program, as reported in "Supplemental Findings of Fact," brief submitted to U.S. District Court by attorneys for plaintiffs, *Evans v. Buchanan.*

In June 1978, the State Board released school-by-school statewide achievement test scores for 1972–1977. Among elementary schools, seven of the top ten schools were in the Alfred I. duPont school district; the three remaining schools were in the Mt. Pleasant, Stanton, and Alexis I. districts. Eight of the lowest ten were in Wilmington; a ninth in De La Warr. Eight-grade results showed a similar pattern. See Larry Nagengast, "Delaware's Top and Bottom Ten," *Evening Journal*, June 25, 1978, p. A8.

12. Herbert R. Barringer, "Integration in Newark, Delaware: Whatever Happened to Jim Crow?" in *Our Children's Burden*, ed. Raymond W. Mack (New York: Vintage Books, 1968), pp. 141–187.

13. 1975–1976 pupil transportation figures are as follows (Delaware Department of Public Instruction, "Report of Educational Statistics—1975–1976," prepared by Dr. Wilmer E. Wise, Nov. 1976, p. 63):

School District (Enrollment)	Number Pupils Transported	Percentage of Pupils Transported
Alexis I. duPont (3,254)	3,144	96.6
Alfred I. duPont (10,280)	4,875	47.7
Appoquinimink (2,358)	1,808	76.7
Claymont (3,261)	383	12.1
Conrad (5,227)	2,183	41.8
De La Warr (3,073)	1,650	53.7
Marshallton-McKean (3,655)	2,930	80.2
Mount Pleasant (4,805)	2,257	47.0
New Castle–Gunning Bedford (6,890)	6,445	72.5
Newark (16,878)	11,773	69.8
Stanton (5,206)	2,537	48.7
Wilmington (13,877)	2,100	15.1
Total (82,455)	43,625	52.9

14. "September Enrollments" and "Racial Enrollments" are issued annually by the Delaware Department of Public Instruction. DPI also reports private and parochial school enrollments, which are analyzed in Chapter 8. In 1975–1976, 15,070 New Castle County children went to private or parochial schools. About a quarter (3,713) of them lived in Wilmington. About 95 percent of the students in these twenty six Roman Catholic and thirteen private schools are white. Within the state, only 12 percent of the nonpublic-school enrollees attend non-Catholic religious schools (e.g., Fundamentalist, Jewish, Quaker). Among the private schools are the prestigious Wilmington Friends, Tatnall, Tower Hill, and Sanford. All but Tower Hill are located in

the suburbs. They account for almost all of the students in the county in private schools. Several are funded, in part, with DuPont family funds. By far the most students in nonpublic schools in the county are in the Roman Catholic schools. Catholic school enrollments reached their peak in 1963–1964 and decreased through 1975–1976. Private school enrollment increased during this period. Most of the school districts in the county also had enrollment declines because of a lower birthrate. This is discussed in Chapter 8 in relation to preimplementation white flight.

15. Mark Shedd et al., "The Wilmington Public Schools: A Preliminary Needs Assessment," report to the Wilmington Board of Education, April 1973.

16. Ibid., p. 30.

17. Ibid., p. 22.

18. Ibid., p. 10.

19. Dolan and Soles, Delaware Government, pp. 170–171.

20. "School Board Member Says She's Quit," Evening Journal, Feb. 21, 1974.

21. "City Students Show Achievement Gains," Evening Journal, June 30, 1975, p. 9.

22. League of Women Voters of Delaware, Delaware Government (Wilmington: The League, 1976), p. 75:

	Alexis I. duPont District	De La Warr District
Total enrollment	3,311	3,302
Amount of state money	$2,770,598	$2,812,344
Total local tax money	2,045,885	598,913
Amount of federal money	31,318	350,894
Local tax rate per $100 assessment valuation	1.24	1.30
Equalization from state in dollars per student	5.07	52.70
Total amount spent per student per year	1,400	1,173

23. See Robert D. Reischauner and Robert W. Hartman, Reforming School Finance (Washington, D.C.: Brookings Institution, 1973).

24. Norton E. Long, "Political Science and the City," in Urban Research and Policy Planning, ed. Leo P. Schnore and Henry Fagin (Beverly Hills: Sage Publications, 1967), p. 254.

25. The desegregation polls were conducted by the University of Delaware College of Urban Affairs and Public Policy. Both were funded by the Delaware Post-Secondary Education Commission and the College of Urban Affairs. The

first also received financial and editorial assistance from the News Journal Company.

The first poll included 901 interviews taken between March 27 and May 1, 1977. The final sample included 317 Wilmington parents who had at least one child in public school; 300 suburban parents with at lease one child in public school; 75 parents of children in private or parochial schools; and 208 people with no children in school. In the 1978 poll, only parents were interviewed, 303 from the suburbs, 195 from Wilmington, and 76 of private and parochial school children. Most of the interviews were conducted by telephone, although Wilmington residents were interviewed in their homes because over half of them lacked telephones.

Those persons interviewed for the survey were selected through the University of Delaware's random sampling of households in New Castle County. Because there is little recent census information on the characteristics of parents in northern Delaware, it is difficult to determine the accuracy of the sample. However, the sample generally reflects the actual population of parents. A racial breakdown, for example, shows that the first sample had a slightly higher percentage of black parents than the actual enrollment of black students in Wilmington. In the sample, 87 percent of Wilmington parents were black; 1976–1977 school enrollments show that 85 percent of Wilmington students were black. The sample also had a good representation of white parents in the suburbs as school enrollment figures indicate. Ninety-three percent of the suburban parents were white; 91 percent of suburban students were white in 1976–1977.

Given sampling error, the results of questions for both the first Wilmington and both suburban parents groups should be accurate to within ± 5.5 percentage points, and ± 7 points for the second city sample.

Each survey included about 150 questions on school quality, racial attitudes, opinions on school desegregation and background of those interviewed. Interviews averaged thirty minutes.

The surveys were directed by Barry R. Morstain and the author.

The News Journal hired David Armor, a sociologist at the Rand Corporation in Santa Monica, California, to help develop the spring 1977 poll (see Chapter 1, note 8). The News Journal was not involved in the winter 1978 poll.

The following table shows the correspondence between the distribution of public school parents in the suburban school district sample and the actual student enrollment in suburban public school districts. The enrollment figures are from the Department of Public Instruction, Sept. 30, 1977.

A number of reports have been issued by the College of Urban Affairs and Public Policy, University of Delaware, Newark, Delaware, describing the results of these polls. See: Barry R. Morstain, "Parent Views on School Desegregation and Related Educational Issues," March 1978; Jeffrey A. Raffel, "Compliance," Oct. 1977; Jeffrey A. Raffel, "Sources and Levels of Information about Desegregation," Oct. 1977; and Barry R. Morstain, "Parents Who Support Magnet Schools: Some Distinguishing Characteristics," June 1977.

District	Total Public School Children		Parents in Sample	
	No.	%	No.	%
Alexis I. duPont	3,342	5.7	8	2.6
Alfred I. duPont	8,733	14.8	37	12.2
Claymont	2,819	4.8	21	6.9
Conrad	4,344	7.4	19	6.3
De Le Warr	2,388	4.0	11	3.6
Marshallton-McKean	3,136	5.3	22	7.3
Mt. Pleasant	4,514	7.7	23	7.6
New Castle–Gunning Bedford	8,580	14.5	45	14.9
Newark	16,657	28.2	101	33.3
Stanton	4,468	7.6	16	5.3
Total	58,981	(100%)	303	(100%)

Results of the surveys are also reported in the following: John Felton and Larry Nagengast, "Busing and You," *Morning News*, May 15–18 1977; Marlene Z. Bloom, "Parents Admit Buses Will Roll," *Sunday News Journal*, April 23, 1978, pp. A1, A10; and *Sunday News Journal*, April 30, 1978.

26. Gary Orfield, *Must We Bus? Segregated Schools and National Policy* (Washington, D.C.: Brookings Institution, 1978), p. 113. The 1975 Gallup Poll found similar percentages—18 percent in favor and 72 percent opposed to busing. Among blacks, 40 percent were in favor and 47 percent opposed. See "A Busing Turnaround," *Evening Journal*, Oct. 23, 1975, reprinted from *Congressional Quarterly*.

27. *Evening Journal*, Oct. 23, 1975, p. 114.

28. Ibid., p. 115

29. John B. McConahay and Willis D. Hawley, "Is It the Buses or the Blacks? Self-Interest versus Symbolic Racism as Predictors of Opposition to Busing in Louisville," working paper, Duke University, Center for Policy Analysis, Institute of Policy Sciences and Public Affairs, presented at the annual meeting of the American Psychological Association, San Francisco; Aug. 28, 1977.

30. Everett F. Cataldo, Michael W. Giles, and Douglas S. Gatlin, *School Desegregation Policy: Compliance, Avoidance and the Metropolitan Remedy* (Lexington, Mass.: Lexington Books, 1978).

31. Ibid., p. 100.

32. Gary Orfield, "The State of Public Knowledge Concerning Desegregation and Busing" (unpub. paper).

33. To assess the determinants of attitudes toward busing, the responses of white parents to the following questions were combined with responses to the pro-con busing operation: (1) [Have you] joined a group which supports your position? (Won't do, might do, will do, have done). (2) [Have you] participated

in a rally or demonstration? (Won't do, might do, will do, have done). (3) The desegregation plan should be obeyed if ordered by the courts. (Strongly agree, agree, disagree, strongly disagree). The following table shows the correlation of the items with attitudes toward busing among white parents (spring 1977 poll). Figures marked with an asterisk are significant at the .05 level. (The correlation coefficient measures the relation between two variables: -1.0 is a perfect negative relation and $+1.0$ is a perfect positive relation.)

Indicator of Attitude Toward Busing	Index	Two-way Busing	Join Group	Participate in Rally	Obey Order
Two-way busing	.43*	1.00			
Join a group	.77*	.10*	1.00		
Participate in a rally or demonstration	.71*	.05	.44*	1.00	
Obey the order	.61*	.19*	.23*	.25*	1.00

As the table indicates, the index hangs together only in a limited way. The two action items (joining a group, participating in a rally) are not statistically related to the basic attitudinal item on feelings about busing. Similarly, feelings that the court order should be obeyed were only related in a modest way to the three other index items.

34. The *News Journal* printed the following summary of the results of the spring 1977 poll (John Felton and Larry Nagengast, "Busing and You: Suburban Parents Got Higher Marks," May 15, 1977).

Q. The U.S. District Court has ruled that schools in Wilmington are illegally segregated. *True.* Wilmington, 49 percent correct; suburbs, 57 percent correct.

Q. There are 14 school districts in the desegregation area. *False:* There are 11 districts. Wilmington, 15 percent; suburbs, 46 percent.

Q. Desegregation will mean that some white students will be attending mostly all-black schools. *False:* The desegregation ruling says no grade at any school will be more than 35 percent black. Wilmington, 35 percent; suburbs, 47 percent.

Q. The Delaware State Legislature could pass a law to stop court-ordered busing. *False:* State laws cannot supersede federal court orders. Wilmington, 24 percent; suburbs, 54 percent.

Q. The Interim Board of Education has at least one member from every school district in the desegregation area. *True:* Wilmington, 32 percent; suburbs, 54 percent.

Q. The U.S. Supreme Court has already turned down appeals of the Wilmington desegregation case. *True.* Wilmington, 32 percent; suburbs, 53 percent.

Q. The Interim Board of Education recently voted to do away with the present school districts and make just one countywide district for next year. *False:*

The Interim Board's plan would not change the number of school districts until 1978–1979, and the Interim Board favors having six school districts. Wilmington, 19 percent; suburbs, 58 percent.

Q. The added cost of busing alone would be over $10 million per year. *False*: While total desegregation-related costs could exceed $22 million, busing costs are estimated at between $1 million and $2 million. Wilmington, 14 percent; suburbs, 21 percent.

Q. The State Board of Education's reorganization plan would lead to three districts in the desegregation area. *True*. Wilmington, 26 percent; suburbs, 75 percent.

Q. The Interim Board's "center plan" would have students in grades one to eleven go to Wilmington schools next fall. *False*: The plan would assign students in grades five and nine to schools in Wilmington or De La Warr. Wilmington, 36 percent; suburbs, 85 percent.

Following is a summary of correct answers of public school parents to the winter 1978 poll:

Q. A single school district will replace the city and suburban school districts. *True*. Wilmington, 20 percent; suburbs, 65 percent.

Q. Some white students will be going to schools where *most* of the students are black. *False*. Wilmington, 45 percent; suburbs, 48 percent.

Q. All teachers will remain at their current schools. *False*. Wilmington, 51 percent; suburbs, 72 percent.

Q. Most property owners in the desegregation area will have to pay *three* times as much in taxes as a result of the plan. *False*. Wilmington, 24 percent; suburbs, 51 percent.

Q. All schools will have *about* one-quarter black students and three-quarters white students. *True*. Wilmington, 45 percent; suburbs, 62 percent.

Q. School property tax *rates* will be made the same throughout the desegregation area. *True*. Wilmington, 23 percent; suburbs, 40 percent.

Q. The New Castle County Planning Board of Education will decide which schools will be closed. *True*. Wilmington, 52 percent; suburbs, 79 percent.

Q. The *added* cost of *transporting* the students next year will be more than 10 million dollars. *False*. Wilmington, 17 percent; suburbs, 16 percent.

Q. How many years will most Wilmington and De La Warr students spend in suburban schools? *9 years*. Wilmington, 35 percent; suburbs, 62 percent.

Q. How many years will most suburban students spend in Wilmington or De La Warr schools? *3 years*. Wilmington, 34 percent; suburbs, 71 percent.

35. For Wilmington and black parents, the low category referred to those without a high school degree, moderate to those with a high school degree, and high to those with at least some college. For suburban and white parents low referred to a high school degree, moderate to some college education, and high to at least a college degree. The following table gives the percentage in each educational group who were high in desegregation knowledge:

Race	Low	Moderate	High
White	15%	32%	60%
Black	8%	15%	29%

It should be noted that the white "lows" are thus comparable to the black "moderates." Fifteen percent of white and black high school graduates had high information levels.

36. Despite those specific misperceptions, the overall level of desegregation knowledge was not related to attitudes about busing among whites.

The correlation between the knowledge index and the opposition to busing index was not statistically significant among suburban whites ($\gamma = -.05$). However, among Wilmington blacks, opposition to busing was related to information level ($\gamma = -.26$).

Correlation of determinants of busing opposition to the antibusing index can be seen in the following table. Among whites, opposition to busing was measured on the opposition index and the Pearson correlation coefficient is reported. Among blacks, opposition was measured on the pro-con question (1 = Favor, 2 = No Position, 3 = Oppose), and the Gamma correlation is reported. Statistically significant correlations are identified with an asterick.

	Simple Correlation with Opposition to Busing	
Independent Variables	Whites (N = 494)	Blacks (N = 313)
Knowledge/information index	−.05	−.26*
Number of children in public school	.17*	.17
Children's school (1 = public school, 2 = private or parochial, 3 = no children)	−.23*	−.24
Homeownership (1 = Own, 2 = Rent)	−.07	−.14
Racial attitude index	.27*	.05
Age	−.18*	.06
Spouse's education	−.17*	−.18
Income	−.09	−.10
Occupation	0	−.09
Education	−.15	.02

37. The table below summarizes the relation of the independent variables for whites with the opposition to busing index in the relevant multiple

regression. Items marked with an asterisk are significant at the .05 level. The standard error is 2.86; R^2 = .16; F = 6.088.

Variable	Simple R	Beta	Change in R^2
Racial attitude index*	.27	.25	.07
Children's school*	−.23	−.16	.05
Age*	−.18	−.16	.02
Spouse's education	−.17	−.10	
Home ownership	−.07	−.05	
Income	−.09	−.05	
Racial composition of neighborhood	.03	−.04	
Number of children in public school	.17	.02	
Knowledge/information index	−.05	.01	
Occupation	.0	.01	
Education	−.15	.01	

38. Like general attitudes toward busing, threats of flight were related to racial attitudes. Suburban public school parents fell into three categories: "keepers," those who said they would not change their child's school under either circumstance; "flighters," those who would remove their child under either condition; and "contingents," those who would remove their child under one of the two contingencies. As the table below indicates, parental willingness to consider future flight was highly related to the feeling that the government had been paying too much attention to blacks (γ = −.60). Half the "keepers" (50% of 140), three-quarters of the "contingents" (76% of 107), and almost all of the "flighters" (94% of 32) agreed with the statement.

39. McConahay and Hawley, "Is It the Buses or the Blacks?" p. 50.

Chapter 3

1. See James S. Coleman et al., *Trends in School Segregation, 1968–73* (Washington: Urban Institute, 1975); National Institute of Education, "School Desegregation in Metropolitan Areas: Choices and Prospects," conference brochure, March 15–16, 1977; U.S. Commission on Civil Rights, *Statement on Metropolitan School Desegregation* (Washington, D.C.: The commission, Feb. 1977).

See Gary Orfield, *Must We Bus? Segregated Schools and National Policy* (Washington, D.C.: Brookings Institution, 1978), Ch. 12 ("Metropolitan Desegregation"), for a good discussion of various metropolitan segregation cases including Indianapolis, Louisville–Jefferson County, and Detroit. Some advocates of serious consideration of metropolitan desegregation are: Gordon Foster, "Desegregating Urban Schools: A Review of Techniques," *Harvard Educational Review* 73 (Nov. 1975): 417–450; Everett F. Cataldo, Michael

Giles, and Douglas S. Gatlin, "Metropolitan School Desegregation: Practical Remedy or Impractical Ideal?" *Annals of the American Academy of Political and Social Sciences* 422 (Nov. 1975): 97–105; and Orfield, *Must We Bus?* including his discussion of Rep. Preyer's and Sen. Ribicoff's metropolitan desegregation bills on pp. 442–445. For more recent arguments supporting metropolitan desegregation, see the National Project and Task Force on Desegregation Strategies, *School Desegregation and the State Government* (Washington, D.C.: Education Commission of the States, Feb. 1979), and National Project and Task Force on Desegregation Strategies, *Metropolitan School Desegregation: A Report and Recommendations of the National Task Force on Desegregation Strategies* (Washington, D.C.: Education Commission of the States, March 1979).

2. See Foster, "Desegregating Urban Schools"; Marian Wright Edelman, "Winson and Dovie Hudson's Dream," *Harvard Education Review* 45 (Nov. 1975): 417–450; William J. Kritek, "Voluntary Desegregation in Wisconsin," *Intergrated Education* 15 (Nov.–Dec. 1977): 83–86; and Joseph M. Cronin, "City School Desegregation and the Creative Uses of Enrollment Decline," *Integrated Education* 5 (Jan.–Feb. 1977): 10–12.

Robert L. Crowson in "*Hills v. Gautreaux*: Implications for Education," *Phi Delta Kappan* 58 (March 1977): 550–552, concludes that this decision will not greatly increase metropolitan desegregation through housing policy. Orfield in *Must We Bus?* argues that "any major gain in residential desegregation in the near future is unlikely" (p. 89).

3. See Harrell R. Rodgers, Jr., "On Integrating the Public Schools: An Empirical and Legal Assessment," in Rodgers, ed., *Racism and Inequality: The Policy Alternatives* (San Francisco: W. H. Freeman, 1975), pp. 125–160. Things have not been clarified much since Rodgers wrote, "The most important issue presently unanswered by the Supreme Court is exactly how much authority the courts have to devise desegregation plans that cross political boundaries."

4. Orfield, *Must We Bus?* p. 167

5. *Brown v. Board of Education*, 347 U.S. 483 (1954) and 349 U.S. 294 (1955).

6. Richard Kluger, *Simple Justice* (New York: Alfred A. Knopf, 1975), ch. 18 ("Jim Crow, Inc."), p. 540.

7. Ibid., pp. 543, 544.

8. Robert J. Taggart, "Desegregation in Delaware, 1950–1967," *UPDATE* (processed handbook; Newark, Del.: Delaware Committee on the School Decision, fall 1976), pp. 2–3.

9. Kluger, *Simple Justice*, ch. 18.

10. Taggart, "Desegregation," p. 3.

11. Ibid.

12. Ibid.

13. Herbert R. Barringer, "Integration in Newark, Delaware: Whatever Happened to Jim Crow?" in *Our Children's Burden*, ed. Raymond W. Mack (New York: Vintage books, 1968), p. 181.

14. Taggart, "Desegregation," p. 4.

15. Ibid.

16. H. Albert Young, "1954–A Climactic Year in Delaware Educational History," paper presented at the Conference on History of Desegregation in Delaware, University of Delaware, June 1976, p. 6. Young's son was cochairman of the National Conference of Christians and Jews and an active member of a group to work for peaceful implementation appointed by the county executive during Delaware's latest school desegregation crisis (see Chapter 6).

17. Ibid., p. 15.

18. *Evans v. Buchanan*, Civil Action Nos. 1816–1822.

19. See Julie A. Schmidt, "School Desegregation in Wilmington, Delaware: A Case Study in Non-Decision-Making," M.A. thesis, Political Science Department, University of Delaware, June 1979.

20. "Supplemental Findings of Fact," brief submitted to U.S. District Court by attorneys for individual and intervening plaintiffs, Feb. 25, 1974, p. 3.

21. Ibid., p. 64.

22. Ibid., p. 62.

23. Delaware State Code, Title 14, ch. 10 ("Reorganization of School Districts") subch. I ("Reorganization") sec. 1009 ("Salary Schedules"), p. 31.

24. "Supplemental Findings of Fact," attorneys for plaintiffs, p. 66.

25. "Supplemental Findings of Fact," brief submitted to U.S. District Court by State Board of Education, Feb. 22, 1974.

26. *Evans v. Buchanan*, 379 F. Supp. 1218 (D. Del. 1974).

27. Ibid., pp. 12, 13–14.

28. Ibid., Gibbons' dissent, pp. 2, 5–6, 8, 22.

29. *Milliken v. Bradley*. 42 L.W. 5249 (July 25, 1974).

30. Ibid., p. 5258

31. *Evans v. Buchanan*, 393 F. Supp. 428 (D. Del. 1975).

32. Ibid., pp. 8, 13. Also Judge Layton, dissenting, concluded that "in all important respects except size, the facts of *Milliken* and this case are strikingly similar. But *Milliken* is not a rule of size, it is a rule of law" (p. 14). Therefore Judge Layton saw no need for an interdistrict remedy:

"In my view, the majority's findings, so sweeping in effect, so heavy with inferences but so lacking in concrete, relevant substance, have fallen far short of fixing the responsibility for inter-district racial discrimination upon Defendant's shoulders. What the majority does not face up to is that there seems to be no definitive explanation for the huge tide of black immigration into the nation's cities, and the white flight therefrom, in the past two decades.

The evidence to support the contention that state action caused the situation fell flat. Even the Educational Advancement Act should not be considered discriminatory state action, for the limits it drew on Wilmington School District consolidation were based on reasonable principles, and even if one were to view the Act as unconstitutional, it had no interdistrict effects, for it left the status quo" (pp. 5–6).

33. Ibid., p. 13.

34. Ibid., p. 20.

3. The Wilmington School District would be treated fairly for its pupil loss.

4. A sincere effort would be made to attract whites into the Wilmington School District with a magnet program that blacks could attend and not be eliminated by testing.

Wilmington rejected the "compromise" (Larry Nagengast and Sandra Dawson, "Wilmington Rejects Compromise Plan for Desegregation," *Morning News*, July 28, 1977).

64. *Washington v. Davis*, 426 U.S. 229 (1976).

65. Tyll Van Geel, "Two Models of the Supreme Court in School Politics," in *The Politics of Education*, ed. Jay D. Scribner (*Seventy-sixth yearbook of the National Society for the Study of Education*, pt. 2; Chicago: University of Chicago Press, 1977), pp. 124–163. Mary Von Euler, "Meeting the Courts' New Research Needs," *Education and Urban Society* 9 (May 1977): 277–302, argues that the Supreme Court does not see modern America as a land of pervasive racism and therefore requires great proof to show the need for a remedy. The District Court's actions suggest that it shared this optimistic view.

66. Judges Caleb M. Wright and Caleb R. Layton had much in common beyond their names. Both were appointed by President Eisenhower. (Judge Gibbons was a Nixon appointee.) Both were from southern Delaware and had been involved in the Delaware desegregation case since the early 1950s. See "3 GOP Judges, 2 from Sussex County, Reach Decisions," *Evening Journal*, May 20, 1976, p. 14.

67. *Evans v. Buchanan*, 447 F. Supp. 982 (D. Del. 1978), p. 43.

68. Another consequence was that the legal process was a long, time-consuming, and costly battle. One early estimate of the lawyers' fees was $200,000. but the cost of school officials' time and attention was probably far greater.

Chapter 4

1. Julie A. Schmidt, "School Desegregation in Wilmington, Delaware: A Case Study in Non-Decision-Making," M.A. thesis, Political Science Department, University of Delaware, June 1979.

2. "State Vows to Obey Antibias Orders," *Morning News*, Dec. 20, 1974.

3. A modest literature on metropolitan arrangements for school governance exists. See, for example, Basil G. Zimmer and Amos H. Hawley, *Metropolitan Area Schools: Resistance to District Reorganization* (Beverly Hills: Sage Publications, 1968).

The issue of reorganization inspired the legal intervention of the New Castle County Vocational District School Board. This board had authority over Delcastle High School. The Vocational School Board argued that the other vocational schools in the county—that is, the new vocational high schools in Newark and Wilmington—should be merged with the current vocational school into an expanded vocational school district. Although the court was never sympathetic to this request, the State Legislature passed legislation for this merger after Judge Schwartz's final order.

35. Ibid., p. 40, 45.

36. Ibid., pp. 22–24.

37. *Evans v. Buchanan*, 423 U.S. 963 (1975).

38. U.S. Supreme Court, Jan. 19, 1976.

39. This sets the Wilmington, Delaware, case apart from the cases c ton, Dayton, Chicago, etc.

40. *Evans v. Buchanan*, U.S. Supreme Court, Nov. 29, 1976.

41. Orfield, *Must We Bus?* pp. 36 and 398.

42. William Trombley, "Possible Metropolitan Desegregation Plan, *Angeles Times*, Jan. 21, 1979, pt. 1, p. 3.

43. *Evans v. Buchanan*, 393 F. Supp. 428 (D. Del. 1975).

44. See Chapter 4 and the texts of these plans in Delaware Departme Public Instruction, "Desegregation Plans Submitted to the State Boaℓ Education," Aug. 1975.

45. *Evans v. Buchanan*, 424 F. Supp. 875 (D. Del. 1976).

46. Ibid., p. 63. The dissenting judge, Caleb Layton, called the major plan "overkill" because he estimated that 15,000 of the 80,000 students in desegregation area would have to be bused.

47. Memorandum for the United States as *amicus curiae*.

48. *Evans v. Buchanan*, 555 F.2d 373 (3d Cir.); cert. denied, 46 U.S.L 3220 (U.S. Oct. 4, 1977); *Swann v. Charlotte-Mecklenburg*, 402 U.S.1 (19: p. 11.

49. *Evans v. Buchanan*, 3d Cir., p. 8.

50. Ibid., pp. 10–11.

51. Ibid., p. 12.

52. Ibid., Judge Garth's dissent.

53. "Report of the State Board of Education" required by the Opinion aℓ Order of the Circuit Court of Appeals in this case (*Evans v. Buchanan*), Ju 1977.

54. Ibid., p. 9.

55. *Evans v. Buchanan*, 435 F. Supp. 832 (D. Del. 1977).

56. Ibid., pp. 21, 23.

57. Ibid., pp. 31, 42.

58. Ibid., p. 49.

59. *Evans v. Buchanan*, Jan. 9, 1978.

60. *Evans v. Buchanan*, 424 F. Supp. 875 (D. Del. 1976).

61. In Boston, for example, Judge Arthur Garrity had appointed four mas ters and two experts. See Charles W. Case, "History of the Desegregation Plaℓ in Boston," in *The Future of Big City Schools*, ed. Daniel U. Levine and Rober J. Havighurst (Berkeley: McCutchan Publishing, 1977), pp. 153–176.

62. *Evans v. Buchanan*, 424 F. Supp. 875 (D. Del. 1976), pp. 85–86.

63. According to an August 12, 1977, State Board memo, Judge Schwartℓ sought a compromise plan based upon the following:

1. No white children would be bused into Wilmington.
2. The Wilmington School District would survive with black children having a liberal opportunity to attend school in the suburban districts.

4. See Educational Research, Inc., "Summary of Research on Size of Research of Schools and School Districts" (Arlington, Va.: ERS, 1974). This report concludes that the "appropriate size of . . . school districts" will vary from locality to locality, but the professional literature suggests 9,800 to 50,000 as the optimum. The literature on responsiveness, decentralization, community control, and related topics is vast. See Harry L. Miller and Roger Woock, *Social Foundations of Urban Education* (Hinsdale, Ill.: Dryden Press, 1973), ch. 10, for an introduction to this literature. L. Harmon Ziegler, M. Kent Jennings, and Gordon W. Peak, in *Governing Local American Schools: Political Interaction in School Districts* (North Scitnate, Mass.: Duxbury Press, 1974), also offer some interesting conclusions. For an introduction to the issue of equity in school finance see Miller and Woock, *Social Foundations*, ch. 3, and Robert D. Reischauer and Robert W. Hartman, *Reforming School Finance* (Washington, D.C.: Brookings Institution, 1973).

5. U.S. Commission on Civil Rights, *School Desegregation in Ten Communities* (Washington, D.C.: The Commission, June 1973).

6. For example, the "Interim Board Task Force on Finance Report," Dec. 1976, table 1, made the following estimates:

Cost to level up teachers' salaries	$8,873,082
Cost to level up teachers hired from local funds	2,965,934
Cost to level up support personnel salaries	2,439,216
Cost to level up fringe benefits	7,726,719
Total	$22,004,951

7. Tom James, "Teachers, State Politics, and the Making of Educational Policy," *Phi Delta Kappan* 58 (Oct. 1976); 165–168.

8. Gordon Foster, "Desegregating Urban Schools: A Review of Techniques," *Harvard Educational Review* 73 (Nov. 1975); 417–450.

9. In court, one suburban school district strongly argued that the Wilmington School District could be desegregated without them. Newark argued that it was its own metropolitan area, outside the immediate influence of Wilmington. Further, the Newark School District argued that including it in the remedy would hardly affect the average percentage of black students in the schools (24 vs. 20 percent). Two other districts responded that Newark would become a haven for white flight if left out of the plan. (The State Board at first had essentially excluded Newark by combining it with Appoquinimink; later, under pressure from the affected districts, it included Newark.)

The District Court included Newark in its opinion of May 19, 1976, but it said that not all schools had to fall within the 10–35 percent ratio. Factors other than race (such as distance) could lead to some schools being excluded. Of course the problem of drawing an exclusion line remained politically impossible. How could the school farthest from the city be excluded and the one only a mile closer be included? The Newark School Board informally decided to include all its schools if any one school was to be included in a mandatory plan.

The lawyer representing the Wilmington School Board, Louis Lucas, used the conflict between the suburban boards to his client's advantage. Newark, trying to avoid being included in a desegregation plan, used much of its court time to show how a desegregation plan without it would work. Mt. Pleasant, trying to avoid the high percentages of blacks planned for its school in the Wilmington Metro Plan, tried to show how Newark was not too far away from Wilmington to be involved in a busing plan. Lucas showed that both of these approaches supported Wilmington's contention that an interdistrict desegregation plan would be quite feasible. Thus the harder the suburban districts argued their individual cases, the more their evidence helped their major adversary's case.

10. Larry Nagengast, "5–2 Wilmington OK Sends Desegregation Plan to State," *Evening Journal*, June 12, 1975, p. 2.

11. Committee for the Improvement of Education, petition for *amicus curiae* status, Jan. 1976. The Spanish-speaking community intervened in the suit in order to protect the interests of the Spanish-speaking students. Their primary concern was maintaining bilingual programs in the county schools, and the court and parties to the suit agreed to their desires.

12. Charles V. Hamilton, "Race and Education: A Search for Legitimacy," *Harvard Educational Review* 38, no. 4 (Fall 1968): 669–684; and William R. Grant, "Community Control v. Integration—The Case of Detroit," *The Public Interest* 24, (Summer 1971): 62–79. Even one of the original plaintiffs was upset with the final desegregation plan. See Sandra Dawson, "Black Pupil Bus Plan Irks Deseg Leader," *Philadelphia Sunday Bulletin*, Feb. 12, 1978.

13. Interim Board of Education, "Criteria to Measure the Feasibility of Various Administrative Structures," Sept. 30, 1976, pp. 15–17.

14. See William L. Boyd and David W. O'Shea, "Theoretical Perspectives on School District Decentralization," *Education and Urban Society* 7 (Aug. 1975): 375–376, for similar problems in applying the rational model to decentralization alternatives.

15. Research for Better Schools, Inc., *Management Plan for the Court-Ordered Reorganization and Desegregation of a Designated Area of New Castle County* (Philadelphia; RBS, 1976). See also Larry Nagengast, "1½-Inch-Thick Tome Is the County Desegregators' Bible," *Evening Journal*, Nov. 3, 1976, p. 37.

16. See James Q. Wilson and Edward C. Banfield, "Public Regardingness as a Value Premise in Voting Behavior," *American Political Science Review* 58, no. 4 (Dec. 1964): 876–887.

17. One school observer claimed that notices advertising the position of administrative director were not placed throughout the districts. He claimed that the descriptions were concentrated in Newark so that a Newark administrator could be chosen to balance out the power of the rival Alfred I. duPont School District. Throughout the desegregation process the superintendents of these districts battled for the county superintendency.

18. Marlene Z. Bloom, "Desegregation Board Approaches a Nail-Biting Deadline," *News Journal*, Jan. 11, 1977.

19. Larry Nagengast, "Dispute Could Force Merger of 11 School Districts into One," *Evening Journal*, March 7, 1977.

20. Marlene Z. Bloom, "Fighting, Rather Than Planning, Is One Vow of Interim Board," *Morning News*, May 19, 1977.

21. Marlene Z. Bloom, "Court Denies Bid to Delay Desegregation," *Evening Journal*, May 9, 1977.

22. Editorial, "Pick a Plan," *News Journal*, Jan. 9, 1977.

23. Larry Nagengast, "Interim Board Wavers on Plan," *Evening Journal*, March 17, 1977.

24. Wendell Howell, "Statement on Pupil Assignment Plans," Jan. 13, 1977, processed.

25. Isabel Spence, "Integration: Work for a Small Army," *Philadelphia Inquirer*, Dec. 5, 1976.

26. "Values Questioned in Desegregation Decisions," *News Journal*, Feb. 9, 1977.

27. Marlene Z. Bloom, "Suburban Grades 5, 9 to Be Bused," Feb. 11, 1977.

28. Editorial, "Pick a Plan," *News Journal*, Jan. 9, 1977.

29. See Thomas F. Pettigrew, *A Profile of the Negro American* (Princeton, N.J.: Van Nostrand, 1964), for a discussion of the problems of white views of black leadership. For one view of Howell, see Duane Gray, "Howell Reaches for Goals," *Philadelphia Sunday Bulletin*, Jan. 30, 1977. For less sympathetic views, see note 36 below.

30. Wilmington Mayor Maloney and Judge Schwartz both tried to help the parties to the suit find a mutually acceptable plan. Both failed.

31. See Harman Ziegler, Harvey J. Tucker, and L. A. Wilson II, "Communication and Decision Making in American Public Education: A Longitudinal and Comparative Study," in *The Politics of Education*, ed. Jay D. Scribner (*Seventy-sixth Yearbook of the National Society for the Study of Education*, pt. 2; Chicago; University of Chicago Press, 1977), for a discussion of the superintendent as broker.

32. Marlene Z. Bloom, "Carroll Biggs: Man of Many Faces," *Evening Journal*, May 9, 1977.

33. Larry Nagengast, "Closed-door Desegregation Debate Opens Wounds," *Morning News*, Aug. 31, 1977, and Ralph Moyed, "They're Doing Our Business in the Boys' Room," *Evening Journal*, Sept. 1, 1977.

34. *Evans v. Buchanan*, U.S. District Court, Del., Jan. 1978, pp. 81–85.

35. Al Smith, Anthony Downs, and M. Leanne Lachman, *Achieving Effective Desegregation* (Lexington, Mass.: Lexington Books, for the Real Estate Research Corp., 1973).

36. Ralph S. Moyed, "School Deal? Heavens No: An Educational Experience," *Evening Journal*, Jan. 6, 1978; Bill Boyle, "Biggs Gets School Job, Names 8 Aides," *Morning News*, Jan. 5, 1978; Ralph S. Moyed, "Deseg. 'Shuffle' in the Cards for 78?" *Evening Journal*, Jan. 2, 1978.

37. See Isabel Spencer, "Biggs' Methods Assailed by Alexis I. Board Head,"

Morning News, Feb. 2, 1978, and Bill Boyle, "Biggs' Style—A Tight Grip," *Evening Journal*, Feb. 8, 1978.

38. See the description of the Citizens Alliance for Public Education, "Community Communications Plan," Oct. 12, 1976, in Chapter 6.

39. Delaware State Congress of Parents and Teachers, *PTA Newsletter*, vol. 4, no. 4 (Convention Issue; April 1976).

40. Bill Boyle, "Urban and Suburban Parents Join to Get City School Ready," *Evening Journal*, Aug. 23, 1978.

41. Paul Dolan and James R. Soles, *Delaware Government* (Newark: University of Delaware, 1976), p. 167.

42. Affidavit of Carroll W. Biggs, October Term, 1978, U.S. Supreme Court, No. A-188, Sept. 7, 1978. Wilmington Representative Jim Sills filed a brief opposing a stay. See Bill Boyle, "Sills Files Opposition to Delay Busing," *Evening Journal*, Sept. 8, 1978.

43. See Norman R. Luttbeg and Richard W. Griffin, "Tying Elites and Public Opinion Differences to Levels of Public Support: Defeat for the Unrepresentative?" *American Politics Quarterly* 3, no. 2 (April 1975): 107–129. They found that public support was linked to school officials' views only on busing.

Chapter 5

1. See William L. Boyd and David W. O'Shea, "Theoretical Perspectives on School District Decentralization," *Education and Urban Society* 7 (Aug. 1975): 357–376.

2. Special Legislative Committee on Desegregation, "Report to Governor Sherman W. Tribbitt and the Members of the 128th General Assembly" (Dover, Del.: The Committee, Sept. 15, 1975), p. 1.

3. Ibid., app. 4.

4. Ibid., app. 8.

5. Ibid., p. 13.

6. "Senate Kicks Off Amendment to Freeze School Districts," *Evening Journal*, May 1975.

7. "Delaware Citizens Dislike All Desegregation Plans," *Evening Journal*, May 28, 1975.

8. "Battler against Busing," *Philadelphia Inquirer*, April 4, 1976.

9. House Bill 567, July 29, 1977.

10. Kurland recommended Fred Gray—state senator and former attorney general of Virginia and an experienced lawyer on desegregation matters—to help the General Assembly. Gray did speak to the legislature and was also a restraining force.

11. Transcript of the appearance of Philip B. Kurland before the Delaware State Legislature, March 15, 1976.

12. House Bill 1198, signed by Gov. Tribbitt on June 25, 1976.

13. See Robert B. Bresnahan and Hazel I. Showell, "Report on Voluntary Student Transfer Program" (Dover, Del.: Department of Public Instruction, Feb. 1977).

14. Senate Bills 173 and 264, signed by Gov. du Pont in June 1977.

15. Lynn A. Rankin, "Deseg Questions Abound," *Evening Journal*, Sept. 14, 1976.

16. Allen H. Zelon, "Report to the State Legislature: Magnet Schools for New Castle County" (Dover, Del.: Special Legislative Committee on Desegregation, Jan. 1977).

17. Paul Geisel, "Reform in Education: Desegregation as an Opportunity for Change," paper presented to the annual meeting of the Council of University Institutes of Urban Affairs, March 4, 1977, New Orleans.

18. One group ranked the Delaware State Legislature as the third worst state legislature in the nation in 1971. See the Citizens Conference on State Legislatures, "Evaluation of State Legislatures," in *Dimensions of State and Urban Policy Making*, ed. Richard H. Leach and Timothy G. O'Rourke (New York: MacMillan, 1975) pp., 176–189.

19. Special Legislative Committee on Desegregation, "But For Plan."

20. John Felton and Richard Sandza, "Legislators Snub Du Pont's Deseg Bill," *Morning News*, Dec. 14, 1977.

21. Ibid.

22. Ralph S. Moyed, "Howell: '77's Man of the Deal, "*Evening Journal*, Dec. 26, 1977.

23. John Felton, "Vote on Schools Was Victory for Anti-busing Group," *Evening Journal*, Dec. 19, 1977.

24. Lynn A. Rankin and John Felton, "School Tax Formula Set by Senate," *Evening Journal*, Jan. 27, 1978.

25. Sheldon Richman, "House Acts to Form Four Deseg Districts with Units on Taxes," *Evening Journal*, Feb. 9, 1978.

26. Marlene Z. Bloom and Isabel Spencer, "One-District Deseg Plan Is Upheld," *Morning News*, Feb. 17, 1978.

27. *Evans v. Buchanan*, 582 Fed. 2nd 750 (July 24, 1978), p. 51.

28. U.S. Commission on Civil Rights, *Desegregating the Boston Public Schools: A Crisis in Civic Responsibility* (Washington, D.C.: The Commission, 1975); David K. Dunaway, "Urban Desegregation: The Mayor's Influence in the Schools," *Integrateducation* 15, no. 1 (Jan.–Feb. 1977): 3–9.

29. "County Is Unique in Social Services Aid from Sharing," *Evening Journal*, Jan. 16, 1974.

30. See Jeffrey A. Raffel, "Desegregation Dilemmas," *Integrateducation* 14 (Nov.–Dec. 1976): 38–41.

31. "Slawik Opposed to Busing," *Evening Journal*, Feb. 12, 1975. For a discussion of Slawik's legal problems see Ralph S. Moyed, "Slawik Learned about Political Survival the Hard Way," *Evening Journal*, Sept. 15, 1977.

32. Letter dated Feb. 11, 1976, from James A. Venema, president, PAC; response from the governor to Venema on March 24, 1976.

33. Letter from Gov. Sherman W. Tribbitt to constituents, May 3, 1976.

34. Robert L. Durkee, "A History of the State Information Center—1976," unpub., Department of Public Instruction. PAC had accused officials of trying to brainwash the public by means of the Information Center.

35. Murray Dubin, "Court Orders Desegregation of Wilmington Schools," *Philadelphia Inquirer*, July 13, 1974.

36. "Maloney Invokes Tom Paine on Rebellion against Forced Busing." *Evening Journal*, Jan. 5, 1976, p. 6.

37. Advertisement, *Evening Journal*, Oct. 28, 1976.

38. See Ron Williams, " 'Hustler' Maloney Revels in Tempests," *Evening Journal*, Dec. 31, 1975, for a description of Maloney's style.

39. Henry Folsom served as acting county executive after Slawik's removal and before Jornlin's victory. As an interim executive, he took little part in the desegregation process.

40. William Frank, "A New Mayor and His Open Door Policy," *Morning News*, Jan. 10, 1977.

41. Editorial, "Mayor Sees the Danger," *Evening Journal*, May 24, 1977.

42. Hugh Cutler, "Governor Tones Down Wording of Tax Notice," *Evening Journal*, July 16, 1978. The original wording said, "Your school taxes may have substantially increased." The accepted wording eliminated the word "substantially."

43. Edward C. Banfield, *Political Influence: A New Theory of Urban Politics* (Glencoe, Ill.: Free Press, 1961).

44. The Delaware Association for Public Administration, a professional association of public administrators, held a conference (which I arranged) on "The Impact of School Desegregation on State and Local Government in Delaware" to encourage government officials to plan for desegregation. One of the major pluses of the conference was a long discussion between one of Jornlin's top advisors and a guest speaker, Mr. William Belanger, assistant to the county judge (an office like the county executive) in Jefferson County, Kentucky. Christine Rossell was also an influential invited speaker.

45. Gov. Pierre S. du Pont IV, Statement on the Circuit Court of Appeals Desegregation Decision, processed, undated.

46. Gov. Pierre S. du Pont IV, Statement on School Desegregation, speech delivered at the Calvary Baptist Church Banquet, Sheraton Inn, Dover, Del., July 24, 1977.

Gov. du Pont's statements are even more striking when compared with those issued by other political leaders. Harrell R. Rodgers and Charles S. Bullock III ("School Desegregation: A Multivariate Test of the Role of Law in Effectuating Social Change," *American Politics Quarterly* 4, no. 2, [April 1976]: 153–176) gathered some significant quotes from past Southern governors. Gov. Griffin of Georgia said, "Come hell or high water races will not be mixed in Georgia schools"; Gov. Wallace launched his political career with statements like "I draw the line in the dust and toss the gauntlet before the feet of tyranny and I say segregation now, segregation tomorrow, segregation forever." Christine H. Rossell ("The Mayor's Role in School Desegregation Implementation," *Urban Education* 12, no. 3 [Oct. 1977]: 247–270), criticizes Mayor White for saying: "We are all faced with the unpleasant task of implementing a court order. The order must and will be carried out. . . . Compliance with law does not require acceptance of it: tolerance does not require endorsement of law. People who would boycott schools are asked to weigh the decision carefully, but it is their decision to make."

47. "Officials Plan Quietly for Smooth Desegregation Transition," *Evening Journal*, July 14, 1977.

48. Robert McBride, "Information Report—Period Ending September 10, 1978," memo to members of the Effective Transition Commission, processed, Sept. 1978.

49. Bill Boyle, "First String Joins Deseg Commission," *Evening Journal*, Aug. 23, 1978, p. 1.

50. It should be noted that no official's actions will fit only in a single category. I have tried to place each executive according to the major thrust of his or her actions.

51. Everett F. Cataldo, Michael W. Giles, and Douglas S. Gatlin, *School Desegregation Policy: Compliance, Avoidance and the Metropolitan Remedy* (Lexington, Mass.: Lexington Books, 1978), p. 1.

52. Gary Orfield, *Must We Bus? Segregated Schools and National Policy* (Washington, D.C.: Brookings Institution, 1978), pp. 422–423.

53. Dunaway, "Urban Desegregation."

54. Ibid., p. 6.

55. Harrell R. Rodgers' and Charles S. Bullock's application of the cost benefit concept to compliance involves a similar problem (*Coercion to Compliance: Or How Great Expectations in Washington Are Actually Realized at the Local Level, This Being the Saga of School Desegregation in the South as Told by Two Sympathetic Observers—Lessons on Getting Things Done* [Lexington, Mass.: Lexington Books, 1976].

56. Dunaway, "Urban Desegregation," p. 6.

57. Ibid.

58. Rossell, "Mayor's Role," p. 265.

59. "Roth Asks for Delay of Integration Busing," *Evening Journal*, June 30, 1975; and Celia Cohen, "Roth Seeking Anti-Bus Bill Supporters," *Newark Weekly Post*, Feb. 16, 1977.

60. Sen. William Roth, letter to the editor, *Evening Journal*, Sept. 9, 1978.

61. See Orfield, *Must We Bus?* for a discussion of Biden's role in the U.S. Senate on this issue. See Orfield, p. 263, for a discussion of this particular bill.

62. Norman Lockman, "Biden's Excessive Reaction," *Evening Journal*, Dec. 19, 1974, p. 30.

63. Orfield, *Must We Bus?* pp. 106, 273.

64. Jim Panyard, "Busing Cost Small, Biden Says," *Philadelphia Sunday Bulletin*, April 24, 1977.

65. Orfield, *Must We Bus?* p. 354.

66. Ibid.

67. Ibid., p. 316–317.

68. "Administration Enters Desegregation Case," *News Journal*, April 23, 1977.

69. Pat Ordovensky, "Carter: Biden's Deseg Bill 'Unnecessary,' " *Evening Journal*, July 21, 1977.

70. See Pat Ordovensky, "More Deseg Funds Available?" *Morning News*, March 10, 1978; "Officials Closer to Deseg Monies," *News Journal*, April 8,

1978; and Pat Ordovensky, "HEW Will Help Pay the Freight for Deseg," *Evening Journal*, May 5, 1978.

71. Ralph S. Moyed and Pat Ordovensky, "Venema Tests the Waters; Biden's Plans Uncertain," *Sunday News Journal*, May 15, 1977.

72. Peter Leo, "He Seeks Harmony on Civil Battlefields," *Evening Journal*, Oct. 27, 1977.

73. See Ben Holman, "Desegregation and the Community Relations Service," *Integrateducation* 13, no. 1 (Jan.–Feb. 1975): 27–29.

74. The suburban districts did utilize the services of the University of Pittsburgh center in the final year, but suburban criticism of the center was harsh. Some thought the center staff were simply not competent; others thought that they did not understand the situation enough to be able to help.

75. Isabel Spencer, "District Gets Busing Funds," *News Journal*, Sept. 9, 1978, p. 17.

76. In general, the county and municipal councils tried to stay clear of the desegregation controversy. County Council did pass a resolution favoring a county school district and a single property tax, but this brought on unwanted pressure and from then on it tried to keep aloof from the issue.

Chapter 6

1. Al Smith, Anthony Downs, and M. Leanne Lachman, *Achieving Effective Desegregation* (Lexington, Mass.: Lexington Books, 1973).

2. The NCCJ is considered as a religious organization because the three cochairpersons were selected from Protestant, Roman Catholic, and Jewish religious groups in Delaware; the offices were located in a church; its primary goal involved human interaction and relations; its central motivating force seemed to be a moral one; and a majority of its leaders had strong religious ties. The NCCJ was not entirely a religious body, however, in that prominent business and professional leaders also played an important role in its activities and provided financial support. Similarly, DEEP was an outgrowth of the Urban Coalition but once on its own feet it seemed primarily powered by religious motives.

3. For an earlier statement, see "Delmarva Churches Act to Ease Desegregation Fear," *Evening Journal*, Feb. 5, 1975; for a later one, see "Call to Peaceful Desegregation," *Morning News*, Nov. 18, 1977.

4. Among the activities: the Roman Catholic Church published strong rules and regulations to minimize the use of its parochial schools as a means of white flight. Individual congregations of different churches held coffees or discussion groups and informational meetings across city/suburban lines to illuminate the desegregation situation. One interfaith council of fourteen congregations of various bodies issued a statement on the decision, encouraged meetings at individual churches and synagogues, contributed funds for a newsletter on desegregation, and distributed information to member congregations. The more conservative unaffiliated churches were not involved in these efforts.

5. Raymond A. Bauer, Ithiel de Sola Pool, and Lewis Anthony Dexter, *American Business and Public Policy* (New York: Atherton Press, 1963), and James Phelan and Robert Pozen, *The Company State* (New York: Grossman Publishers, 1971).

6. Bauer, Pool, and Dexter, *American Business*, p. 265, 267, 270, 275.

7. Ralph Nader, "Introduction" in Phelan and Pozen, *Company State*, p. ix.

8. Ibid., p. x; see Kenneth Dolbeare, "Public Policy Analysis and the Coming Struggle for the Soul of the Postbehavioral Revolution," in *Power and Community: Dissenting Essays in Political Science*, ed. Philip Green and Sanford Levinson (New York: Vintage Books, 1970), pp. 85–111 for a similar discussion concerning the study of the political process vs. the effects of policy.

9. See, for example, William E. Connolly, *The Bias of Pluralism* (New York: Atherton, 1973).

10. Phelan and Pozen, "Urban Renewal Incorporated: Greater Wilmington Development Council," *Company State*, pp. 177–203.

11. See Timothy K. Barnekov and Daniel Rich, "Privatism and Urban Development: An Analysis of the Organized Influence of Local Business Elites," *Urban Affairs Quarterly* 12, no. 4 (June 1977): 431–460. The GWDC generalizations are based in part on their work, the specifics on the work of Phelan and Pozen.

12. Barnekov and Rich, "Privatism," p. 441.

13. Larry Nagengast, "Business Group Counsels Peaceful Integration," *Morning News*, June 13, 1976; Phelan and Pozen, *Company State*, p. 242.

14. See Smith, Downs, and Lachman, *Achieving Effective Desegregation*, on the need for business assistance; on the nonparticipation of business, see Lorraine M. McDonnell and Gail L. Zellman, "The Roll of Community Groups in Facilitating School Desegregation," paper presented at the 1978 annual meeting of the American Political Science Association, New York City, Aug. 31–Sept. 3, 1978. McDonnell and Zellman studied 131 community organizations located in 40 school districts throughout the country. New Castle County was one of the communities studied and so their results are based partly on the Wilmington metropolitan case. Among their conclusions: "In a majority of communities undergoing school desegregation, the business community has avoided involvement in the process."

It should also be noted that McDonnell and Zellman omit religious groups or universities from their list of groups most often involved in desegregation (pp. 4–5). They do list "traditional civil rights organizations, namely the NAACP and Urban Leagues; public interest groups, notably the League of Women Voters; civic or business elite groups like the Chamber of Commerce or area development councils, umbrella organizations which are usually *ad hoc* coalitions of a variety of community groups; court-appointed monitoring bodies; social service delivery organizations."

15. John Egerton, *Promise of Progress: Memphis School Desegregation, 1972–1973* (Atlanta: Southern Regional Council, June 1973), p. 9.

16. Mimeographed materials from Greenville Chamber of Commerce supplied by SANE, Inc., of Delaware.

17. Entry of PRO-Detroit, 32nd Annual Silver Anvil Awards Competition.

18. Charles W. Case, "History of the Desegregation Plan in Boston," in *The Future of Big City Schools*, ed. Daniel U. Levine and Robert J. Havighurst (Berkeley: McCutchan Publishing, 1977), pp. 153–176.

19. Phelan and Pozen, *Company State*, p. 115.

20. Anyone who wishes to convey information about Delaware to Delaware faces a difficult task because the state lacks its own commercial television station. Although Philadelphia television stations occasionally cover a Delaware news story and Delaware's educational channel has a nightly news program, most residents of New Castle County get their local news from radio or the Wilmington News Journal papers, the *Morning News* and *Evening Journal*. The spring 1978 poll indicated a great reliance on the newspapers for desegregation news among all kinds of New Castle County residents.

The *News Journal*'s editorials supported desegregation through busing, the establishment of a county school district, and peaceful implementation. Its news columns, however, gave much space to PAC and its activities as well as to groups seeking a smooth desegregation process. The *News Journal*, like other papers, found news in conflict. With only occasional lapses, the *News Journal* covered all desegregation events. As the start of busing approached, the paper reported the details of the student assignment plan in a special supplement, passed along the telephone number of the countywide desegregation Information Center, and gave special prominence to the answer of each week's most frequently asked question. During the first week of desegregation the paper assigned over thirty reporters to the story. Reporters checked with the principal of each school twice a day.

Local radio stations through their talk shows provided easy access for those on all sides of the issue, but their newscasts often suffered from factual inadequacies and were over-dependent on official spokespersons and newspaper sources. The local educational television station covered the issue fully and presented lucid analyses, but the percentage of Delawareans who watched the educational channel was not high. Before September 1978, the Philadelphia television stations produced a few panel shows on the issue, but more were shown at 6 A.M. than in prime time. During the first week of school each of the Philadelphia channels rode the bus with specific black and white children on the way to their new schools (my daughter, Allison, was one of the children).

21. Marlene Z. Bloom, "Deseg Ad Campaign Arouses Criticism," *Morning News*, July 14, 1977.

22. Bloom, "Deseg Ad Campaign," and Larry Nagengast, "Business Group Counsels Peaceful Integration."

23. Although GWDC pressed for a plan that would create a county district and the religious community pressed for a plan fair to blacks, a specific proposal was not a major concern of either sector.

24. Most of the generalizations about the religious and business sectors applied to groups active in other areas. The positive roles played by the following organizations should be noted.

Both the Greater Wilmington and Newark League of Women Voters kept their members informed through written information and meetings. Both supplied leaders to community organizations and coalitions. The Newark League helped to establish CARE, a Newark School District group for peaceful implementation. Both leagues supplied scores of volunteers for the Information Center.

The University of Delaware's College of Education conducted teacher training programs through the Desegregation Institute, an arm established for the New Castle County School situation. The college also conducted a program in community education, which helped parents to organize around this issue. The College of Urban Affairs at the University not only supported my activities but also helped to develop and operate the computer work necessary to complete the student assignment plan. Pupil information from the eleven school districts had to be merged before a plan could be put in place. Staff at the college also provided technical assistance on this issue to the Wilmington Home and School Council through the Parent Education Resource Center.

25. Executive Order No. 65.

26. Jeffrey A. Raffel, "Coffee, Tea, or Busing," unpub. paper, University of Delaware, 1978.

27. Robert Salisbury, "School Politics in the Big City," *Harvard Educational Review* 37 (Summer 1967): 408–424, made this argument with respect to city schools and administrations, but it seems to have held for the DCSD as an advisory body at the state and local level.

28. Senate Joint Resolution No. 25, June 8, 1977, sponsors: Sen. Thomas Sharp and Rep. William Oberle.

29. For an analysis of community coalitions in other communities and a report of this conference see Community Relations Service, U.S. Department of Justice and National Center for Quality Integrated Education, *Desegregation without Turmoil: The Role of the Multi-Racial Community Coalition in Preparing for Smooth Transition* (New York: National Conference of Christians and Jews, 1977).

30. See the Citizens Alliance for Public Education, "Community Communications Plan," Oct. 12, 1976.

31. See Marlene Z. Bloom, "State PTA Schucking Its Tea-and-Cookies Image," *Evening Journal*, Nov. 1975; and Lisa Monty, "Betty Lewis Is Positive about Desegregation," *Morning News*, May 7, 1978.

32. McDonnell and Zellman argue that past researchers have "side-stepped the issue of measuring the actual impact of a group and have instead examined the internal effectiveness of organizations" ("The Role of Community Groups," p. 20).

33. McDonnell and Zellman view such changes as more significant than others (ibid., p. 22). They argue that causing changes beyond an organization's

contacts, influencing a governmental agency to deliver service, and causing institutional change are significant impacts that may be achieved by community organizations.

34. Christine H. Rossell, "The Mayor's Role in School Desegregation Implementation," *Urban Education* 12 (Oct. 1977): 247–270.

35. See Steven V. Roberts, "Leaders of Wilmington, Del., Seek Smooth Start of Busing," *New York Times*, Feb. 2, 1978, and William Trombley, "Strike Perils Busing Plan in Delaware," *Los Angeles Times*, Oct. 30, 1978, pt. 1 p. 3.

Chapter 7

1. For a description of Venema and other PAC leaders see Peter Leo, "Specter of Busing Hits Raw Suburban Nerve," *Evening Journal*, Dec. 21, 1975, and Bob Frump, "Antibusing Group Leader Sold Cosmetics," *Philadelphia Sunday Bulletin*, July 20, 1975.

2. James A. Venema, "Robin Hoodism and Its Perils," *Evening Journal*, Aug. 9, 1977.

3. "PAC Say Officials Go Too Far in Desegregation Planning," *Evening Journal*, June 29, 1977.

4. Leo, "Specter."

5. William D'Onofrio, "Citizen Column," Newark *Weekly Post*, Dec. 15, 1976.

6. Leo, "Specter."

7. Ibid.

8. Bill Oberle, letter to the editor, *Evening Journal*, Jan. 7, 1976.

9. Bob Whitcomb, "Desegregation Planning Looks toward September," *Evening Journal*, July 23, 1975.

10. "Mr. Venema's Welcome Words" (editorial), *Evening Journal*, Nov. 1975.

11. "PAC Say Officials Go Too Far."

12. "Antibusing Group Raps Legislature," *Evening Journal*, Aug. 1974.

13. Marlene Z. Bloom, See "Deseg Hearing Stirs Wide Spectrum," *Morning News*, Sept. 29, 1976; and "34 Give Views on Deseg. Plan: 25 Are Opposed," *Evening Journal*, June 3, 1975.

14. "Group urges Voluntary Pupil Shifts," *Evening Journal*, June 12, 1975.

15. See Peter Leo, "Name Revealed, Cover Blown for 'Busing Coverup' Author," and "Where Is Author's $2 Million in Grants?" *Evening Journal*, June 14 and 20, 1977. See also Edward P. Langerton, *The Busing Coverup* (Cape Canaveral: Howard Allen Enterprises, 1975).

16. Lynn A. Rankin, "Venema Admits Trip Aid from Allegedly Racist Fund," *Morning News*, Oct. 21, 1977.

17. Marlene Z. Bloom, "Boston Antibusing Rally Draws 50," *Sunday News Journal*, Aug. 21, 1977.

18. Letter from James A. Venema, president, PAC to "All United States Senators," Dec. 1, 1975.

19. See Paul E. Peterson's description of ideological conflict, in *School Politics: Chicago Style* (Chicago: University of Chicago Press, 1976), pp. 51–53.

20. A fascinating but difficult question arises from this analysis of the characteristics of those active in PAC: did their strong antibusing attitudes and actions, which differentiate them from their suburban peers, cause or follow from their PAC activity? That is, did those suburban parents who felt most strongly against busing join the antibusing organization to show their opposition, or did those who happened to come into contact with PAC become hardened against busing as a result? Given the cross-sectional nature of the poll, we do not know the extent to which either possibility is true.

21. See Murray Edelman, *The Symbolic Uses of Politics* (Urbana, Ill.: University of Illinois Press, 1964).

22. This has been true in other communities. See John Hillson, *The Battle of Boston: Busing and the Struggle for School Desegregation* (New York: Pathfinder Press, 1977).

23. Gail Stuart, "Legislators Stand Steadfast against Busing," Newark *Weekly Post*, Dec. 1–7, 1976.

24. My conclusions raised a stir when they were publicized by the Newark *Weekly Post* in June 1977. One retort was that PAC's influence was stronger than that of other interest groups like teacher organizations and unions. That may have been true; the small influence involved was difficult to measure. Certainly the election results did not bear out statements such as one by PAC's president, Jim Venema: "In some cases, we've been told, the lack of a PAC endorsement will be the 'kiss of death' come November." See Celia Cohen, "Study Claims PAC Had Little Election Influence," Newark *Weekly Post*, June 1, 1977; William D'Onofrio, "Citizen Column," Newark *Weekly Post*, June 22, 1977; and my reply, "Citizen Column," June 29, 1977.

25. See "Venema Gets Top Regional GOP Post," *News Journal*, Dec. 9, 1978; and Richard Sandza, "Baxter, Venema Still Feuding," *Evening Journal*, Nov. 8, 1978.

26. Ralph Moyed, "Ironically Venema Must Get Credit for the Smooth Busing," *Sunday News Journal*, Sept. 17, 1978.

In spring 1978, Concerned Parents for Childrens' Rights was formed as a result of the student demonstrations. Leaders promised that their group would be a more aggressive alternative to PAC, especially in using demonstrations. Although they staged a few small protests, the group ultimately worked within the school district citizen committee system. No other antibusing group could gain any momentum.

Chapter 8

1. Karen Shofield, "Desegregation Begins Quietly, Peacefully," Newark *Weekly Post*, Sept. 13, 1978, p. 1; "School Opening Draws High Marks," *Morning News*, Sept. 12, 1978; Phil Milford, "Police 'Happily Bored' with Deseg Implementation," *Morning News*, Sept. 14, 1978; "Teachers, Students

Delighted," *Evening Journal*, Sept. 12, 1978, p. 3; "First Day Is Breeze: 4th R Is for Routine," *Evening Journal*, Sept. 12, 1978; "Busing: 3 Days' Practice Makes (Almost) Perfect," *Morning News*, Sept. 13, 1978.

2. "A Lesson in Wilmington," KYW–TV 3/KYW Radio editorial, broadcast Sept. 13–14, 1978. National networks also praised Delaware and interviewed officials in Los Angeles, where desegregation began a few days later, who indicated that Delaware showed them the peaceful way.

3. "Early-bird Earl Boards, Bides Time," *Morning News*, Sept. 12, 1978.

4. "Busing: 3 Days' Practice."

5. Ray Goldbacher, "50% of Pupils Stay Away from Conrad," *Evening Journal*, Sept. 15, 1978.

6. Gary Orfield, *Must We Bus? Segregated Schools and National Policy* (Washington, D.C.: Brookings Institution, 1978), pp. 3, 5.

7. James S. Coleman, "Integration, Yes; Busing, No," *New York Times Magazine*, Aug. 24, 1975, p. 10.

8. James S. Coleman, Sarah D. Kelley, and John A. Moore, *Trends in School Segregation, 1968–73* (Washington, D.C.: Urban Institute, Aug. 1975); and Thomas F. Pettigrew and Robert L. Green, "School Desegregation in Large Cities: A Critique of the Coleman 'White Flight' Thesis," *Harvard Educational Review* 46, no. 1 (Feb. 1976): 1–53.

9. Everett F. Cataldo, Michael W. Giles, and Douglas S. Gatlin, *School Desegregation Policy: Compliance, Avoidance and the Metropolitan Remedy* (Lexington, Mass.: Lexington Books, 1978).

10. John Egerton, *Promise of Progress: Memphis School Desegregation, 1972–1973* (Atlanta: Southern Regional Council, June 1973), p. 7.

11. W. Vance Grant and C. George Lind, *Digest of Educational Statistics, 1977–78* (Washington: National Center for Educational Statistics, 1978).

12. Peter J. Bachman, *Dropout Follow-up Report* (Dover, Del.: Dept. of Public Instruction, May 1978).

13. For examples of cohort analysis see James Bosco and Stanley Robin, "White Flight from Court-Ordered Busing?" *Urban Education* (April 1974), pp. 87–98, and "White Flight from Busing? A Second, Longer Look," *Urban Education* (Oct. 1976); pp. 263–274.

14. David J. Armor, "White Flight, Demographic Transition, and the Future of School Desegregation" (Santa Monica, Calif.: Rand Corp., Aug. 1978).

15. There were 19,917 whites 4 years old or less in New Castle County in 1950. In 1960 the cohort—those whites aged 10–14 years—numbered 24,555. The corresponding figures were 32,390 and 35,591 for 1960 and 1970. In Armor's terms, the retention rate decreased from 1.23 to 1.10 but remained positive.

16. The minutes of the Nov. 22, 1978, meeting of the Population Consortium of WILMAPCO describe the methodology for the Bureau of the Census projections.

17. See U.S. Bureau of the Census, "Estimates of the Population of Delaware Counties and Metropolitan Areas: July 1, 1976 (Revised) and 1977

(Provisional)," ser. P-26, nos. 77–78, issued July 1978, and the corresponding publications for Pennsylvania and New Jersey.

18. Armor, "White Flight."

19. Several analysts have used projection methods based on enrollment history rather than breakdowns of birthrate and private school enrollments. Edward C. Ratledge of the College of Urban Affairs and Public Policy at the University of Delaware made two such projections for 1978 based on 1972–1977 enrollments for the new school district. Ratledge projected enrollments of 66,238 to 66,776 for September 1978. The actual enrollment in the county district was 63,558, about 3,000 or 5 percent less. This is a loss of about 6 percent of the white enrollment, the lower white flight estimate derived in the text.

20. Armor, "White Flight," p. 38.

21. Jack McCurdy, "Desegregated L.A. Schools Lose 15% of Their White Students," Evening Journal, Oct. 27, 1978.

22. One analysis found that flight was greater during the years suburban students were to be bused. See Larry Nagengast, " 'White Flight' Trend Tied to School Busing Years," Sunday News Journal, Feb. 25, 1979, p. 1.

23. Sandra Dawson, "Black Pupil Bus Plan Irks Deseg Leader," Philadelphia Sunday Bulletin, Feb. 12, 1978. Mrs. Richardson died soon after this interview and before the desegregation plan began.

24. Committee on Excess School Capacity, "Interim Report," submitted to the New Castle County Board of Education, Dec. 12, 1977.

25. As a result of the lowering of the high city property tax rate financing the schools, Mayor McLaughlin proposed reducing property taxes by 20 cents per 100 dollars. The mayor also proposed reducing the controversial city wage tax, which was disliked by suburban residents and their legislators. Finally, the mayor proposed spending some of the school tax saving on other municipal services. It was estimated that 1.25 million dollars would be tied to the property tax cut, 1.65 million would be tied to the lowering of the wage tax, and 0.6 million would be diverted to other services. See "City's Budget Gives Suburbs Tax Break Too," Evening Journal, April 4, 1978.

It should be noted that the De La Warr tax rate in 1977–1978 was an anamoly and was later reduced. The voluntary transfer plan led to extraordinary expenses for De La Warr, which had to pay "tuition" to the districts into which its students transferred. Later in the year the State Legislature appropriated additional funds for the De La Warr district, allowing De La Warr to lower its tax rate.

26. For a more complete analysis of the teachers' strike in New Castle County in fall 1978, see Jeffrey A. Raffel, "Teachers' Strike," College of Urban Affairs and Public Policy, University of Delaware, Feb. 1979, processed.

27. Research on the impact of desegregation in New Castle County is continuing. In spring 1979, for example, I directed a third poll of suburban and city public and private school parents. Approximately 200 parents who transferred their children out of the public schools, 400 suburban parents

previously interviewed in 1977 or 1978, and 200 city parents were interviewed.

Chapter 9

1. Richard Nelson, *The Moon and the Ghetto: An Essay on Public Policy Analysis* (New York: W. W. Norton, 1977).

2. Aaron Wildavsky, "The Political Economy of Efficiency: Cost-Benefit Analysis, Systems Analysis, and Program Budgeting," *Public Administration Review* 26 (Dec. 1966): 292–310.

3. Robert Sowell, "Linear Programming Systems for Pupil Assignment Planning," paper presented to the Council of University Institutes of Urban Affairs, New Orleans, March 4, 1977.

4. John A. Finger, Jr., "Why Busing Plans Work," in *School Desegregation: Shadow and Substance* ed. Florence H. Levinsohn and Benjamin D. Wright (Chicago: University of Chicago Press, 1976), pp. 58–66.

5. Charles Dolezal, Ray Cross, and Ronald Howard, "The Use of Computers for Student Assignment in Desegregation," *Integrateducation* 14 (July–Aug. 1976): 8–10; and Ronald Ozio, "Corpus Christi," *Integrateducation* 15 (Nov.–Dec. 1977): 5–8. See Gary Orfield, *Must We Bus? Segregated Schools and National Policy* (Washington, D.C.: Brookings Institution, 1978), pp. 136–137, 144, 187, for a discussion of computer modeling for desegregation.

6. Nelson, *Moon and Ghetto*, p. 75.

7. Recommendations based upon the organizational model are strongly emphasized in William H. Banks, Jr., "What to Do until the Court Order Comes," *Phi Delta Kappan* 58 (March 1977): 557–561, and Alan C. Ornstein, *Reforming Metropolitan Schools* (Pacific Palisades, Calif.: Goodyear Publishing, 1975), ch. 5 ("School Desegregation"), pp. 157–192.

8. Dale Mann, "The Politics of Representation in Educational Administration," *Education and Urban Society* 6 (May 1974): 297–317.

9. U.S. Commission on Civil Rights, *Desegregating the Boston Public Schools: A Crisis in Civic Responsibility* (Washington, D.C.: the Commission, 1975).

10. U.S. Commission on Civil Rights, *Fulfilling the Letter and Spirit of the Law: Desegregation of the Nation's Public Schools* (Washington, D.C.: The Commission, Aug. 1976).

11. Al Smith, Anthony Downs, and M. Leanne Lachman, *Achieving Effective Desegregation* (Lexington, Mass.: Lexington Books, for the Real Estate Research Corp., 1973).

12. Garley A. Forehand and Marjorie Ragosta, *A Handbook for Integrated Schooling* Washington, D.C.: U.S. Office of Education, July 1976).

13. Gary Orfield, "How to Make Desegregation Work: The Adaptation of Schools to Their Newly-Integrated Student Bodies," *Law and Contemporary Problems* 39 (Winter 1975): 314–340.

14. Ibid., p. 316.

15. U.S. Office of Education and the Council of Chief State School Officers, *Take a Giant Step: Recommendations of a National Conference on Successful Desegregation* (Washington, D.C.: U.S. Government Printing Office, 1977).

16. Roscoe C. Martin, "School Government," in *Governing Education: A Reader on Politics, Power, and Public School Policy*, ed. Alan Rosenthal (New York: Anchor Books, 1969), pp. 278–279. For a more recent study confirming many of Martin's conclusions see L. Harmon Ziegler, M. Kent Jennings, and Gordon W. Peak, *Governing Local American Schools: Political Interaction in School Districts* (North Scituate, Mass.: Duxbury Press, 1974). For similar conclusions regarding school systems in large cities see Marilyn Gittell and T. Edward Hollander, *Six Urban School Districts: A Comparative Study of Institutional Response* (New York: Frederick A. Praeger, 1968); Marilyn Gittell, *Participants and Participation: A Study of School Policy in New York City* (New York: Frederick A. Praeger, 1967); and David Rogers, *110 Livingston Street: Politics and Bureaucracy in the New York City School System* (New York: Vintage Books, 1969).

17. See Christine H. Rossell, "The Mayor's Role in School Desegregation Implementation," *Urban Education* 12, no. 3 (Oct. 1977): 250–251.

18. Horst W. J. Rittel and Melvin M. Webber, "Dilemmas in a General Theory of Planning," *Policy Sciences* 4 (1973): 155–159.

19. For a view explaining education's focus on process and the effects of this orientation, see Willis D. Hawley, "If Schools Are for Learning, the Study of the Politics of Education Is Just Beginning." in *Politics of Education*, ed. Jay D. Scribner (*Seventy-sixth yearbook of the National Society for the Study of Education*, pt. 2; Chicago: University of Chicago Press, 1977), pp. 319–334. A literature of the politics of implementation is just emerging. See, for example, Erwin C. Hargrove, *The Missing Link: The Study of the Implementation of Social Policy* (Washington, D.C.: Urban Institute, 1975); Jeffrey L. Pressman and Aaron Wildavsky, *Implementation* (Berkeley: University of California Press, 1973); and Jerome T. Murphy, "Title I of ESEA: The Politics of Implementing Federal Education Reform," *Harvard Educational Review* 41 (Feb. 1971): 35–63.

20. Kenneth M. Dolbeare, "Public Policy Analysis and the Coming Struggle for the Soul of the Postbehavioral Revolution," in *Power and Community: Dissenting Essays in Political Science*, ed. Philip Green and Sanford Levinson (New York: Vintage Books, 1970), pp. 85–111.

21. See, for example, Robert L. Crain, *The Politics of School Desegregation* (Chicago: Aldine Publishing Co., 1968); David Kirby et al., *Political Strategies in Northern School Desegregation* (Lexington, Mass.: D. C. Heath 1973); and Paul E. Peterson, *School Politics: Chicago Style* (Chicago: University of Chicago Press, 1976).

22. Kirby et al., *Political Strategies*, p. 34.

23. Harrell R. Rodgers, Jr., and Charles S. Bullock III, *Coercion to Compliance: Or How Great Expectations in Washington Are Actually Realized at the Local Level, This Being the Saga of School Desegregation in the South as Told by Two Sympathetic Observers—Lessons on Getting Things Done* (Lexington, Mass.: Lexington Books, 1976); Frederick M. Wirt. *Politics of Southern Equality: Law and Social Change in a Mississippi County* (Chicago: Aldine Publishing, 1970); J. W. Peltason, *Fifty-Eight Lonely Men: Southern Federal Judges and School Desegregation* (New York: Harcourt, Brace, and World,

1961). For an analysis of individual rather than school district compliance, see Everett F. Cataldo, Michael W. Giles, and Douglas S. Gatlin, *School Desegregation Policy; Compliance, Avoidance and the Metropolitan Remedy* (Lexington, Mass.: Lexington Books, 1978).

24. See Beryl A. Radin, *Implementation, Change, and the Federal Bureaucracy: School Desegregation Policy in H.E.W., 1964–1968* (New York: Teachers' College Press, 1977); and Gary Orfield, *The Reconstruction of Southern Education* (New York: Wiley-Interscience, 1969).

25. Jay D. Scribner and Richard M. Englebert, "The Politics of Education: An Introduction," in *Politics of Education*, ed. Scribner.

26. Graham Allison, *Essence of Decision* (Boston: Little, Brown, 1971).

27. My discussion of pluralist and ideological concepts here owes much to Peterson, *School Politics*.

28. Ibid., especially chs. 2 and 4.

29. Ibid., especially chs. 2, 3, and 7.

30. Julie A. Schmidt, "School Desegregation in Wilmington, Delaware: A Case Study in Non-Decision-Making," M.A. Thesis, Political Science Department, University of Delaware, June 1979.

31. Hargrove, *Implementation*, p. 69.

32. Uncertainty was also reduced by the change in atmosphere in Washington. With Carter's election and actions (Amy went to a desegregated school although she was not bused), Delawareans found it difficult to maintain that relief was certain at some point.

33. William Trombley, "Dallas" *Integrateducation* 15 (Nov.–Dec. 1977): 20–23.

34. David K. Dunaway, "Urban Desegregation: The Mayor's Influence in the Schools," *Integrateducation* 15, no. 1 (Jan.–Feb. 1977): 3–9, argues that taking a positive position on implementing school desegregation plans would be political suicide for some mayors.

35. Murphy, "Title I."

36. Norton E. Long, "The Local Community as an Ecology of Games," *American Journal of Sociology* 64, no. 3 (Nov. 1958): 251–261.

37. Lewis Anthony Dexter, "The Representative and His District," in *New Perspectives on the House of Representatives*, ed. Robert L. Peabody and Nelson W. Polsby (Chicago: Rand McNally, 1963), pp. 3–32.

38. Trombley, "Dallas."

39. David I. Bednarek, "Milwaukee," *Integrateducation* 15 (Nov.–Dec. 1977): 36–37.

40. William E. Connolly, *The Bias of Pluralism* (New York: Atherton, 1973).

41. Trombley, "Dallas," and Bednarek, "Milwaukee."

42. Nelson, *Moon and Ghetto*, pp. 17, 75.

43. John B. McConahay and Willis D. Hawley, "Is It the Buses or the Blacks? Self-Interest versus Symbolic Racism as Predictors of Opposition to Busing in Louisville," working paper, Duke University, Center for Policy

Analysis, Institute of Policy Sciences and Public Affairs, presented at the annual meeting of the American Psychological Association, San Francisco, Aug. 28, 1977, p. 50.

44. Elisabeth Kubler-Ross, *On Death and Dying* (New York: MacMillan, 1972).

45. Gary Orfield, "Desegregation in the National Context," talk to the DEEP Community Workshop on School Desegregation, Wilmington High School, March 6, 1976.

46. On the effect of time on desegregation conflict see William R. Grant, "Detroit," pp. 2–4, Muriel Cohen, "Boston," pp. 9–10, and Art Branscombe, "Denver," pp. 11–13, in *Integrated Education* 15, no. 6 (Nov.–Dec. 1977).

47. Many authors have questioned this commitment under the Nixon and Ford administrations. See Orfield, *Must We Bus?* and Radin, *Implementation.*

48. For a description and analysis of the Civil Rights Act, Title IV, programs, see Stephen Crocker et al., *Title IV of the Civil Rights Act of 1964: A Review of Program Operations* (Santa Monica: Rand Corp., Aug. 1976). See also Orfield, *Must We Bus?* pp. 427–30.

Lorraine M. McDonnell and Gail L. Zellman criticize ESAA's support of community groups that tutor students but play no advocacy role in the local community ("The Role of Community Groups in Facilitating School Desegration," paper presented at the 1978 annual meeting of the American Political Science Association, New York City, Aug. 31–Sept. 3, 1978). For a general description of the federal role in school desegregation see Frederick S. Edelstein, "Federal and State Roles in School Desegregation," *Education and Urban Society* 9, no. 3 (May 1977): 303–326. For a general discussion of federal roles in education, see Michael W. Kirst, "The Future Federal Role in Education: Parties, Candidates, and the 1976 Elections," *Phi Delta Kappan* 58, no. 2 (Oct. 1976): 155–158.

49. William W. Wayson, "ESEA: Decennial Views of the Revolution; the Negative Side," *Phi Delta Kappan* 57, no. 3 (Nov. 1975): 151–156.

50. Both Christine Rossell and William Balanger, assistant to the county judge, Jefferson County, Kentucky, made this point at the Delaware Association for Public Administration Conference, "School Desegration and State and Local Government in Delaware."

51. The conference in Washington co-sponsored by CRS on coalition building (see Chapter 6) and the U.S.O.E.–Urban Coalition conference in Houston on community participation in desegregation both helped Delaware's community leaders to learn the desegregation ropes.

52. Crocker et al., *Title IV,* reach similar conclusions for different reasons.

53. See Orfield, *Must We Bus?* pp. 442–445.

54. Harrell R. Rodgers and Charles S. Bullock III, "School Desegregation: A Multivariate Test of the Role of Law in Effecting Social Change," *American Politics Quarterly* 4, no. 2 (April 1976); 153–176, and *Coercion to Compliance.*

55. Peltason, *Fifty-Eight Lonely Men,* p. 96.

56. See Crocker et al., *Title IV*, for some relevant examples.
57. Rittel and Webber, "Dilemmas."
58. Orfield, *Must We Bus?* p. 427.

Glossary

Breakfast Group: unpublicized, informal, regular meeting of school, governmental, and community leaders responsible for desegregating the New Castle County Schools under the federal court orders.

CIE (Committee for the Improvement of Education): organization of black parent leaders in the City of Wilmington, which filed an *amicus* brief against busing city children.

Citizens Alliance for Public Education (the Alliance): coalition of groups and individuals supporting peaceful and effective desegregation, public involvement, and quality education in New Castle County schools.

Committee of Twelve (later the Delaware Committee on the School Decision): Committee appointed by County Executive Slawik to advise the county government on how to deal with federal school desegregation court orders.

CRS (Community Relations Service): agency of the U.S. Department of Justice charged with reducing racial tensions in school desegregation cases and other areas.

DCSD (Delaware Committee on the School Decision): fifty-person committee appointed by the governor, the mayor of Wilmington, and the county executive to work to implement whatever school desegregation plan was ordered by the federal courts; successor to the Committe of Twelve.

DEA (Delmarva Ecumenical Agency): council of Christian denominations on the Delmarva peninsula working for interfaith harmony.

DEEP (Delaware Equal Education Process Committee): prodesegregation and probusing organization, an offshoot of the Urban Coalition of Metropolitan Wilmington.

DPI (Department of Public Instruction): state education department in Delaware under the jurisdiction of the State Board of Education.

EAA (Educational Advancement Act): legislation passed by the Delaware State Legislature in 1968 to consolidate school districts, later judged unconstitutional by the federal courts.

Evans v. Buchanan: the 1960s Delaware school desegregation case reopened in 1971.

ETC (Effective Transition Committee): a blue-ribbon committee appointed by Governor du Pont to coordinate and oversee the beginning of busing.

GWDC (Greater Wilmington Development Council): area development council funded by Delaware's corporate sector; it helped to establish SANE of Delaware, Inc.

Intergovernmental Task Force on Desegregation: a staff committee appointed by the governor, the mayors of Wilmington and Newark, and the county executive to plan and establish institutions and programs needed to help in the process of school desegregation.

Interim Board of Education: thirteen-member board appointed after the May 1976 court order, as modified by the State Legislature, to plan for the desegregation and reorganization of the schools in New Castle County.

ITF (Interfaith Task Force): committee established by Delaware's religious leaders to bring together religious efforts and resources toward achieving peaceful desegregation.

NANS (National Association for Neighborhood Schools): national coalition of groups working against busing.

NCCJ (National Conference of Christians and Jews): local committee of the national organization working to improve relations across racial, religious, and other societal divisions.

New Board (New Castle County Planning Board of Education): five-member board established by the court and appointed by the State Board of Education to plan for school desegregation within a single reorganized school district.

PAC (Positive Action Committee): antibusing organization in New Castle County working to stop or limit busing in Delaware.

SANE of Delaware, Inc. (not an acronym): committee of four people established by the corporate community of Delaware to work for the peaceful implementation of federal school desegregation court orders.

Special Committee on Desegregation: committee established by the Delaware State Legislature to consider what it should do about school desegregation.

Wilmington Home and School Council: parent organization of the Wilmington School District, independent of the PTA.

Index